Praise For *The Assist*

"Team sports, like life, are never simple. Beneath the concrete final score, there are games within games, small plays leading to big plays, a melding of diverse talents and personalities into a cohesive (or disparate) unit. Rarely is that tapestry revealed as fully, and as convincingly, as in Neil Swidey's *The Assist*."

—*Boston Globe*

"This is a fine piece of journalistic literature; do not make the mistake of thinking it is for sports fans only."

—*School Library Journal*

"Basketball may be the soul game, but, as Swidey deftly reveals, it's often played and coached by wounded souls . . . There's triumph, tragedy, and salvation in this story. Not to mention a movie. GRADE: A-."

—Steve Wulf, *Entertainment Weekly*

"Thankfully, *The Assist* isn't a formula sports story where everything leads up to 'The Big Game' that's won in overtime. It's an absorbing examination of at-risk, inner-city youths who succeed against all odds. GRADE: A."

—*Rocky Mountain News*

"[Swidey] builds narrative momentum and details his subjects with the touch of a skilled novelist. This is a prodigiously reported, compulsively readable book that readers (sports fans or not) will savor."

—*Publishers Weekly*

"A classic . . . This book made me laugh. This book made me cry. This book made me think."

—Michael Holley, author of *Red Sox Rule* and *Patriot Reign*

"Swidey, an award-winning journalist for the *Boston Globe Magazine*, quickly converts his readers into genuine fans of these young men. Like [Coach Jack] O'Brien, he shows a fanatical devotion to his subject. He follows the team off the court and into the projects, to pizza parties and prestigious tournaments. *The Assist* will prove indispensable to anyone interested in the art of coaching at any level or in any sport. And by distracting us from the sordid, steroid-fueled headlines, Swidey reminds us why we enjoy watching sports in the first place."

—Andrew Ervin, *Washington Post Book World*

"One does not have to be from Boston to appreciate Swidey's writing skills. His characters are real and have a story to tell. It's a tale that pulsates with the intensity of a full-court press."

—*Tampa Tribune*

"[Swidey] uses practically unfettered access to detail the ups and downs of O'Brien's powerhouse program and the coach's fierce dedication to the players."

—*New York Times Sports Magazine Play*

"Neil Swidey might have started out trying to tell the tale of an exceptionally successful high school basketball team and their coach, but as he spent time with the subjects of his story, he realized that they could help him explore a much larger story. His book is about basketball, certainly, but it is also about education, race, the hypocrisy with which our games are riddled, and a collection of young men trying to figure out who they are and who they can be."

—Bill Littlefield, host of NPR's *Only a Game*

"He shoots, it's good . . . Swidey masterfully deploys his observations to make his points."

—*New York Post*

"Like *Hoop Dreams*, this captivating account transcends its time and place."

—*Booklist*

"With a powerful, moving narrative, Neil Swidey has delivered the rarest of transcendent sports books. Coach Jack O'Brien and his Charlestown players will bring you to your feet, and they'll bring you to tears. Most of all, they'll make you care about a game so much bigger than winning and losing. This is a brilliant book, one that will stay with you."

—Adrian Wojnarowski, author of
New York Times bestseller *The Miracle of St. Anthony*

"A noble debut."

—*Kirkus Reviews*

"The Celtics may have reached thirty wins in fewer games than any team in NBA history, but the best story to come out of Boston this season is *The Assist* by Neil Swidey."

—Mark Kriegel, author of *Pistol:*
The Life of Pete Maravich

"A must-read."

—*Las Cruces Sun-Times*

"368 pages of fast reading. Turn the TV off and dig into *The Assist*. Once you do, you'll realize just how high the stakes are for every jump shot, rebound, and game."

—*Dime Magazine*

"Set in compact, feisty, history-haunted Charlestown, this book is a powerhouse work of literary journalism about a powerhouse basketball program and the coach who wouldn't take no for an answer."

—Madeleine Blais, Pulitzer Prize–winner
and author of *In These Girls, Hope Is a Muscle*

"Swidey is there for it all."

"So much of Boston's history, good and bad, can be seen through Charlestown. So much of our basic humanity can be seen through the games we play. Neil Swidey brings all of that forward with a shrewd eye, a wide-ranging mind, and an uncommon gift for illuminating our common humanity."

"A must-read . . . The second-best book about inner-city high school basketball behind Darcy Frey's *The Last Shot.*"

"What happens when a tough-as-nails Boston basketball coach dedicates his life to helping inner-city teens? Success."

"This isn't a great basketball book. This is great literature."

"Like *Hoop Dreams*, this captivating account transcends its time and place."

"With a powerful, moving narrative, Neil Swidey has delivered the rarest of transcendent sports books. Coach Jack O'Brien and his Charlestown players will bring you to your feet, and they'll bring you to tears. Most of all, they'll make you care about a game so much bigger than winning and losing. This is a brilliant book, one that will stay with you."

"A noble debut."

"The Celtics may have reached thirty wins in fewer games than any team in NBA history, but the best story to come out of Boston this season is *The Assist* by Neil Swidey."

"A must-read."

"368 pages of fast reading. Turn the TV off and dig into *The Assist*. Once you do, you'll realize just how high the stakes are for every jump shot, rebound, and game."

"Set in compact, feisty, history-haunted Charlestown, this book is a powerhouse work of literary journalism about a powerhouse basketball program and the coach who wouldn't take no for an answer."

"Swidey is there for it all."

—*NCAA Champion Magazine*

"So much of Boston's history, good and bad, can be seen through Charlestown. So much of our basic humanity can be seen through the games we play. Neil Swidey brings all of that forward with a shrewd eye, a wide-ranging mind, and an uncommon gift for illuminating our common humanity."

—Charles P. Pierce, NPR commentator and author of
Moving the Chains: Tom Brady and the Pursuit of Everything

"A must-read . . . The second-best book about inner-city high school basketball behind Darcy Frey's *The Last Shot*."

—Bill Simmons, ESPN

"What happens when a tough-as-nails Boston basketball coach dedicates his life to helping inner-city teens? Success."

—NBC's *Today Show*

"This isn't a great basketball book. This is great literature."

—Yahoo Sports

THE ASSIST

THE ASSIST

HOOPS, HOPE, AND THE
GAME OF THEIR LIVES

NEIL SWIDEY

PublicAffairs
New York

Set in 9 pt. Lucida by the Perseus Books Group.
Designed by Pauline Brown.

PublicAffairs books are available at special discounts for bulk purchases in
the U.S. by corporations, institutions, and other organizations. For more
information, please contact the Special Markets Department at the Perseus
Books Group, 2300 Chestnut Street, Suite 200, Philadelphia, PA 19103, call
(800) 255–1514, ext. 5000, or e-mail special.markets@perseusbooks.com.

Library of Congress Cataloging-in-Publication Data

Swidey, Neil.
  The assist : hoops, hope, and the game of their lives / Neil Swidey.
     p. cm.
  HC ISBN: 978-1-58648-469-9 (hardcover : alk. paper)
  PB ISBN: 978-1-58648-666-2
     1. Charlestown High School (Boston, Mass.)—Basketball. 2. O'Brien,
Jack. 3. Basketball—Massachusetts—Boston. 4. School sports—Massachu-
setts—Boston. I. Title.
  GV885.43.C57S95 2007
  796.323'620974461—dc22
                                          2007035826

10 9 8 7 6 5 4 3 2 1

For Denise, my partner in everything I do,
And for my parents, Samuel and Mary Swidey,
my first and finest teachers

CONTENTS

PROLOGUE

Jack O'Brien knelt down, and his index finger began tracing the etching in the black granite. It moved quickly through the curves of the numeral 3, the straight line of the 1, but lingered when it arrived at the detailed image of a basketball sailing through a net.

He closed his watery brown eyes. His large forehead, made to look even larger by the way he brushed his brown hair up and back, became as deeply grooved as the granite.

He stood up and stepped back, taking in the full image of the stone. Then he turned to the two boys he'd brought with him. "Nice, huh?" O'Brien said.

Between the 31 and the basketball net, there was a face. Laser-etched onto the granite, it belonged to a handsome young man who wore his hair closely cropped, diamond studs in each ear, and a slightly crooked smile.

Below the face, a name:

JONES
RICHARD L.

O'Brien's mind flashed back five years, to the fall of 1999, when Richard Jones first crossed the threshold of his gym. O'Brien had made it his job to be aware of every teenage boy in the city of

1

Boston who ever picked up a ball. But Richard, a tall laid-back junior, had bounced around enough schools in and out of Boston to have eluded O'Brien's detection. The kid with the electric smile and spot-on Eddie Murphy impersonation was so friendly he was impossible not to like instantly, even for O'Brien, who had learned the power of withholding warmth. But Richard also had a habit of making excuses for himself. During his years coaching in Boston, O'Brien had heard more excuses than a highway cop clutching a radar gun. His reaction was always the same: ride the kid so hard that exhaustion wore down any reflex to pass the buck. Yet somehow Richard had inspired O'Brien to be more creative. Once when he showed up late for practice, O'Brien got Richard a chair and sat him down in the center of the court, making sure he was comfortable. Then he made the rest of the team run grueling "suicide" sprints around him. Richard was never late for practice again. Better yet, he turned into a leader, holding himself and everyone else around him accountable. He, more than anyone, helped O'Brien guide Charlestown High School to the first of its four back-to-back state titles. In turn, O'Brien helped Richard score an athletic scholarship to a Division I college in Buffalo, where he became a model on and off the court. He was on track to graduate a semester early and begin graduate school—hardly a typical trajectory in the world of Division I basketball, where graduation rates tend to clock in well below field goal percentages.

Staring straight ahead, O'Brien extended an arm in either direction. The boys on either side of him, his co-captains for the upcoming season, clasped their hands with his, and bowed their heads. "Dear Lord," O'Brien began. "Please watch over Richard and his family, especially his mother. And let us meet again someday in Paradise."

O'Brien's eyes fixed on the dates etched into the granite: November 5, 1982–May 5, 2004. Richard Jones had been gone for nearly four months now, but his stone had just been erected. Then

O'Brien glanced at the dates on the gravesites on either side of Richard's. To the left, a sixty-four-year-old; to the right, a seventy-eight-year-old. There's grief in every death, for sure. But there had to be a special sadness reserved for the death of a twenty-one-year-old who had overcome the long odds imposed by life in the inner city, only to drop dead on a basketball court in college. The cause of death for Richard, whose warmth and love of life seemed to be boundless, was an enlarged heart.

If O'Brien could find any hint of comfort in Richard's death, it was that at least he had died of natural causes. Oak Lawn Cemetery sat atop a Boston hill between a boarded-up Ford dealership and a battered Stop & Shop supermarket. Across the street was the larger, more established Mt. Calvary Cemetery, where the gravestones dated back more than a century and carried the names of Boston's Irish-Catholic past. That was O'Brien's past, but because he was closer to his players than to most of his own family, O'Brien knew the contours of Oak Lawn better. There, the names were a mix of black Boston, the Washingtons and Morrisons first attached to the sons of sharecroppers, the Baptistes and Campbells attached to newer arrivals from Haiti and Jamaica. Given its tether to the city's black neighborhoods, Oak Lawn also offered a visual profile of the stretches of recent history when it was most dangerous to be a young black man growing up in Boston. The cemetery, only fifteen years old, had already logged more than 3,000 burials—and far too many of them belonged to the young. There were clusters of head-stones memorializing teens cut down in the early- and mid-1990s, but far fewer as the decade wore on, when Boston's murder rate for the young had decreased so sharply that it was branded the "Boston Miracle." Yet even before the criminologists acknowledged the shift in the narrative, a rush of new names and dates etched into granite at Oak Lawn documented the miracle's demise.

O'Brien had come to Boston as an outsider, a white guy from the suburbs whose success as a coach defined him and whose main goal was racking up more wins. But during more than a decade coaching in Charlestown, a Boston neighborhood that was almost entirely white, he worked almost entirely with black kids bused in from the city's high-crime neighborhoods. Somewhere along the way, his priorities changed. He was still obsessed with winning, but more and more he saw his relentless pursuit of state titles as a means to an end: an insurance policy against having to spend any more time at Oak Lawn.

O'Brien led his co-captains to an adjacent section of the cemetery. An afternoon shower had left the grass moist, though it had done little to improve the humid August air. They walked in silence, except for the sounds of the Canada geese squawking from an adjacent field, and the players' high-top sneakers squishing in the soil and the occasional droppings left by the flock. Thirty yards from Richard Jones's stone, O'Brien stopped and looked down at a rectangular bronze slab laid into the ground. It read: PARIS G. BOOKER, February 19, 1988–August 5, 2003. At the top-right corner of the marker, there was a covered picture frame. O'Brien knelt down and gingerly opened it to reveal a photo of a tall boy, wearing clear aviator glasses and a blue pin-striped suit. The boy looked to be a high school senior. In fact, he was only fifteen. In his hand, he was holding his middle school diploma.

While Richard had made it out, Paris was just beginning his climb. He was 6-foot-2 in the eighth grade, destined to be a star. Even his name—Paris Booker—sounded tailor-made for the loudspeaker at an NBA game. One year earlier, just a few weeks before he would start his freshman year at Charlestown High, Paris was riding his bike in the Dorchester neighborhood of Boston. An SUV hit him and then dragged him 30 feet. The driver fled. Paris's mother buried her boy with a Charlestown jersey in his arms.

O'Brien put his head down and his arms out. Once again his co-captains joined him in prayer. "Dear Lord, please watch over Paris and his mother," he said. "I never got the chance to coach him, but he was part of Charlestown, and we miss him." O'Brien's new co-captains were both seniors, so Richard had graduated by the time they joined the Charlestown program, and Paris had never suited up as a member of their squad. Still, in the family O'Brien forged, they were all brothers. The coach had Paris's initials sewn onto the shoulders of the team uniforms and Richard's jersey framed and hung on the gym wall. Before every game, he led a locker room prayer asking Jesus to watch over Richard and Paris. And as soon as the players took to the court, they would perform the same rocking, swaying, pre-game huddle chant that Richard had introduced during his Charlestown days.

O'Brien let his arms drop to his side. Then he stepped back, so he could make eye contact with both co-captains, Ridley Johnson and Jason White. O'Brien had taken a gamble in pairing them: although they had played together for three years, they weren't at all close. Ridley was a 6-foot-3 wire with a soft voice and a demeanor as gentle as the slope of his profile, Jason a muscular 6-footer with piercing eyes and a penchant for icy stares. "Remember," O'Brien told them, "no matter how tough life may get, these guys would do anything to change places with you."

I

THE PRE-SEASON

1

—

HOOD

THE DODGE CARAVAN STUTTERED ALONG Washington Street in the Roxbury section of Boston as O'Brien slowed down at each intersection to squint at the street signs.

"Is this the turn?"

"Nah, the next one, Coach," said the kid riding with him.

"This one?"

O'Brien lived in Medford, a small suburban city 5 miles northwest of Boston, with his elderly mother in the same house he had grown up in. When he'd taken the Charlestown High coaching job, he'd had no idea that none of his players would actually live in the neighborhood of Charlestown. Soon enough, he learned an important legacy of Boston's public school desegregation wars of the 1970s: Because there were virtually no white students left, the schools were more segregated than ever. So O'Brien got used to driving his white minivan, with the Evergreen air freshener dangling from the mirror, around the black neighborhoods of Boston that other middle-aged white guys from the suburbs long ago decided to avoid.

He turned up Townsend Street and pulled in front of a cluster of freshly built townhouses painted in the hues of spring. The New

Academy Estates. The complex had just opened, and O'Brien could hardly believe the transformation. Old Academy had been one of Boston's most treacherous housing projects, a warren of flat-roofed cement buildings flanking expansive courtyards that had turned into shooting galleries where even the cops feared to tread.

O'Brien beeped his horn, and out sauntered Jason White. The kid had grown up in old Academy and then shuttled between apartments during the years it took to raze and replace the project. When O'Brien had picked him up for the cemetery visit two weeks earlier, Jason was living in a tired three-decker on a residential street. But a week after that—actually, it was on September 3, the same day Jason turned nineteen—he and his family turned the key on their new townhouse.

Jason emerged wearing a blue baseball cap with the manufacturer's 59Fifty label purposely left on the brim and an oversize black quilted jacket. It was 72 degrees outside. On the basketball court, he moved with such ferocious speed that the ends of his cornrows bobbed behind his head, struggling to keep up. But everywhere else, he favored a leisurely, defiant strut. O'Brien knew that many adults at the high school looked at the kid's posture, his clothes, and his stare and saw nothing but a thug. The nickname Jason went by—Hood—only strengthened the impression. O'Brien liked knowing that his vision was better than theirs.

Hood shook hands with O'Brien without saying anything, and climbed into the minivan.

"Whatup, Spot?" Hood said, extending his hand to the teammate who had been O'Brien's first pickup of the day. Lamar Brathwaite had a Hollywood smile and a nickname he owed to an oval-shaped birthmark on the right side of his head and the threat a former teammate once made to "smack that spot onto the wall." He was wearing washed-out baggy jeans, a bright-white extra-long T-shirt, and a black nylon do-rag.

On the drive back to Washington Street, O'Brien spotted a pair of kids, maybe ten years old, shooting jumpers at a broken hoop. "I want you to get me the names of those kids," he told Hood, chuckling. "They're working on their fundamentals. Most kids in the inner city just wanna play games."

O'Brien drove past a liquor store with a mural of famous black faces painted onto the side wall, the once proud images now crowded out by graffiti, then on past a used car lot encased in barbed wire, the brightly colored triangular flags strung above the clunkers now torn and faded, flapping in the wind. He drove past clusters of idling teenagers who, like Hood, wore black coats too warm for the weather, and past idling adults who sat in cars on blocks, blasting hip-hop through open windows. Across this landscape of resignation, there were flashes of renewal—a lovingly restored three-decker bathed in a fresh coat of bright turquoise, a storefront church unmistakably in expansion mode. But in a neighborhood where the billboards continued to carry the peeling campaign messages of candidates defeated years earlier, the signs of optimism were rationed. Even the storefront churches had thick security gates over the doors and windows.

O'Brien looked back at Hood and Spot through his rearview mirror. "You guys got your contacts in?" They shook their heads. So did he. A while back, he had arranged for them to get fitted with contact lenses, made sure they got to their eye doctor appointments, even cobbled together some money to help cover the costs. The only thing he couldn't do was put the lenses in their eyes. He laughed. "Imagine how good we'd be if our players could actually see."

As always, O'Brien was wearing one of his Charlestown warm-up suits, which he owned in a rainbow of colors. He was taking Hood and Spot to visit a college on the North Shore of Boston. Unlike many other high school coaches, O'Brien could handle a weekend task like this without having to miss his son's soccer game or saddle his wife with the kids for the day. He had never been married and his only kids were the ones on his roster. The absence of family commitments allowed him to build his program with complete devotion, investing endless hours and emotional energy in his players' lives off the court. To them, he was both a shoulder and a scold. He rode them about their homework and drove them to check out colleges. He arranged their doctors' appointments and rearranged their class schedules. He ran them hard, until every one of their muscles ached. And then he stopped by the Foodmaster to get them the plastic produce bags they preferred for icing their sore joints.

During his tenure, the forty-six-year-old O'Brien had helped nearly every one of his players who stuck with his program through their senior year get to college. The majority of them made it there without the benefit of a big-time athletic scholarship. Most years, at least one of his kids would grab some glory, getting a full ride to play ball at a Division I college. But it was finding a path for all the other kids that took the most work. O'Brien, a phys ed teacher who had struggled to earn his own degree from a not-very-competitive state college, was never much of a student himself. Still, he'd learned what it took to get kids to the next level. Among other things, it required lots of Saturdays like this one.

Nearly an hour after being picked up, Hood was staring out the window as the minivan hugged the coast, winding past the majestic estates of Beverly Farms before gliding onto the campus of Endicott College. The small liberal arts college, coed for only a decade, had been building up its athletic programs in the hopes of attracting more young men. O'Brien was an eager supplier. He'd already sent three former players there. A Division III school, Endicott offered no athletic scholarships. But athletic ability helped students get admitted, and the poor backgrounds that most of O'Brien's kids came from often allowed them to receive nearly full financial aid.

O'Brien led Hood and Spot into an office near the gym. There, the college coach spoke about his team's winning record and its up-tempo style of play. He talked up the college's internship program and asked Hood and Spot what they wanted to major in. Hood said "business." Spot said the first thing that popped into his head: "electrical engineering." The coach winced. So did O'Brien. Endicott didn't offer engineering.

"We see you guys fitting in here really well," the coach said, moving on.

By the end of the afternoon, it was clear Hood and Spot did not agree.

While O'Brien chatted with the Endicott coach, Hood and Spot walked around campus with the hesitancy of Japanese tourists who had been separated from their American guide. They stayed for the first half of the Saturday afternoon football game, long enough to see the home team get crushed. Around them, the bleachers were a sea of white.

O'Brien could sense the discomfort in Hood and Spot. But he wanted them—needed them—to get past it. As they climbed back into the minivan, he pointed left and right. "Lookit, everything is right here for you—your dorm, the gym, the library. You won't have to take no more trains and buses to get to class."

"It looks boring," Hood said flatly.

"The problem is you want to stay home," O'Brien said. "Not for anything, but you'd get here faster from your house than it takes you to get to Charlestown."

O'Brien, who loaded up his players' days with practices, summer leagues, study halls—anything to keep them off Boston's streets—was so focused on seeing the streets as the enemy that he sometimes forgot they were also his players' home.

A few minutes later, the minivan was back on the highway, passing a sign that read, "Boston 28 miles."

"You can always go back to Boston," O'Brien said. "This is your future we're talking about here."

Closer to home, O'Brien asked, "Hey, Hood, with your new apartment, will it be easier to get to school on time?" The ride to Charlestown High from his last apartment took more than an hour each way.

"Nah, harder," Hood said. "The 42 never runs."

"Why can't you take the 22?"

"That's not my neighborhood. That's Jackson. I can't go there."

O'Brien shot a disbelieving look into the rearview mirror. "What do you mean? It's only five minutes from your house."

Hood stared straight ahead. "I'd get killed."

•   •   •

HOOD'S MOTHER, PEARL WHITE, first made her way up to Boston from her native Alabama after she graduated from high school in 1973. Plenty of her relatives had made the move before her, part of the large-scale migration of Cotton Belt blacks to the North that more than quadrupled Boston's black population between 1940 and 1970.

For many Southern blacks, Boston held a special appeal. Massachusetts was a birthplace of the abolitionist movement, where William Lloyd Garrison issued his fiery call to end slavery, and the birthplace of W. E. B. Du Bois, whose soaring brilliance helped found the National Association for the Advancement of Colored People (NAACP). It had been a hub of the Underground Railroad, ferrying escaped slaves to safety in Canada. Even centuries ago, Boston had had a small, thriving population of educated, cultured blacks—mostly Massachusetts-born or natives of the West Indies—who were accorded privileges that blacks in other parts of the country could have hardly imagined.

But Boston also had a complicated racial past. Many of New England's leading families had made a mint ferrying slaves from Africa to the West Indies. True, Massachusetts' highest court banned slavery in 1783. But that same court later hatched the noxious "separate but equal" legal foundation on which the U.S. Supreme Court based its 1896 decision in *Plessy v. Ferguson*, which sanctioned segregated public schools for the first half of the twentieth century. As Boston's black population grew, largely because of the influx of rural migrants from the South with limited education, tensions increased within the black community, and racism increased among the city's whites. Sure, Boston was responsible for putting the doctor in Dr. Martin Luther King and electing the first black U.S. senator since Reconstruction. But its underlying racism also radicalized many of the blacks who lived there, notably Louis Farrakhan and Malcolm X, who served part of a six-year sentence for armed robbery at the Charlestown State Prison.

Pearl White's initial distaste for Boston had little to do with racism, though. It was just too different from the slow pace of the Birmingham area where she had grown up. So she headed back home. After three years, she tried Boston again and liked it enough to stay for good. Pearl kept mostly to her relatives' apartments in the thoroughly black Mission Hill housing project in Roxbury, and it was around Mission Hill that she met a smooth-talking young amateur boxer with a high-wattage smile and an easy laugh. His name was Willie Barnes, but, on the streets, they called him Chill Pill.

Willie was born in Virginia, but when he was about four, his father moved him and his bevy of sisters to New York to live with him and his girlfriend. When he was nine, his father woke him and his sisters up in the middle of the night and told him they were going to move to Boston with their mother, who had cleaned up her act and shown up to retrieve her kids. "All I know," Willie would later recall, "is some lady with glasses had her arms around me, saying 'son.'" She told the kids about the great life they'd have in Boston, how there was a swimming pool and horses—amenities that sounded like a fairy tale. The fairy tale ended as soon as they pulled up to their new home in a scraggly housing project where the only horses were the play structures in the park.

Willie spent his teenage years shuttling between New York and Boston. He was a natural player. He'd get tight with the security guards at the old Boston State College, making them laugh and going on runs for them to the store. They, in turn, would let him into the basketball games for free, where he would swipe people's wallets and use the proceeds to pay his way to New York.

By the time Willie and Pearl got together in 1984, she had a son from a previous relationship and he had a couple of kids. The next year brought Jason, their first child together. When Jason was about two, he chased a ball into the street. A crackhead going for her fix ran over him, breaking one of his legs. She then tried to back up, and ended up breaking his other leg and his pelvis. She fled, parking her car a few blocks away. But she eventually returned to the scene because that's where her dealer was. Her actions were too much even for drug dealers; a couple of them held her until the cops came.

Jason spent two months in the hospital in a body cast. By the time Pearl was able to wheel him out, she had a young daughter strapped to her chest and was pregnant with another son. Jason now had screws in his legs, and it wasn't clear if he would walk unimpaired.

The family bounced around apartments in Boston and Providence, Rhode Island, before settling in 1994 in a Roxbury project called Academy Homes II. The 315-unit complex had been built nearly three decades earlier, just after the adjacent 200-unit Academy I complex. Rising where the Catholic archdiocese's Notre Dame Academy had once stood, the two projects were billed as the future of subsidized housing, a signature achievement for the city's urban renewal program. The architect won a prestigious award for his innovative design using pre-cast, pre-stressed concrete slabs that allowed for rapid, low-cost construction. Racially integrated construction crews built what were intended to be homes for an integrated community of residents.

But everything about Academy Homes turned out to be a disaster. Within the first year, the roof on one of the long, rectangular buildings blew off in high winds. The concrete expanded and contracted, leaving large openings in the walls, allowing in colonies of roaches and rodents. Drafts blew through fist-wide cracks in the cold concrete, and mold grew on the walls. In Academy II's nine-story tower, there was no working elevator. The out-of-state owners who had been showered with federal funding were nowhere to be found. In 1974, the Department of Housing and Urban Development foreclosed on the project. The goal had been to turn it over to tenant ownership, but the tenants were wise enough not to take on the burden until the most grievous problems were fixed. They weren't, and conditions continued to deteriorate for decades. In the mid-1990s, HUD officials admitted as much, calling Academy II the most dilapidated project in Massachusetts.

Not surprisingly, crime became a blistering problem, as gangs of poor kids from Academy came together to battle the poor kids from nearby projects, most notably the one across Columbus Avenue called Bromley Heath. Even here, Academy's design made matters worse. Hoping to avoid the darkness and density associated with so many urban projects, the Academy architects arrayed the apartment buildings around sweeping courtyards. But when crime descended on the project, so much gunfire crackled across the courtyards that residents were scared day and night to leave their apartments for fear of getting caught in the crossfire. The cops had enough trouble keeping peace on the streets, so the courtyards became a land for outlaws.

On Halloween night, 1994, the same year Pearl and Willie moved their family into the project, a couple of gang-bangers drove by

Academy I and fired shots into the courtyard. When the smoke cleared, a nine-year-old boy fresh from a night of trick-or-treating lay dead.

Still, Jason loved the courtyard by his apartment. There, he glimpsed his future as a star athlete. Although he had no lingering problems with his legs, in pickup football games his puny size made him one of the last kids to be chosen for teams. But one rainy day when he was eleven and playing in a two-on-two game, he made a dazzling catch to score the winning touchdown.

After that, he never had trouble getting picked again.

For much of the time Jason was in elementary and middle school, his father was an erratic presence in his life. Willie had become hooked on drink and drugs, and feeding his needs, rather than providing for his kids, became his top priority. But that didn't stop him from breezing into their apartment every once in a while, giving Jason lectures about what he should and shouldn't be doing, and then breezing right back out. Jason let it go in one ear and out the other. He turned into the archetype of the angry young black male, a hardened kid with a quick temper, icy glare, and fists always at the ready. He became only more steely after two of his cousins, who had gotten caught up in the street life, were killed. All around him was unfairness he was helpless to combat. When he was in the eighth grade at Grover Cleveland Middle School, he joined the basketball team. Only then, on the court, did he find a sense of control.

Sometimes just getting to the game was an achievement. Bright when he wanted to be, Jason was usually too cool for school, doing just enough work to keep a C average so he could play ball. His hair-trigger temper got him suspended so often that the assistant principal took to keeping him in his office for the whole day leading up to a basketball game so he would remain eligible to play. One of his middle school coaches was friendly with Jack O'Brien, whom he invited to come see his dynamic eighth-grader on the court.

Afterward, O'Brien pulled Hood aside and told him about Charlestown's winning program, about all the guys who had found discipline at Charlestown and a path to college. Jason listened, occasionally responding with a "yeah," managing in his practiced cool to stretch two or three syllables out of that one four-letter word. Then he walked away, confident of two things: That O'Brien guy sure could talk. And Jason had no intention of ever going to Charlestown High.

In Boston Public Schools, the parents of eighth-graders were asked to rank their top choices for the high school they wanted their children to attend. There were twelve district high schools, as well as three more competitive schools that required an entrance exam for admission. More than a decade earlier, this "choice" system had replaced the more rigid race-based assignment process that had governed Boston schools under court-ordered desegregation since 1974.

Like many eighth-graders, Jason based his choices simply on where his friends were going. He told O'Brien he would be going to either Boston English or Jeremiah E. Burke High School. But, as he would soon learn, the Charlestown coach did not take no easily. O'Brien called Jason's mother, telling Pearl all the potential he saw in her son—she had never seen one of his games—and all the reasons she should consider sending him to Charlestown. With Willie largely out of the picture, Pearl had worried that Jason's trouble-making ways might only get worse if he went to Boston English or Burke. She'd heard around the neighborhood that fights were always breaking out at those schools. In O'Brien she saw someone who would stay on top of her son.

She took the form, wrote down Charlestown High as Jason's first choice, and dropped it in the mail. She never told her son what she'd done.

When August rolled around, Hood received a notice telling him to show up for his first day of ninth grade at Charlestown High.

Charlestown? He was fuming. He'd never been to that part of Boston, didn't even know where it was. But Pearl would brook no debate. She had made her decision, had put her trust in Coach O'Brien. Reluctantly, Jason checked out a subway map to figure out how to get to his new school.

None of his eighth-grade friends went to Charlestown, but Jason did know one kid heading into his sophomore year there. Tony Lee had the huge, sweet eyes of a basset hound and the mean, rippled build of a bulldog. He was considered one of the toughest kids to come out of one of the roughest projects in town, Mission Hill, the same place where Jason's parents had first connected. He and Tony first met at an anger management class in middle school. They later ran into each other at a summer camp in Mission Hill and quickly came to blows. The fight migrated around the project and ended with Jason and Tony trading punches on top of a car. After that, they weren't friends or enemies, but acquaintances who enjoyed each other's mutual respect.

Tony Lee also happened to be on the Charlestown basketball team, one of the many hardened guys who by and large had accepted the law laid down by its intense, overbearing, nagging, but devoted coach. As a freshman, Tony had clashed with O'Brien, and after bringing a knife to school, he almost ended his Charlestown hoops career before it began. But after some intense lobbying from his assistant coaches, O'Brien had given him a second chance.

When Jason joined the team, he looked around in wonder at how O'Brien had managed to hold sway over these guys. One of the biggest and toughest was Alray Taylor, whose 6-foot–3, 220-pound frame gave him the nickname "Horse," but whose gentle ways inspired the cafeteria ladies to slide him extra desserts. It was Alray who, seeing Jason trying to look tough through squinted eyes, the hood of his black sweatshirt pulled over his head, first named him "Hood." The nickname stuck. Jason became Hood.

Hood quickly determined that there were two Coach O'Briens. Off the court, the man was usually soft-spoken and helpful, if always relentless. But on the court, he was a monster, throwing balls, making the guys get on the line to run sprints for the slightest infraction or when someone tried to challenge him or correct something he said. Hood would think to himself, *Man, he hate to be wrong.*

Hood listened to O'Brien just enough so he could remain on the team and play, but no more. O'Brien obviously saw something in him, calling him up to the varsity team from the junior varsity squad during his freshman year. But all the coach's talk about the importance of getting good grades, like Willie's lectures of the past, went in one ear and out the other.

For two years, Hood recoiled from O'Brien's intense scrutiny and rigid standards. Then there were the coach's phone conversations— monologues, really—that never seemed to end. But toward the end of his sophomore year, he began to change. He started doing better in his classes and found that he liked how that felt. And he noticed how the older guys on the team were not afraid to cut their own path—how Tony Lee would eat by himself in the cafeteria rather than surround himself with the thugs from his neighborhood.

During Hood's sophomore year, Willie Barnes began working to build a real relationship with his son, using basketball as the base. The two had the same piercing eyes and both wore their hair in tight braids. Willie had been drug-free for a few years. He'd become evangelical about Narcotics Anonymous, and had gotten a steady construction job. Speaking the language of recovery, he moved back in with the family and began faithfully attending every one of his son's games. He'd post the Charlestown schedule on the window of the truck he drove for his job, making it clear to everyone which days he would need to leave early for a four o'clock game.

Most of the other Charlestown players' fathers were absent from their son's lives, so Willie immediately stood out. He usually arrived with a Canon T70 slung over his shoulder, snapping action shots of Hood and all his teammates. He had a gregarious way of connecting with the strangers next to him in the bleachers. And although he often came in beat-up work clothes, he sometimes arrived dressed for a night out, wearing sharp leather suits in shades of red and tan and square-toed leather shoes. Eventually he began having red rally T-shirts printed up, with "Charlestown" on the front, and Hood's number 3 on the back. He'd wear his and give others to anyone who asked for one.

The other Charlestown players would smile and greet him with a, "Hey, Mr. Hood." Hood himself was wary. Willie had blown in and out of his life too many times before. He'd seen some of his teammates' fathers come back into their sons' lives only long enough to soak up the glory associated with a winning team. He wanted to make sure Willie was in it for the long haul.

As Hood's high school years wore on, Willie's commitment became clearer. At games, Hood would scan the stands and often see that he was the only player whose father was there. Though Hood almost never showed warmth in public, he knew he was lucky to have his father back in his life. He began to listen more when Willie offered him advice on everything from what to wear to why it didn't cost him anything to smile at strangers.

O'Brien could see positive changes in Hood, and he encouraged him to rebuild that relationship with Willie. Willie Barnes reciprocated, encouraging Hood's deepening connection with O'Brien. He knew the coach had his son's best interests in mind. When O'Brien would scream at Hood on the court, Willie would smile and tell others around him in the stands, "After the game, there's a whole lotta love. But during the game," and then he would break out into a deep-bellied laugh.

•   •   •

A S'THE CHARLESTOWN BASKETBALL program became more embedded in Hood's life, it changed the kind of company he kept. Instead of hanging with the Academy kids he traveled with during middle school, he began spending more time off the court with his Charlestown teammates, especially Tony Lee.

Still, there was a permanence to Boston's housing project turf lines. Even though he was no longer living in Academy while it was being rebuilt, Hood had to continue to steer clear of the territory held by rival housing-project gangs, which extended beyond just the grim apartment buildings of their project to include the local subway station and bus stops and commercial districts. Once an Academy kid, always an Academy kid. Not that he tried to hide his affiliation. Hood often wore baseball hats that carried the "A" associated with Academy. For him, anything less would have been disloyal and could be dangerous, because free agents could be particularly vulnerable. Kids crisscrossed the city every day on subway and bus lines to get to one high school or another, but people still managed to sniff out who came from where, who was an ally and who was an enemy. Stabbings and shootings sometimes sprang from nothing more than a kid providing the wrong response to the question, "Where you from?"

Much of that madness disappeared during the second half of the 1990s, when the city became a national model for reducing gang violence. The key was something called Operation Ceasefire, a coming together of the many layers of local, state, and federal law enforcement, as well as black clergy and youth outreach workers. Together, they identified the most violent offenders. Together, they showed gang members how a crime committed by one of their members would bring down the combined Ceasefire apparatus on the entire gang. There was credible follow-through behind the tough talk. They literally presented slideshows, documenting how whole slates of other gangs had been put away on a variety of federal charges. The approach was stunningly successful. From 1996 to 1997, Boston's homicide rate was cut in half—by two-thirds for victims under age twenty-five. Not long after that, it became known as the "Boston Miracle."

It may have been too successful. As the miracle drew national media attention, many of the cops and ministers behind it were called to the White House, to Congress, and to other cities to share their secrets. The fact that some people got a lot more credit than others strained the program's remarkable interagency cooperation and drained it of its singular focus. During the years the Miracle dog-and-pony show continued its national tour, the streets of Boston slipped back to their treacherous ways. Murders and shootings spiked, the vast majority of them unsolved. In one year, Boston Police failed to even identify a suspect in more than two-thirds of the city's homicides, and an appalling 96 percent of its nonfatal shootings.

As a tribute to his two cousins who'd been slain and other friends lost to gang violence, Hood began writing "Tha Sqad" in marker on the sides of his basketball high-tops. He found the best way to stay out of the line of fire was to stay indoors. After practice, he would come home, eat some supper, and drink as much soda as the refrigerator could supply. His girlfriend would come over and they'd talk while she braided his hair.

LaTia "Tia" Martin had met Hood during their freshman year at Charlestown, when they were assigned to the same homeroom. She thought he was conceited. While others avoided the apparently angry young athlete, Tia preferred to make fun of him. Hood probably never expected that from her, but he was amused. Tia had grown up in a subsidized apartment in Columbia Point, a mixed-income housing development near the John F. Kennedy Presidential Library on Dorchester's waterfront, and her half-brother had played for O'Brien a few years earlier. As the school year progressed, so did the relationship between Tia and Hood. During the summer, things turned romantic.

As Hood's popularity rose in direct relation to his increased role as a star tailback on the football team and starting guard on the basketball squad, some of Charlestown's A-list girls—who had shapelier figures and better dating resumes than Tia—questioned why he stayed with her. But Hood paid little attention to that. He and Tia were real. On nights when she didn't come over to his house, they'd stay on the phone until they both fell asleep. Neither of them wanted to be the one to hang up first.

During her junior year, Tia was hanging out at Hood's house just about every day. When he wasn't there, she would sit with his mother. In February of that year, Pearl had to go into the hospital for a procedure. She didn't say much about it, so Hood figured it was minor, but when he and Tia went to visit her that night, they found Pearl with tubes going in and out of her body. Worry washed over Hood. He slumped down in a chair and pulled the brim of his hat down over his eyes, but Tia could see tears sliding down his cheek. Pearl had been under heavy sedation during surgery, and as Hood, Tia, and Hood's brother sat across from her, they saw her drifting in and out of consciousness. When she was lucid, she down-played the surgery she had just gone through. But what really gave Hood a scare was what his mother told him on his way out the door.

"I love you," she said. Her love for him had always gone without saying. Pearl wasn't the type to put words to it. He knew he didn't have the whole story. Back at home, he told Tia, "There's something my mother isn't telling me."

Hood had missed it when his mother mentioned the reason for her surgery. Pearl had said it quickly so as not to alarm her son. In-stead, she lingered on the more optimistic point that her doctors felt they had caught things in time. "She said she had lung cancer," Tia explained. The surgeons had removed cancerous tissue.

Hood didn't believe it. He called his brother to ask him if he had heard their mother say it.

Listening to his brother, Hood let the phone drop from his ear and began to sob.

Later that night, when his coach called to check in on him, Hood was crying so much that O'Brien could barely tell what he was saying. Hood would eventually make the painful experience the focus of his college-application essay. "It made me realize how much I love her," he wrote. "She means the world to me, and I hate that it took me so long to realize it."

• • •

A FEW WEEKS AFTER HIS VISIT TO ENDICOTT COLLEGE, Hood sat with his mother in their living room. Pearl held the phone up to her ear while Hood watched Meredith Vieira ask contestants questions on *Who Wants to Be a Millionaire.* Pearl had her own question, which she posed to Willie, who was on the other end of the line.

"Jason's here waiting for you to come home so he can drive to Charlestown. Where you at?" Everyone on the basketball team may have called her son Hood, but she sure wasn't about to.

Willie made a suggestion that Pearl quickly shot down. "You know I ain't going to give that boy my car. No, I need my car!" There was a pause. "He's right here," she said, handing the phone over. "Jason, it's your daddy here."

Hood sat expressionless as he listened to his father talk, occasionally offering up one of his drawn-out *ye-ah*'s. As Hood entered his make-or-break senior year, which would determine whether he got a college scholarship and rose above the bleak neighborhood that kept so many good kids down, Willie had made a decision. He didn't want to see his son blow his big chance because he accidentally crossed some stupid, gang-imposed turf line while taking the subway to school. "Just to become twenty-one around here today is a real blessing," Willie would say. So he gave Hood the keys to his car, a twelve-year-old Mitsubishi Diamante. Still, it was Willie's car—his sweat as a construction worker paid for it, not his son's. They would share it—on Willie's terms.

As soon as Willie came bounding in, Hood grabbed the keys and hopped in the gray sedan. As he pulled out of the parking lot, he passed a couple of people unloading a U-Haul. Residents were still moving into New Academy Estates, marveling at how spiffy the attached brick-and-clapboard townhouses looked, with their sloping roofs and bay windows and tiny front and back yards. What a difference from the old godforsaken project. And the changes ran deeper than just appearance. In addition to pumping nearly $60 million into the project, HUD had managed to turn the complex over to tenant ownership. The tenant board brought in a private security firm and worked with housing and law enforcement officials to "broom out" the former residents who had lengthy criminal records. It truly would be a fresh start.

Well, almost. Despite the extermination treatments that had taken place before the new buildings went up, residents found that plenty of the rodents soon returned. Like many residents, Gloria Bowers, the tenant board president, took matters into her own hands. She got a cat. The management company that the tenant board hired to run the complex specified "no pets" on the lease. Bowers told them, "When you get rid of the mice, I'll get rid of the cat."

Yet cats were of no help in stopping the other old problem that had resurfaced. Even though most of the thugs with lengthy rap sheets had been broomed out, many of them quickly made the new complex their preferred hangout space. The familiar, menacing faces were back, in packs.

2

—

RIDLEY

CHARLESTOWN HIGH SCHOOL SAT NEAR THE WATER on the northern edge of Boston's northernmost neighborhood. Charlestown itself sat on a peninsula between two rivers leading to the Atlantic Ocean. The high school, an example of the boxy, graceless architecture that gained traction in the 1970s, was actually two hulking brick structures. On one side of Medford Street was the five-story school; on the other side, the gym and pool. The school's 1,200 students used an enclosed walkway high above the street to travel between the two structures.

After the final period had ended on a day when the new school year was one month old, Ridley Johnson made his way through the second floor of the main building, glided across the enclosed walkway, descended a flight of stairs, and arrived in the dimly lit lobby outside the gym. There was a wall of glass at one end of the lobby, providing views of the swimming pool one story below. No matter how much time Ridley and his basketball teammates spent in this building, they never showed any interest in looking in on the pool. The senior co-captain took a right and headed straight for the royal-blue doors with the block letters spelling GYM sideways.

The gym was big and bright, especially in contrast to the dark lobby. Sunlight found its way in through the skylights sandwiched into the ceiling, between heating ducts the size of water-park slides, and through a bank of windows near the top of the tiled back wall. When the blonde-wood bleachers were pulled out on both sides of the court, the place could seat 800 people. In addition to the main glass basketball hoops on either end of the court, there were two pairs of white wooden backboards facing each other from the sidelines, for use in practice and gym class. An electronic scoreboard hung on the red front wall, just to the left of the royal-blue doors. Painted onto the floorboards at center court was a picture of the Bunker Hill Monument. The 221-foot granite obelisk, which stood a few blocks from the school, dominated Charlestown's skyline, commemorating the American Revolution blood-bath that for centuries had defined Charlestown's identity of defiance in the face of long odds. Below the picture was the word "Townies," which was the team's official name, though none of the players ever used it.

At one time, the Charlestown gym must have looked sleek. But the years had taken their toll. The windows were clouded with grime, the bleachers decorated with graffiti. The red wall paint was faded, and the tiles on the far wall were gray enough to make you wonder if they had ever been white. Several swaths of plaster were gone, leaving only exposed insulation. Gone too were the doors to the stalls in the nearby boys' bathroom.

None of that mattered to Ridley. All he had to do was glance over at the four rectangular banners hanging on the tiled back wall. The white letters on the red fabric said it all. *Charlestown High School Boys Basketball: State Champions.* The banners celebrated not just victory, but dominance. For four seasons, the string was unbroken: 1999–2000, 2000–2001, 2001–2002, 2002–2003. Ridley, who had been called up to the varsity squad during his freshman year, was proud to have been part of two of those title-grabbing squads. Yet, for him, the fact that there wasn't a state-championship banner from 2003–2004 still stung. The fact that people in basketball circles were predicting there wouldn't be one at the end of the up-coming season either—when Ridley and Hood would be in charge—stung even more.

There would be plenty of time in the coming months to worry about proving everyone wrong. Today, Ridley had more immediate pressures to deal with. He headed for the bleachers, where he un-hooked his belt and let his jeans drop to the floor. He and his team-mates always went to school wearing basketball shorts under their pants, so they wouldn't have to bother changing in the locker room. Ridley, who had a faint goatee, boasted a stunning vertical leap that on the court made him seem half-a-foot taller than his 6-foot–3 frame.

Yet in other ways, he seemed young for his age. He wouldn't turn eighteen for another two months. When he took off his shirt to change into his basketball jersey, he revealed a chest so devoid of definition that it might have belonged to a twelve-year-old boy. It was a reminder that for all the athleticism coursing through com-petitive high school leagues, there was a reason it was still called *boys* basketball. Even Hood—who was a full calendar year older than Ridley, had much more developed biceps, and seemed forever in search of the pose that would make him appear meaner and more mature—even he had a boy's chest.

Ridley sat on the edge of the bleachers and laced up his white Nike Jordans with the red soles. "I'm nervous," he told a kid sitting next to him. "One mistake, man. . . "

He watched as they arrived. One by one, a dozen coaches in polo shirts strode over the Bunker Hill Monument painted onto the floorboards and settled into the bleachers to the right of the cham-pionship banners. They'd come from as near as Northeastern Uni-versity, just a short subway ride away, and as far as the University of Toledo, near the banks of Lake Erie some 800 miles away. A good showing, but Toledo's Stan Joplin was the only head coach in the bunch. Ridley spotted O'Brien and could tell his coach was not pleased. Head coaches make the final recruiting decisions; O'Brien had wanted more of them present.

O'Brien had arranged this "open gym" showcase, where the Charlestown players would run through drills and light play as college coaches with notepads looked on. To avoid running afoul of high school league rules prohibiting off-season practices, O'Brien had to hand his whistle over to someone else and stay outside. He also had to make it a truly open gym, allowing in any interested student, even special needs kids who had no shot of playing high school basketball, never mind scoring a college scholarship. They lined up for the drills right behind O'Brien's varsity starters. No matter. The college coaches all had their eyes fixed on Ridley.

It was Ridley's graceful jump shot, combined with his vertical leap, that put him on the radar of college recruiters. But he had more than his game going for him. A steady if unexceptional student, he was in the best academic shape on the team. O'Brien had spent the last weeks of summer rearranging his and the other players' course schedules. When O'Brien ran down his schedule for him, Ridley protested when he heard he'd been signed up for a fourth year of science.

"You only need three," Ridley complained.

O'Brien cut him off. "That's just the requirement to graduate. Colleges want to see more than that."

In a chaotic urban high school, good grades were often less about command of a subject matter than rewards handed out to students who showed up and didn't cause trouble. Ridley was clearly one of the guys, and he liked to joke around. But there was something about his easy disposition that managed to endear him to even the most hardened, battle-weary teachers. They all seemed to reach for the same words to describe him. "That Ridley," they would say, "he's the nicest kid."

He hadn't posted a great basketball season last year. O'Brien celebrated his friendly ways off the court but kept repeating that he had to get a lot meaner on it. No basketball player ever got ahead by being polite under the boards. Yet ever since Ridley had excelled at a couple of invitational tournaments in the off-season, his cell phone had been ringing with college scouts telling him they liked his game and asking him what he wanted to major in.

His dream school had always been Boston College, which was the closest thing Boston had to NCAA royalty. The thicket of coaches in the Charlestown bleachers included a BC assistant named Pat Duquette. But his appearance indicated courtesy rather than strong interest. Duquette confirmed that, far from getting a hometown advantage, Ridley would be judged more carefully than a player of similar talent from another part of the country. "We pay special attention to a local player, and are *very* careful to make sure they are the right fit," he said. "We don't want to have a local player who will end up sitting on the bench, so it's a different pressure."

It's an open secret in college basketball circles just how easy it is to get rid of a recruit who doesn't work out. With a lot of neglect and precious little playing time, the kid will likely be gone by the end of the season—quitting in a huff or bombing out academically. Either way, that would open up his scholarship slot for a new recruit who might have a bigger upside. But leaving a well-known local kid to languish on the bench would embarrass the team as well as the player.

The NCAA assigns college basketball programs to one of three divisions, based primarily on the resources devoted to their athletic program. Division I teams, like BC's, tend to be well funded, with lots of athletic scholarships covering the full cost of tuition, room and board, and other resources for players, such as tutors and first-rate travel accommodations. Division III colleges offer no athletic scholarships, though at many of them, athletic talent is the ticket in, and then financial aid can take over from there.

Division II programs occupy the space in between, usually providing some full scholarships and some partial ones, and travel accommodations that tend to be more Red Roof Inn than Hyatt Regency. Even within those categories, though, there's lots of variation.

But to the kids who grew up on the courts of any big city in America, nursing their hoop dreams, D-I is the only one that counts. Only Division I teams have a shot at being invited to the Big Dance, the NCAA tournament whose games are broadcast on network television during "March Madness" and become the preoccupation of office-pool bettors everywhere. Never mind that most low- and mid-D-I teams have as good a chance of scoring one of the sixty-five coveted invitations to the Big Dance as an average schmo does showing up at the box office to buy Super Bowl tickets. The point is, at least they have a shot, and every year there's usually one Cinderella arrival from Gonzaga or George Mason or some other basketball program no one has ever heard of, going toe-to-toe with a powerhouse like Indiana or Kentucky.

Of the handful of seniors on the Charlestown team, only Ridley was a D-I prospect. But given BC's perch in the upper reaches of D-I, the school seemed out of Ridley's grasp, especially in early fall, when most programs were still chasing their dream players. Standing beside the bleachers, C. J. Neely, an assistant with Division II Stonehill College, a small Catholic school located half an hour away, watched as the star of the day tossed up beautiful jumpers. "We'd love to get Ridley," Neely said, "but I think he'll go higher." As for Hood and Spot, the other players O'Brien was hoping to help snag scholarships, Neely wasn't impressed.

Although many of the assistant coaches were content to hang toward the back of the bleachers, Toledo's Stan Joplin made sure he got the best view of Ridley, sitting right near the baseline. He'd gotten lost trying to navigate his rental car through the confusing side streets of Boston, doing battle with the city's infamously gnarled traffic and unforgiving drivers, an experience that stretched a fifteen-minute drive into more than an hour. After watching Ridley, he would be hopping in the car and heading back to the airport. He was dreading the return journey. Ridley had better be worth it. Joplin had made the trip at the urging of one of his assistants, who had coached Ridley a few months earlier at the Eastern Invitational Tournament in New Jersey. That tourney was one of the biggest meat markets of the summer, bringing together high school athletes looking for their big break and college coaches looking for choice cuts to help them keep their jobs.

For the first time in a long while, Joplin's mind was also on keeping his own job. He'd been a star during his own playing days at the University of Toledo, leading the team to the Sweet 16 round of the NCAA Tournament in 1979, the best performance in school history. But the team's postseason record during his eight years as head coach had been less impressive. He was feeling the heat, and knew he had very little margin of error for his next class of freshman recruits.

After the drills were done, the Charlestown players took turns using a Gatorade towel to wipe the sweat from their faces. Then they pulled their jeans back up over their shorts and walked across the court to shake hands with each of the coaches before leaving the gym. After years of prodding from O'Brien, the players automatically said goodbye to strangers with a handshake—even those strangers who held no power to determine their college futures. The handshakes with strangers were always brief and usually wordless, unlike the elaborate hand and body gestures the guys would use when they "dapped up" each other. But they were handshakes nonetheless.

Afterward, Joplin found O'Brien. "I'm not disappointed," he said.

• • •

ONE MONTH LATER, AT 5:50 AM, Ridley rolled out of bed. His room was near the front entrance of a first-floor apartment in a three-decker with gray, peeling paint. He and his mother shared the place with the people she took in that no one else would. At this point, the roster included a pair of young brothers who were her godchildren and a former neighbor in his seventies who could no longer afford his rent and now slept on their living room couch.

Ridley shuffled down the hall to the bathroom, past the dining room that his mom decorated by hanging twenty-four framed plaques her boy had collected over the years, from basketball awards to perfect-attendance certificates. He returned a couple of minutes later, grabbed the Right Guard, chose a pair of Jordans from the stack of a dozen Nike boxes near his bed, and pulled up his jeans. He showered at night to make the mornings less brutal.

By 6 AM, he was outside with his black hood over his head. He walked fifteen minutes in the dark along the side streets of Dorchester to catch the 21 bus on Blue Hill Avenue, which would take him to the Orange Line subway stop at Forest Hills, which would take him to the 93 bus in Sullivan Square, which would, if everything went well, deposit him a block from Charlestown High, nearly an hour and twenty minutes after his commute began.

Just an ordinary weekday, but this one was different. The night before, the Boston Red Sox, who had broken hearts for generations, had miraculously captured their first World Series in eighty-six years. The city would operate in dazed exhilaration for weeks, but Ridley was oblivious to all that. Like his teammates, he followed the NBA, not major league baseball, and his team loyalty was always based on individual players, not hometown geography. Something completely different was on Ridley's mind as he walked in the middle of a side street with one of the boys who was crashing at his house.

During the weekend, he had made an official recruiting visit to the University of Toledo and he had liked what he saw of the com-

puter science program. (His Charlestown teammates all had Play-
Station 2 consoles in their bedrooms, but no computer. Ridley was
the opposite.) He liked the campus. But most of all he liked what
Stan Joplin and Toledo were offering: a full four-year Division I
scholarship worth well over $100,000.

There are two "signing periods" when the NCAA allows colleges
to get their recruits to commit, one in the fall and one in the
spring. O'Brien usually advised his players entertaining high-level
offers to sign early and settle their heads. But with Ridley, he
wasn't certain. He didn't know much about the Toledo program. BC
was noncommittal. And the other Division I school showing the
most interest, Robert Morris University outside Pittsburgh, already
had three of O'Brien's former stars competing for playing time. So
he recommended that Ridley wait until the spring to see what
opened up.

Ridley, though, was nervous. What if he got injured? What if he
had another lackluster season? A few days after returning to
Boston, he called Toledo and told them he would sign. "I knew that
scholarship would go to someone else if I waited," he said as he
crossed Blue Hill Avenue, "and I didn't want that to happen."

By the time the 93 bus exited Sullivan Square, the morning light
had risen behind the Schrafft's candy factory, which, after the Bunker Hill Monument, was the most familiar fixture on the Charlestown skyline. For decades, Schrafft's, with its Willy Wonka-like
clock tower, had been a pillar of the town's bustling industrial corridor along the Mystic River. Now it provided vanilla office space
for generic small companies. The bus stopped in front of a Spanish
variety store a block from Charlestown High. Dozens of kids
shoved their way off and piled into the cramped market. Ridley
bought his regular breakfast, an empanada meat patty and a 20-
ounce bottle of Mountain Dew, and then made his way to school.

From the Spanish store, Ridley could walk down either Elm
Street or Polk Street to get to the high school. Elm Street brought

him by restored row houses that had gone condo, with flower boxes under the windows and Saabs in the sloped driveways. This was the typical housing stock of contemporary Charlestown now that white yuppies had largely replaced the white working class. Polk Street brought him along the edge of the Bunker Hill housing development, Boston's largest project, where almost all of Charlestown's black and Hispanic residents lived. The kids in school called the project "the bricks" because its 1,100 grim units were spread across a host of flat-roofed brick buildings. Some of the kids who lived in the bricks went to Charlestown High, but many others traveled to some other part of the city. Pretty much none of the kids who lived in the restored row houses went to Charlestown High.

Ridley took Elm Street. Once inside the school, he climbed the stairs to get to the cafeteria, where, as usual, O'Brien and his assistants were waiting for him. All the players were expected to check in with the coaching staff in the morning before heading to their first class. Ridley shook hands with O'Brien and dapped up assistant coach Hugh Coleman, an exuberant twenty-six-year-old former Charlestown star who had graduated from Bowdoin College, married Ridley's favorite aunt, and then returned to teach at his alma mater.

Ridley hustled through the crowded stairwell to get to his Forensic Science class on the third floor. He was a few minutes late, but plenty of other kids, including Hood, filed in after him. The class was designed to convert the popularity of shows like *CSI* into interest in science. Ridley never watched *CSI*, but he liked the class because it was a lot easier to take first thing in the morning than English or Pre-Calculus. His teacher, a stocky forty-year-old with a goofy laugh, knew how to keep the kids' interest. The makeup of the class mirrored that of the overall school: about half black, and the rest split between Hispanics and Asians, with a white kid here and there.

A chatty Hispanic girl named Janice sat across from Ridley, complaining about her Spanish class. She said it was a waste of time because she knew more of the language than her teacher.

"I know, me too," Ridley said.

Janice raised one eyebrow, and then her voice. "You? You Spanish?"

"Yep," Ridley said. "Both my mother and father."

"What kind?"

"Honduran."

Janice wasn't buying it. Like a jeweler using a loupe to find inclusions in a precious stone, she trained her eyes on Ridley's complexion, just a shade lighter than their black slate lab table. Then she pointed to a fair-skinned Hispanic boy at the next table. "He's Honduran, Ridley. You black!"

Ridley knew he didn't fit neatly into any of those race circles they ask you to fill out with a number 2 pencil. Whenever he had to choose one, he chose black, because that part was obvious. His mother would probably have chosen Hispanic, but that's because she still spoke a lot of Spanish. Ridley wasn't a fluent Spanish speaker, but he understood a great deal. Still, the only time he really felt his Latin roots was when he was eating his mother's food.

In English class, his teacher was out, so Ridley spent the period playing Connect Four. The pace was slow in Pre-Calculus class as well. The teacher was an older woman with long white-blonde hair and glasses that seemed to rest permanently on the end of her nose. Even if the subject matter was brutally dull, all the basketball players loved Ms. Raimondi because Ms. Raimondi loved all the basketball players. In a school where faculty members were usually no-shows at the basketball games, Diane Raimondi came to many games and even brought along her own homemade cheering signs. A weary veteran of the Boston schools, Raimondi taught in an old-school manner that contrasted sharply with the newfangled approaches favored by the recent Ivy League grads who had been invading the Charlestown teaching ranks. But O'Brien liked putting his players in her classes because Raimondi had realistic expectations about what they could handle.

Ridley dreaded fourth period the most because it was the slowest of all. That's when he should have been in gym class. But O'Brien, one of two phys ed teachers at the school, had persuaded the headmaster to let his players skip gym in favor of a study hall that O'Brien monitored with ferocious scrutiny. Shortly after arriving at Charlestown, O'Brien instituted a mandatory after-school study hall that was held every day during basketball season. But over the years he noticed his players' biggest academic troubles usually occurred out of season, when he had the least control over their lives. This additional study hall—held during the day, all year long—was his way of extending control. Sitting at the front of the room, wearing one of his warm-up suits, O'Brien insisted on monastic silence. As Ridley did his homework, he plotted in his head when he would take his bathroom break to best keep the boredom at bay.

O'Brien wasn't some jock coach trying to line up gut classes for his stars. He often pushed his guys to stretch, as long as he was sure the teacher would work with them, giving them extra help and making sure they never failed. This year O'Brien had put Ridley in an Advanced Placement U.S. History class, which was a gamble. He knew colleges reward ambition but penalize failure. The class was like nothing else in Ridley's day. In pace, substance, even the look of the classroom, it was like being transported to a competitive school in some affluent suburb.

There were two young, demanding teachers for fourteen students. The classroom was vibrant. The walls were decorated with bumper stickers that read "I think, therefore I'm dangerous" and blown-up quotes from the likes of Malcolm X. There were flip charts and study guides and color-coded assignment sheets and handouts of writings by left-wing historian Howard Zinn. There was even a very verbal white girl with purple hair who repeatedly spoke in affected sentences that always seemed to begin with the word "distinctly."

The lead teacher was a young woman named Amy Piacitelli who wore an extra-long denim skirt and kept a pen hanging on a string around her neck. As she began her lesson on the Whig Party, Ridley took out a piece of loose-leaf notebook paper and wrote "Chapter 14" in block letters at the top. He tried to keep up, turning repeatedly to the black girl sitting next to him. Menda François had her hand up almost from the moment she walked into class, confidently fielding the teachers' questions about nineteenth-century politics. She was smart and talkative and serious, a girl in a hurry. Back when she was a freshman, Menda had treated school like a joke, ending the year with a D+ average and an abysmal attendance record. Not long after that, she heard about a college awareness program in Vermont and applied, but her low grade point average sank her application. That rejection turned out to be all the motivation she needed to transform herself into a straight-A student by her sophomore year. She had remained a high flier ever since.

The class was the closest thing Ridley had to a true college prep experience. If everything went right, it would give him vital skills for next year. But first he had to get through it. By October, his average in the class hovered around a D-minus.

With basketball season still a month away, Ridley didn't have after-school study hall or practice yet. Instead, when the final bell rang, he headed for the weight room, trying to add some muscle to his upper body on his march to get meaner on the court. After the workout, he and Spot hung out in the lobby outside the gym. There, they were met by a dodgy guy named Jermaine, who looked to be in his early thirties. He herded the two high school seniors into his car so they could play for a team he coached in a men's league. It didn't matter that Ridley and Spot weren't exactly men yet. The important point was they were shooters.

As he walked out of the gym, Ridley was stopped by two different girls, each wanting to hug him. Around the school, it was obvious that more and more girls were trying to catch Ridley's rising
star. As the guys drove off in Jermaine's tan luxury sedan with
leather seats and rap blasting on the stereo, they passed a girl
walking alone up the street between the high school and the housing project. Spot rolled down the window and flashed his Hollywood smile. "I love you, baby!" he said, holding his hand up to his
ear. "I'll call you tonight."

Ridley asked Jermaine what restaurant he would be taking them
to after the game.

Jermaine turned down the stereo. "If you niggas don't win, there
ain't gonna be no food." Then he turned the volume way up and
pushed his foot down hard on the accelerator.

$$\bullet \quad \bullet \quad \bullet$$

IN EARLY NOVEMBER, a few dozen people walked into the small café
on the fifth floor of Charlestown High to witness Ridley's signing
ceremony. He would be officially committing himself to the University of Toledo. In truth, the signing was for show, like those giant
cardboard checks the Powerball people hand out for the benefit of
the TV cameras. All the details of Ridley's scholarship had already
been worked out behind the scenes. But O'Brien wanted to give
Ridley a chance to bask in the limelight and, more important, give
his younger players something to strive for. There was pizza and a
huge sheet cake with Ridley's picture on it.

"One of every 10,000 high school basketball players in this country receives a basketball scholarship," O'Brien, dressed in a red
Charlestown warm-up suit, told the gathering of players, teachers,
and Ridley's family. "One out of every 10,000." He had read that sta-
tistic somewhere, or at least he was pretty sure he had. No matter—

he knew no one in the crowd would challenge him on it. He simply wanted to drive home the point that Ridley's achievement was special and had taken lots of hard work.

For most of the players in the audience, who were as familiar with Toledo as they were with Tajikistan, O'Brien made sure to orient them in a language they would understand. "Toledo is in one of the top ten basketball conferences in the country," he said. "Turn on your TV on December 12, and you'll see them playing Duke on ESPN."

O'Brien unfurled a flurry of other figures for the crowd, some of them goosed a little to improve their motivational power: how Ridley's scholarship was worth $145,000 over the next four years; how Division I scholarship athletes needed a minimum combined SAT score of 820, whereas Ridley's was 960; how they needed to have completed fourteen core courses, whereas Ridley had twenty-two under his belt and was an honor roll student. "I hope you younger guys look at him and say, 'You know what, I hope to be in that position some day,'" O'Brien said. "Most of all, he's a real good person."

As the group applauded, Ridley, wearing square zirconia earrings and a gray Charlestown hoodie, walked up to the front of the room. O'Brien then said, "Ridley also brought his honey. Say hi to Rebecca." Wearing a cream-colored top and a black skirt, Rebecca Johnson stepped forward, a smile filling her heart-shaped face. "I'm Ridley's mom," she told the crowd, waving tentatively.

Back at the table, looking a little uneasy, sat a man with short hair, squarish on the top, and a closely cropped salt-and-pepper beard. Ridley's father, McClary Johnson, was dressed stylishly in jeans and loafers. Rebecca had met McClary on one of her trips home to Honduras after the death of her first husband, with whom she'd had a son and daughter. McClary followed her to the United States, where they married and then had Ridley. When Ridley was young, they separated, though the divorce hadn't gone through until last year. McClary lived with his own mother just a few miles away from Ridley, but as the years went by he had seen less and less of his son. That only endeared Ridley more to Rebecca. One evening, as she pointed to McClary across the room, Rebecca said, "My heart don't beat no more for him. Only for Ridley. He's my pride and joy."

As for the signing ceremony, Ridley didn't want to make too much of a fuss and asked his mother not to tell his father about it. "I won't," she had assured him.

Instead, she not only told him but brought him with her in her car. "I wanted McClary to hurt a little bit," she said later. "To see what he missed."

3

THE RULES OF THE ROAD

THE COACH'S SCREAMS WERE AS RAPID-FIRE as the bursts of his whistle. "Get *low!*" "We *don't* pass with one hand!" And finally, in an exasperated bark that exposed the richness of his Boston accent, O'Brien cried, "The sea-zun's STAHTIN!" That meant the nurturing O'Brien with the supportive nods was gone. In his place was the perpetually distressed O'Brien, standing courtside and scrunching his face so tightly that lines blanketed his forehead and shot out from the corner of his eyes. The season was half an hour old; already he was hoarse.

The Monday after Thanksgiving was the first day of the year that Massachusetts high school basketball teams were allowed to practice. Although the season was year-round for serious high school players, who participated in an alphabet soup of summer leagues, summer camps, invitational tournaments, and fall leagues—high school coaches weren't allowed to lead their squads in any organized fashion in the off-season, so O'Brien had to be careful to stay on the periphery before Thanksgiving. Somehow, he managed to remain a hovering presence even from there. Surrounded by shootings and drugs and dead-enders, the Charlestown players lived in

45

perpetual danger of getting pulled off track. Absent O'Brien's regimented schedules and continuous glare, the off-season could become perilous. So O'Brien took no chances. He spent most summer days with one kid or another, playing one-on-one at the YMCA or discussing a book he had assigned as summer reading. He began and ended each day with calls to as many of his guys as he could get to. On weekends in the fall, he sometimes made his calls long-distance, from the driver's seat of his minivan, as he drove all day—he was afraid to fly—to see his former players in faraway colleges.

But now that the season had officially begun, O'Brien abandoned the pretense of being anything but the dominant force in his players' daily lives. Standing at center court, he screamed over the squeaking sounds of sneakers on the gym floor. This first practice was technically the tryout period for the 2004–2005 team. But O'Brien would never leave that much to chance. With the exception of one or two slots, he'd known for months exactly who would be on his squad. Still, there was intense competition for those final slots. And as far as O'Brien was concerned, the veterans needed to be reminded about the fundamentals of Charlestown basketball as much as the newcomers. All the returning veterans were in the gym, with the exception of Hood, who had hurt his back at the end of the football season.

O'Brien pulled out a crumpled 3×5 index card from his pocket. It contained a detailed hand-written list of drills he would run that day. He'd been coaching for twenty years, but still he worried he wouldn't get things right if he didn't prepare harder this year than the last.

When he spied a couple of freshmen spectators in the bleachers trying to get the attention of one of the players, he went wild. "You talk, you're out!" he thundered, pointing to the exits. "We're teaching here!" The gym was a sacred space now. The freshmen had to watch the action from the lobby, peering through the small windows in the royal-blue gym doors.

As he ran through his battery of drills, with ribbons of players flowing on and off the court, he made a big deal of even minor mistakes. He was especially harsh if the slips were the result of showboating or sloth. His message was unmistakable: Wherever else you may have played before, Charlestown basketball was different. When a defender watched the ball sail through the hoop and drop to the floor before he retrieved it, O'Brien pounced. "The ball doesn't hit the floor when it goes in! You *grab* it!" Whenever he saw someone taking it easy, he shouted, "Everybody on the line." Suicide sprints would follow.

Despite all his shouting and his painfully serious expression, O'Brien was hardly the archetypal gruff high school coach. For one thing, he never referred to his players by their last name, preferring their first names or occasionally the nicknames they had given each other. Nearly everyone on the team had a nickname. Some, like Hood and Spot, were more memorable and widely used than others. A slim sophomore guard named Derrick Bowman was called "D-Black" or sometimes "Midnight," on account of his extremely dark complexion. A well-built Haitian sophomore named Phil Jean had a complexion that was just one shade lighter than Midnight's, so he was called "11:59."

In another departure from the archetype, O'Brien was willing to let himself look foolish. Across all the drills, he stressed defense above all else. "The way we play defense," he said, "is you never let an offensive player come to you. You go *at* him." Repeatedly, he demonstrated the Charlestown defensive position by crouching down close to the floor, arms low and out, and doing a crazy manic shuffle across the court. He knew he looked ridiculous, but he didn't care. That proper position was key to his team's smothering defense, which more than anything else was responsible for all those championship banners hanging on the wall.

All afternoon, O'Brien kept his eye on a shorter Jamaican kid running up and down the court. Ricardo "Robby" Robinson had a tattoo of a python with the words "Fear No One" on his left forearm, and one of a cross with his mother's name, Maud, on his right upper arm. Ridley was hoping O'Brien would put his friend Robby on the team. O'Brien was hesitant. Robby was clearly not an impact player and would log a lot of time on the bench. Coaches usually gave those benchwarmer slots to younger guys, as an investment in the future. But Robby was a senior. He had no future with Charlestown after this year. Still, O'Brien was moved by what Robby had endured off the court.

When Robby was three, his father was shot dead. When he was fifteen, his mother died of a brain tumor. He essentially lived on his own now—he could rattle off the costs of each of his monthly utility bills—and he had really begun pushing himself in school, hoping to honor his mother's memory by going to college. Even though all his guys came from difficult circumstances, O'Brien had found over the years that many of them had been babied by their mothers. Nobody babied Robby, that was for sure. O'Brien figured that Robby's mental toughness would be good for the team, even if he never scored a point.

● ● ●

TWO DAYS LATER, TWENTY-EIGHT GUYS—the new varsity and JV squads—sat in Room 319, a chemistry classroom that O'Brien used as his home away from the gym. The walls were covered with fundraising calendars, featuring photos of the basketball squads over the years. "This is the most important meeting we'll have all year," O'Brien said. "We're going to talk about how we're going to live for the next three months." He told them to report there, on time, after school each day for his mandatory hour-long study hall.

"Five bricks for every minute you're late, by *my* watch."

Even the freshmen had already heard about bricks. O'Brien's peculiar brand of punishment, they were worse than suicides. A player had to hold a brick in each hand and run between the hash marks on the gym floor. Sixteen sprints in one minute counted as one brick. If the player didn't make sixteen, he would have to start again.

As O'Brien looked out at the roomful of teenagers sitting behind student desks, one face was out of place. Harry Landry, a short, balding, sixty-something court clerk with a gray bushy mustache, sat at a desk near the back of the room, smiling as O'Brien rattled off the rules of the road.

O'Brien told the players the words he didn't want to hear—"me," "I," or any swearing—and those he did—"thank you," "please," "we." He knew he would be directing many of them to largely white colleges, and people there were inevitably going to talk about them. So let those people talk about their politeness. On this point, O'Brien led by example, always having a "How we doing—everything good?" for the custodians and bus drivers, and never swearing in front of his players. *Damn* and *hell* were the worst they ever heard come out of his mouth. He didn't need to curse to convey his wrath.

Then he told them that every player in the room was expendable. "There aren't too many kids here better than Lamar," he said, causing Spot to flash his smile, which faded as soon as he realized where his coach was headed. "He was a starter his sophomore year, on a team that won the state championship. I threw him off five games into the season."

Spot's offense? Causing trouble in class. O'Brien warned him, but when the teachers' complaints kept coming, he was gone.

O'Brien surveyed the faces in the room. "I guarantee it," he said, "somebody here is going to get thrown off this season." It was hardly an idle threat. Over the years, many guys who started with him didn't last. The room was weighted heavily toward sophomores and seniors, including an elated Robby, who had been given the last spot on the roster. There were only two returning juniors, even though that pair had been part of a pack of seven when they joined the team as freshmen. The other five members of that class had slipped out of O'Brien's grip. One had gotten involved with a girl from Columbia Point, and a couple of the gang members there began threatening him so much that he fled Boston and moved in with a relative out of state. Two others tired of O'Brien's tight leash and transferred to other schools, but soon got involved in street life. As supportive as O'Brien was, once the players were gone, they were gone. Investing more time in guys who refused to commit was like drawing pictures on water. He had no time for it. Being part of the Charlestown program was no guarantee that a kid would become a success. But dropping out of the program dramatically increased the odds that he wouldn't.

Every November, O'Brien used the meeting to hammer the notion that his players needed to follow the example of the Charlestown guys who'd gone before them. Those previous players had surmounted the same seemingly impossible hurdles. To make sure the message got through, each year he dwelt on the example of a recent grad he was sure even his newest players would know. This year he fixed the spotlight on Tony Lee, Hood's best friend and captain of last year's squad. "Tony turned his life around, right here at Charlestown," O'Brien said, looking directly at Hood. "He broke with his troublemaker friends. Talk about guts. He knew he wanted a better life. And look where it got him." Tony was one of the three former Charlestown players on scholarship at Division I Robert Morris University.

O'Brien pulled out a large poster-board chart. All season long, he would reward players with gold stars for achievements that never made the headlines, like having perfect attendance in school and practice (three stars), committing no turnovers in a game (one star), and making the honor roll (five stars). He explained that the winner at the end of the season would receive a large basketball clock and an unrestricted license to gloat.

"Who won last year?" one of the freshman asked.

"Tony Lee," said a sophomore.

"Yeah," piped up another. "He won like three years in a row."

O'Brien turned things over to his assistant coaches. The three assistants were nearly perfect complements to one another, and O'Brien relied on each one for specific skills.

Steve Cassidy was a thirty-year-old history teacher with a round, serious face. He wore his brown hair parted to the side and had a preference for khakis and Oxfords. O'Brien turned to him for sharp basketball strategy and sound academic guidance. Unlike the other two assistants, he'd never played for O'Brien. He'd earned his bachelor's degree from Fordham University and a master's degree from Boston College and was taking more courses so he'd be qualified to become a principal. The players were on a first-name basis with the other assistant coaches, but Cassidy they called strictly by his last name.

Cassidy reinforced O'Brien's message with a story of how, a few weeks earlier, he went to a wedding in Pennsylvania and afterward drove to Robert Morris to see Tony Lee. He found him flourishing in his new environment, a world away from the streets of Mission Hill. "He was playing lacrosse with some white guy from Australia on the quad," Cassidy recalled, smiling. "Some of your friends may be just getting by in their grades. If you want to get out of here, you have to overachieve."

At twenty-six, Hugh Coleman was the youngest coach. He was in his first year teaching at his alma mater and still new to coaching, but he brought other talents to the bench. An inspirational speaker brimming with optimism, Hugh was the only black on the coaching staff, and the only one who had beaten the same long odds of the inner city that the players in the room now faced. "When I was a freshman at Charlestown, I was the last one picked for the JV team," he said, flashing a wide, toothy grin that filled the lower third of his narrow face. "I learned how to work at it, become a better person. Once you do that, the basketball will take care of itself."

Finally came Zach Zegarowski. He'd been with O'Brien the longest. He'd played for him in the late 1980s—before O'Brien made his way to Boston—and had been with him on the Charlestown bench for nearly a decade. Like O'Brien, Zach was a gym teacher at Charlestown High. The pair spent so much time together that they often finished each other's sentences. O'Brien leaned on the wiry thirty-three-year-old for his high-octane intensity and his emotional intelligence in reading and motivating the players.

Bounding to the front of the room, Zach directed his comments to the uninitiated. "If I were one of you freshmen, I would look at Ridley," Zach said. "Forget about LeBron James! He's not in your life. Ridley is right there. On top of being a great basketball player, he's one of the nicest kids in school. Never missed a day of school in four years, isn't that right, Rid?"

In a school where it was seen as cool to skip the first day of classes, and many others as the year wore on, the freshmen seemed incredulous, and turned to look for confirmation in Ridley's face.

Ridley nodded, without emotion.

Then Zach pulled out a laminated newspaper article. Under the headline "Townie Angel Dies," the article had appeared in the *Boston Herald* the day after Richard Jones dropped dead on his college court in Buffalo, from an enlarged heart. "He was a beautiful person," Zach said, pacing. "If you think I'm going to take one *day* for granted, you're in the wrong place."

O'Brien stepped forward again, and for the benefit of the younger players, talked about what the memory of Richard and Paris Booker meant to the program. Then he gave all the players the same message he'd given Hood and Ridley at the cemetery three months earlier: "Those guys would do anything to change places with you."

As devastating as those deaths were to O'Brien, he knew things could be a lot worse. In a dozen years of coaching kids from Boston's toughest neighborhoods, he'd never seen a player under his supervision murdered or incarcerated or, to the best of his knowledge, father a baby out of wedlock. Not that there weren't some close calls.

Halfway through the rules-of-the-road meeting, a chiseled 6-foot-4 sophomore with high cheekbones walked in. Terry Carter wore a brown-and-tan leather jacket. Instead of calculating his tardiness penalty in bricks, O'Brien smiled and extended Terry his hand. He then watched as the boy walked to the back of the room and sat beside Landry, the bald guy with the bushy mustache. O'Brien knew Terry had a good excuse, and that's why he had let Landry sit in on the team meeting. Terry had just been released from Massachusetts General Hospital. The morning before, outside the Spanish market a block from school, where all the guys stopped for their morning meat patties and Mountain Dew, Terry had been stabbed.

The way Terry had explained it, a couple of drug addicts mistook him and his friends for dealers, words were exchanged, and Terry chased them down an alley where they stabbed him in the stomach and arm. Although Terry was a sophomore, it was his first year playing for O'Brien, so the coach didn't know him well enough to trust him implicitly. But he was willing to take him at his word. Terry came from a troubled family and had been in and out of the Department of Youth Services system. Even though Terry was just returning to school, the rest of the guys had heard about what had happened. So O'Brien decided to turn the incident into one more object lesson for the day.

"We had a real scare with Terry. Thank God he's OK," O'Brien said. "But don't feel the need to be macho. If five big dudes come walking down an alley with a bat, you think they're going to play *baseball*?" Laughter rippled through the room. "Get the hell out of there!"

The coach told the guys he knew each of them would, at one point, probably face a challenge from some dead-ender looking to test their toughness. But they all had to be smart enough to pick their spots. "Remember what Michael Jordan says: 'I kill him on the court.'"

•   •   •

O'BRIEN BEGAN THE NEXT DAY'S PRACTICE like all the rest, by pushing a wide gray broom up and down the court. At most away games, at least a couple of strangers would walk up to O'Brien and introduce themselves. They guessed there was glamour in coaching a powerhouse program. They would have never suspected that he handled the daily mopping duties in the gym. Or that he counted to make sure he had all six warm-up basketballs before getting on the bus for road games. Or that he kept a nervous eye on the water cooler outside his gym, hoping it didn't run out before the end of the month in a school where lead levels made the tap water undrinkable.

In fact, as soon as the state titles started coming, people began pressing O'Brien on why he stayed at Charlestown, where his annual coaching stipend was just $6,000. Why not move up to the college level, where the spotlight shone brighter and the checks were a whole lot bigger? O'Brien heard the question enough to have honed a standard response: "This is where I feel I can have the biggest impact." That usually satisfied the questioner's curiosity. A more complete answer would have prompted only more questions.

After completing his sweep of the last column of the court, O'Brien rested his forearm on the top of the mop handle and watched the players file into the gym. Above him hung the four championship banners. But the prime real estate on the wall—the space in the center of the banners—was devoted to a small framed

Charlestown jersey, royal blue with red-and-white trim. The number on the jersey was 31. On the bottom of the frame there was a plaque that read: "Richard Jones: Forever in Our Hearts." O'Brien had hung the jersey to honor Richard's memory. But sometimes when he was feeling down, he would glance up at the jersey and try to remind himself that there was often a positive side to pain. He still struggled to understand Richard's death, but he told himself that things happen for a reason. In his previous coaching jobs, he'd seen incredible highs followed by excruciating lows. When the lows hit, he'd wondered how he would soldier on. But had he been spared those painful endings, he would never have made it to Charlestown. Had he never made it to Charlestown, he would have never gotten the chance to coach Richard and give flight to his short life.

4

O'BRIEN

JACK O'BRIEN FELL IN LOVE WITH BASKETBALL when he was around twelve years old. Every day, he would cut through the woods near his house to get to the blacktop basketball court at Carr Park and lose himself shooting hundreds of baskets at a stretch. When the brutal New England winters tried to stand in his way by dumping snow by the foot, O'Brien would simply bring along a shovel and dig out the space in front of the hoop. Some kids take to basketball for its social component, making friends and finding rivals through the shifting teams of pickup games. Jack was most content on the court alone. Through the sheer discipline of shooting one jumper after another after another, he willed himself to get better. He didn't need anyone's help. He was a loner in love with a game. When there was tension at home between his parents, the blacktop court became even more of a refuge. No matter what was going on elsewhere, on the court Jack worked around it.

When John Adrian O'Brien was born in 1958, his parents, John and Theresa, had just recently moved to a modest one-story ranch-style house in Medford. With nearly 60,000 residents, Medford was technically a suburb of Boston, but it had a rhythm all to itself. It

57

had gracious colonial houses sitting on groomed lawns and dilapidated three-deckers covered in cheap siding. The O'Briens' neighborhood occupied the middle of that spread. The overall feel of the city was more suburban than urban, more working class than professional class, and definitely more white than not. For generations, most of the people who ran the place had last names that were either Irish or Italian.

Like a lot of old-school Irish, O'Brien's father was a hard-working man. He always seemed to be juggling a couple of jobs, from delivering cases of soda to digging graves at the local cemetery. His mother, whom people affectionately called Teddy, was round-faced and sociable. Four years after giving birth to Jack, Teddy delivered a girl and then another boy a few years later. Growing up, Jack was close with his mother and his paternal grandmother—his Nana—who watched him when his mother was working as a waitress at Boston hotel functions. He had a distant relationship with his father, who was often dead tired when he came home and in no mood for father-son bonding. Jack wasn't particularly close with his siblings either.

Over the years, Jack's parents had their share of problems. He inherited his father's sad eyes and long face. But whenever his parents argued, he instinctively sided with his mother, though he tried not to get involved. His father's moods would later be diagnosed as severe depression, although little was known about the disease at that time, especially among the Irish working class, who tended to view it as yet one more luxury available only to the affluent. But depression deepened the divide between father and son.

Jack attended a small Catholic grammar school in Medford called St. Francis of Assisi, and served as an altar boy at the church of the same name. On Saturday mornings, he played in a league held in the school's tiny gym with a flip-chart scoreboard and half-moon-shaped backboards. But it wasn't until he moved on to Medford's public high school that his game came alive. At the time, Medford High had close to 4,000 students. In the school's classrooms and corridors, the introverted kid wasn't much of a student or a socializer. But on the court, he was something else. On his freshman team, all that time he had logged at Carr Park working on his shot paid off, as he quickly established himself as the squad's best perimeter shooter. His coach, Roy Belson, occasionally got frustrated that he didn't penetrate more, but when the kid put his arms up over his head and did his quick wrist-flick to release the ball, Belson knew it was a surefire two. O'Brien captained his varsity team, playing the role of game-maker, a kid who compensated for a lack of natural ability with a searing work ethic.

When high school ended, so did Jack's playing career. He went on to attend Salem State, a mostly commuter college 20 miles north of Medford. But his attendance was in fits and starts, as he alternated between college and full-time work behind the deli counter at the Foodmaster. He never tried out for the Salem State team. Then, during his sophomore year, he had the chance to reconnect with the game. He was tapped to be the freshman coach at Medford High. Over the next few years, he threw everything he had into the job, immersing himself in the lives of his players, connecting most easily with those who came from troubled family backgrounds. He organized summer leagues and after-school study periods. He took his players to camp, to colleges, to church. He was still just a kid himself, and he hadn't found a lot of success in life yet. But somehow he found the confidence to counsel his players—on and off the court. The sight of his students soaking up his intensity and paying attention to what he said boosted his confidence and his drive to be the best coach around. He gave his all, and expected the same from his guys. One day his sister overheard him talking to one of his players on the phone. She could hardly believe the man rattling off demands into the receiver was the same introverted brother she had grown up with.

In the role of coach, Jack O'Brien had discovered himself. After three years, he was promoted to junior varsity coach. In six seasons, he posted a 95–7 record, won six league championships, and spawned a cult of loyal supporters.

Other parts of his life suffered. He lost the drive to finish his degree at Salem State. By this point, he was making day wages as a substitute teacher at Medford High, intending to land a full-time teaching job. But those slots were hard to come by, and impossible if he didn't get his degree. Still, success as a coach was all-consuming. When he wasn't in the Medford gym, he would sometimes slip into the stands at Boston University to watch Coach Rick Pitino lead his team in practices. Pitino was just beginning his climb to the top of the coaching ranks, and O'Brien would sit quietly during practices, a notebook on his lap, trying to divine coaching acumen from the young college hotshot.

In the summer of 1983, O'Brien got his big chance. The head coach of Medford High's varsity squad resigned. Although only twenty-five, O'Brien felt he had earned the promotion. After all, he'd spent six years building a rigorous feeder program for the varsity team.

O'Brien's success as a JV coach had given him the confidence to get past his introverted tendencies. Among the people he had reached out to during this time was Medford's mayor, volunteering to help in his reelection bid. It was a worthwhile investment in a political-machine city where important municipal decisions had the habit of being decided long before any gavel was lifted. The mayor, who was a voting member of the school board, began pushing for O'Brien to get the varsity job. But he ran into a wave of opposition.

Although he had posted an impeccable win-loss record as JV coach, O'Brien had his critics. During one packed school board meeting, the freshman basketball coach stood up and charged that O'Brien cared only about his own players, bent league rules in his pursuit of success, and even once brandished a gun in practice to motivate his guys. O'Brien countered that his critics were hurling half-truths to put the job out of his reach. The weapon, he explained, was an unloaded BB gun one of his players brought to a practice during February vacation. After doing the responsible thing and confiscating the gun for safekeeping, O'Brien said he had briefly held it up and joked, "We better hustle today."

The accusations stuck because they echoed a larger pattern of discomfort some people had with O'Brien. He was twenty-five years old, unmarried, and underemployed, and his life seemed to begin and end with basketball. The other leading candidate for the job, Angel Torres, was a thirty-seven-year-old married teacher at Medford High. At 6-foot-7, he'd been a star during his own playing days. He was also a Vietnam veteran and had head-coaching experience at a local parochial school. What's more, Torres was black. Medford had a small black population going all the way back to the 1700s. But it was growing. As with many school districts in the 1980s, there was a strong push afoot to get more minorities into leadership roles.

To some people in Medford, it was a no-brainer. Torres was simply the better choice. This camp included most of the high school faculty as well as Roy Belson, who had coached O'Brien as a freshman and was by then the school system's No. 2 official, and John Regan, the athletic director. But to the basketball team's most hardcore boosters, it was outrageous to consider giving the job to anyone except O'Brien. No one cared more about these kids, no one had worked harder on their behalf, and no one was hungrier for success than Jack O'Brien. In addition to the mayor, this camp included the players O'Brien had coached, both black and white, and a booster named Tom Regan, who stood up at a meeting to denounce his brother, the athletic director, and question his basketball bona fides.

For weeks, the bitter debate over who would get the $2,200-a-year coaching job dominated talk in coffee shops and space in the *Medford Daily Mercury*. Finally, on November 13, 1983, the school board voted 4–3 to give the job to Torres. Immediately after the vote, Tom Regan approached his brother, the athletic director who had backed Torres, and began to swear at him and shove him. John Regan responded, and the beginnings of a brawl broke out around them. O'Brien stayed above the fray. After the vote, he walked across the meeting room to shake Torres's hand.

The fight echoed similar squalls that had been happening all over Boston since the 1970s. For generations, Irish politicians had been able to take care of their own through the patronage of city jobs—cops, firefighters, teachers, street sweepers. These jobs weren't glamorous, but they were the secret to keeping neighborhoods cohesive and working people on the climb to the middle class. But during the 1970s, at the same time that the white working class was watching a federal judge blow up the Boston school system and force their kids to spend three hours a day commuting to schools in mysterious black neighborhoods, the Irish machine was losing its hold on patronage jobs. Judges and congressmen were pushing through affirmative action programs to open up the workplace and begin making up for centuries of inequality. An admirable goal, for sure, but why, the working-class Irish wanted to know, were the white people on the lower rungs of the economic ladder the only ones being asked to pay the price?

Jack O'Brien felt the same injustice. When he heard leaders in Medford talk about the need to start a new chapter in the city, where people saw blacks in high-profile positions, O'Brien thought to himself, *Hey, I've never discriminated against anybody. So why should it begin with my job?*

Inside, O'Brien was crumbling. He may not have had a harmonious family life or a well-paying day job or a wife or even a college degree. But no one could deny that, as a basketball coach, he had been a raging success. His whole identity was wrapped up in the program.

To move himself forward, he adopted the only approach he knew, the one he had found as a twelve-year-old shooting hundreds of jump shots at Carr Park. Discipline, relentlessness. He decided he had lost his job because of politics and his lack of a college degree. He went back to school. And he kept abreast of the political winds, which soon began to change direction.

A year later, O'Brien applied for the head-coaching job once again. It was an unexpected move, since Angel Torres was now ensconced in the post and had guided the team to a winning record in his first season. But during the year, a few new faces had joined the school board. This time the vote was 4–3 in O'Brien's favor. Torres's supporters immediately charged racism, seeing it as yet another example of the city's white power brokers refusing to let anyone else share in the spoils.

Torres fought back hard. He filed a complaint with the state's commission against discrimination and was granted a temporary restraining order forbidding the school board from implementing the coaching change. He also threatened to file a lawsuit against the city for hefty damages. The saga played out on the front page of the newspaper for a month. Teachers circulated a petition on Torres's behalf, and a couple of coaches for other Medford High teams resigned in protest.

By then, O'Brien had begun to worry that even if he ultimately prevailed in keeping the job, he might never get past the charge that he had won it through cronyism and racism. He stood before a gaggle of local reporters and read a prepared statement.

It was claimed by some that I was too intense in my coaching. If taking basketball players to the Shriner's Institute twice a year to visit children less fortunate can be considered too intense, then I am intense. . . . If taking ball players to colleges for interviews and arranging scholarships at the Kaplan Center in order that they improve S.A.T. scores can be considered intense, then I am intense. . . . I believe that a coach's responsibility does not start at the beginning of the season and end with the last game, but rather is a continuing effort that results in the growth and formation of a well-rounded student/leader. . . . I do not believe in using children and students as pawns in a struggle for a coaching position. . . . Being a lifelong resident of the city, I care for its name and reputation probably more than those who would seize upon an ill-conceived opportunity to drag the city and the School Committee into court. . . .

I have, after long and careful consideration, decided to step aside.

A reporter asked him what he planned to do next. O'Brien allowed a slight smile: "I was thinking about jumping off a bridge."

• • •

A YEAR LATER, the head coaching job opened up at Salem High School. O'Brien was familiar with Salem, a small, scrappy, sports-obsessed city by the sea, because he commuted there from Medford to attend state college. When he applied for the coaching job, he used the Medford fiasco to his advantage, telling Salem officials, "Hey, I had the job, but for the good of the city, I backed away." He had heeded other lessons from his downfall in his hometown, using his free time to finish his course work at Salem State and finally earn his bachelor's degree.

Once he won the Salem slot, he threw everything he had at it, with a passion even greater than he had shown in Medford. He was a force of energy, showing up in his unmistakable warm-up outfits just about anywhere in the city where there was a hoop—from summer leagues to middle-school practices to pickup games at the park. He had his eyes on much more than just leading his high school team to a winning season. He wanted to build a full-fledged *program*, with teams in the lower grades serving as feeders to the varsity level. He also wanted to prove that he was about more than just basketball, and he developed an even more rigorous study hall system than the one he had put in place in Medford. O'Brien was still unable to get a full-time teaching job and had to get by as a substitute teacher in Salem. No matter. He was young and didn't need much in the way of income. And he wasn't interested in any kind of job that would get in the way of putting his all into coaching.

Salem was a complicated city. Although it teemed with high-end history, from restored captain's mansions to the exquisite collections of the Peabody Essex Museum, the city of 40,000 was blue collar at its core. The longtime residents were so crazy about their local sports that coaches who didn't produce learned soon enough about Salem's mean streak. That streak stretched back to 1692, when a group of women and men falsely accused of being witches were executed, a dark chapter in city history popularized on stage and on film in *The Crucible.*

Most of Salem's rabid boosters, who were thirsty for a winning team, were excited by what they saw in O'Brien. He became a celebrity in town. But, as had happened in Medford, some people began to see things they didn't like. The Salem athletic program had always been fairly traditional, with the talented athletes from well-known families tending to be in the starting lineups all year long, from football through baseball season. O'Brien began to shake things up, scouring areas of the city long overlooked in his hunt for fresh talent, including a low-income area where a lot of the Hispanic kids lived, and a home for troubled kids, many of them black. The Medford critics who had dismissed O'Brien as part of the white old-boy network would have been surprised to hear the complaint being whispered about him around Salem: that he favored minority kids over whites. But anyone who really understood O'Brien knew he never saw the world in terms of black versus white. He only saw it as "us versus them," the people who were part of his program—whatever color or creed they might be—and the people who were so threatened by the intense unity he fostered that they sought to destroy it. The minority students he got close to in Medford and Salem could tell that he didn't see color. All he saw were *his* kids. And what made an ideal O'Brien kid? Someone who worked hard and was loyal, for sure. But it also helped if the kid was hurting or damaged in some way. "I've always been a guy that gets closer to the people that have problems," O'Brien once explained. In his efforts in Salem to enlist those kids with problems,

O'Brien had a lot more air balls than swishes. Yet some of these kids went on to be his most dependable performers, taking the starting slots that the more established athletes in town—and their parents—had felt were rightfully theirs.

Early on in Salem, O'Brien received a gift in the form of a sixth-grader who moved with his family to Salem from Rochester, New York. Even as a middle-schooler, Rick Brunson showed signs he was going to be a basketball standout. By the time he was a sophomore at Salem High, the 6-foot-3 shooting guard was leading the team to the 1989 state semifinals, which Salem lost in overtime by one point. The following year, O'Brien's squad, led by Rick, won the state championship—O'Brien's first. Rick would go on to have a journeyman career in the NBA, attributing much of his success to what he learned from O'Brien. "Basketball is one language," Rick said many years later, "and he teaches it."

O'Brien's success in Salem allowed him to heal the wounds of his Medford exit. His hometown team hadn't fared nearly as well. Angel Torres had never been able to shake Jack O'Brien's shadow. When his squads performed well enough but lacked distinction, many people around Medford grumbled about how Angel didn't have Jack's fire in the belly. One summer afternoon in 1989, Torres let himself into the Medford High swimming pool complex. He had begun stepping up his workouts to try to shed some of the pounds he'd added to his 6-foot-7 frame. After setting up his eight-year-old son in an adjoining room, he strapped weights around his ankles and began exercising around the pool. Around 2:30 PM, his son came into the pool area, but couldn't find his father. Then, in horror, he spotted him at the bottom of the 15-foot deep end of the pool. The boy ran to get the custodians. One called for help, while the other jumped into the pool to try to save him. He couldn't. Neither could the firefighters when they arrived. Torres was too heavy. Finally, firefighters used a pole to pull his body from the water. An autopsy indicated he had a preexisting condition of an enlarged heart and had suffered a heart attack during his workout, apparently causing him to fall into the water and drown. He died just shy of his forty-third birthday. A few years after his death, the city named the school's fitness center in his memory.

In Salem, among the players O'Brien rode hardest was Zach Zegarowski, his future assistant coach who didn't become a starter until his senior year of high school. Growing up, Zach was given lots of leeway from his parents, who, he said later, were struggling with their own vices. So he was not prepared for O'Brien's relentless demands. Over time, meeting those demands became Zach's most important goal in life.

But not everyone shared that view. There was a general perception that O'Brien demanded too much of his players, turning a three-month season into a year-round operation with weekend, holiday, and summer commitments and taking the "family" feel of the team too far. The school superintendent pulled O'Brien aside and warned him that he should be careful about making too many enemies. But O'Brien was never someone who hewed easily to authority other than his own. His relentless, critics-be-damned style had gotten him this far, and he wasn't about to ease up.

One of the people O'Brien rubbed the wrong way was the sports editor of the *Salem Evening News*. They had been on bad terms ever since 1990, when O'Brien refused to give him the scoop on which college Rick Brunson had chosen to attend, and then refused to call him off from naming the wrong college in print.

In 1992, the editor splashed a story involving O'Brien across the sports pages. O'Brien had gotten some pushback from one of his star players, so he suspended him. When a Salem reporter pressed O'Brien on why the star was missing from the lineup, O'Brien told him about the suspension. In doing that, the *Salem Evening News* reported, O'Brien had broken a privacy rule that the high school principal had imposed on all coaches. A pretty minor infraction, to be sure. But as soon as the incident hit the paper, things snowballed, fueled by O'Brien's willingness over the years to collect critics as freely as a pocket collects lint.

The school superintendent now told him he'd had enough. Soon the school board was deep in debate over whether to renew O'Brien's contract. As in Medford, there were heated public meetings that attracted the coach's legions of fans. Among them was Zach, who rushed back from college, stood up at a packed meeting, and warned, "You get rid of him, this will be the biggest mistake you ever make." As in Medford, O'Brien eventually saw the handwriting on the wall and resigned.

At thirty-three, O'Brien could lay claim to a 131–30 record, giving him the best coaching record in the state over the previous seven years and the best in Salem basketball history. But he could no longer lay claim to a job.

Many years later, Zach summed it up this way: "He got too big for the town. It's still painful for him, but he believes things happen for a reason."

Anyone watching closely couldn't miss the parallels between O'Brien's overwrought exits from Medford and Salem. In both cases, O'Brien and his tactics divided a town. He became a cult of personality. He sacrificed just about everything else in his life, all in the name of his kids. They, in turn, would go to battle for him. After all, how many other adults would make themselves available at any hour, and be a rock of stability? But in both cities, many people found something unnatural about his level of devotion. O'Brien had no patience for doubters. Why couldn't they see the big picture: that he was busting his tail to help these kids get ahead? What were these critics doing on Saturday mornings and Sunday afternoons and Wednesday nights to help his kids get to college? In his own life, he had paid the price for his lopsided devotion to basketball, when his lack of a college degree was used against him in his pursuit of the Medford job. Who better to motivate kids to avoid making the same mistake? Coaching was his calling; he had committed to it.

•   •   •

THE YEAR AFTER HE LEFT SALEM couldn't have been longer for O'Brien. He picked up a job with a real estate agency renting apartments, but he desperately missed working with his players. In the spring of 1993, he decided to try to get a job coaching in Boston. He knew he worked best with players who needed structure in their lives and weren't getting a lot of it from home. Boston schools, he was sure, had plenty of kids like that. He heard the Charlestown coaching job was vacant. At the time, Charlestown High's headmaster was a black man who had once played ball himself. He told O'Brien he'd consider him. As the start of the 1993–1994 season drew near, O'Brien was working as a substitute teacher at Charlestown but still hadn't been offered the basketball job. He decided to call in a chit. He had gotten to know Temple University coach John Chaney after his former Salem star Rick Brunson went there. He figured a strong endorsement from one of the most famous black coaches in the game might mean a lot. The headmaster never mentioned the call to O'Brien, but he soon gave him the job.

O'Brien thought he'd have no trouble putting together a winning program. The raw talent was there. All he had to do was apply his structure and intensity, and the wins would start coming. He decided to send a message early about who was in charge. The star of the team O'Brien inherited was Shawn Brown, a tough junior with a ripped build and gang affiliations. The son of a single mother, he'd lost a brother to gang violence and already had an infant son. He also had a transcript full of D's and F's. After tryouts, O'Brien announced he would post the roster the next day. When Shawn looked it over, he was stunned not to see his name. Assuming it was a mistake—no new coach would be stupid enough to keep the best player off the team—he showed up at practice anyway. O'Brien stopped him as soon as he walked into the gym. "Hey, if your name's not on the list, you don't belong here." Shawn couldn't believe it. This intense white guy was the first person who ever stood up to him in his life.

They both paid the price. Shawn sat out the year. O'Brien's team lost every game but one. O'Brien nearly quit. He was unprepared for what it takes to coach in the city. Suburban coaches have to contend with meddling parents furious when their kids don't get playing time. They wish the parents would just go away. City coaches get to see what it's like when that wish comes true. It's pretty lonely.

That summer, Shawn went to the movies with his girlfriend and two-year-old son. There, a guy from a rival gang flashed him, showing his gun in an unmistakable provocation. Shawn was on fire. He was about to call his gang friends to help him settle the situation. But then his mind raced back to a conversation he'd had with O'Brien, when the coach told him where his life was headed if he didn't change, and asked him, "Do you want your son to grow up without a father?"

At the time, Shawn had told him, "That is *never* going to happen. I had to live with that, and I'm not going to let my son grow up with that."

So instead of calling his buddies, Shawn called O'Brien. It may have been the most important phone call of his life. The next morning, he met the coach at the gym, and they began working out together. Shawn left the street life behind, helped O'Brien turn around the Charlestown team, and then went on to graduate from Merrimack College, a small, respected Catholic school northwest of Boston. After college, Shawn, who married his girlfriend and went on to have two more kids with her, returned to Boston, founding a mentoring program that helped get scores of other Boston kids out of the street life.

Things happen for a reason.

II

THE SEASON

5

FITS AND STARTS

O'BRIEN SMILED AS HE LED HIS PLAYERS into Salem High School on a sleeting night in December, but it was a distracted smile. Charlestown wouldn't actually be facing the team from Salem for another five weeks—this season opener against Peabody was part of a tournament. But just being in the gym with the white cement walls and the red banners proclaiming "Home of the Witches" was reminder enough of the painful end to the previous season, when Salem had eliminated Charlestown early in the playoffs. That loss, so crushing it left Tony Lee crying in a corner of the locker room, ended Charlestown's four-year state-championship reign. It also re-opened the wounds O'Brien had suffered after being forced out of his Salem job a decade earlier. In the final minutes of the game, the Salem fans had been unable to resist chanting, "Over-rated!" and "Sit down, Ja-ack!"

Still, with the new season about to begin, O'Brien had more immediate concerns on his mind. Would Ridley play tougher? Would Hood find more control? Would the rest of the team play well enough to quiet all the talk in basketball circles that Charlestown's days of dominance were over?

O'Brien was wearing his game-day uniform of black slacks frayed at the cuffs and a stretched-out red Charlestown sweater vest over a white dress shirt. In the locker room, he pulled out his crumpled 3×5 card from his pocket and reviewed the hand signals he would be giving the guys from the sidelines. Then he said, "Let's bring it in," throwing his right arm up toward the ceiling. The players stood up and huddled around him, raising their arms to meet his. "Lord, please bless us tonight," he began. "Please help us to play with confidence. Please help us to dig out there. Please make sure no one gets hurt. Please make sure that everyone's helping each other. Make sure coaches, players, everyone's real attentive." Then he invoked the memory of the two guys who remained members of the Charlestown family in spirit. "Also, please make sure to look over Paris, to look over Richard. In Jesus' name we pray."

Just before tip-off, as the Peabody players took to the floor and licked the bottoms of their sneakers to improve their traction, O'Brien squatted down in front of the Charlestown starting five. Diagramming defensive plays by moving pieces around a white magnetic clipboard, O'Brien told his guys, "We gotta start strong!"

Peabody scored first. "Aaaah!" O'Brien groused, throwing his arms up as his tasseled loafers shuffled along the sideline. When one of his players missed a couple of free throws, O'Brien threw his arms up again.

Charlestown's starting five consisted of senior guards Ridley and Hood, sophomore point guard Paul Becklens, and senior forwards Spot and George Russell. Everyone looked flat, especially Hood, who was still nursing a strained back. It took several minutes before the team posted its first points of the season, and they came from an unlikely source. George, a square-faced, thick-bodied 6-foot-1 plugger, had the habit of tipping his head to change the direction of his body, as though it were a steering wheel. He usually finished games with more rebounds than points. But his layup was enough to awaken Charlestown's offense. Then the team from Peabody, a predominantly white community north of Boston, began to choke in the face of Charlestown's press.

Unlike most high school teams, Charlestown ran a full-court press for all thirty-two minutes of every game—pressuring the ball for the entire length of the court with the aim of causing turnovers. O'Brien had tried this approach five years earlier, and it brought Charlestown its first state championship. He'd stayed with it ever since. Most teams employed the press only at the end of tight games, because it was so draining to sustain. That's why O'Brien and his assistants kept their deep bench in perpetual motion, cycling ten players in and out, with no player typically logging more than five minutes at a stretch. Throughout every game, there were clumps of Charlestown players crouching on the floor in front of the scorer's table, waiting to be waved into the game by a referee during a stop in play. Sometimes the constant substitutions made it hard for the Charlestown offense to find its rhythm. But when the press was working well, it was a thing of beauty, with the players keeping up an intensity that suggested every minute was the game's final one.

Teams facing Charlestown for the first time were surprised to find every play contested, right down to a routine in-bounds pass on the opposite end of court in the early minutes of the game. Even if the opponent managed to get the ball in bounds, his work was just beginning. At every spot on the court, two Charlestown players ganged up on the ball handler, with one pressuring him up close and another hanging back a little to close down his passing lanes. Each time the opponent got off a pass, the Charlestown defense rotated to pressure the new ball handler and close down his passing lanes. Occasionally, the opponent took advantage of this double-teaming, hurling the ball to an open teammate near the hoop. But more often, the intense coverage wore down the other side's stamina and confidence, forcing them to cough up the ball again and again.

That is what happened to Peabody. When Ridley spotted the deer-in-headlights expression on a Peabody guard's face, he pounced. He stole the ball mid-court, bounded to the basket, and sailed into the air to unleash a dunk. The Charlestown bench jumped up to cheer, as did the team's small contingent of fans in the stands. O'Brien, his cheeks and neck glistening with sweat, was already focused on the next play. "Ridley, get back!"

After the slow start, Charlestown dominated the rest of the game. With a few minutes left on the clock, and Charlestown enjoying a wide lead, Terry Carter entered the game, two Band-Aids on his arm the only reminder of his stabbing ten days earlier.

In the locker room after the game, O'Brien was downbeat, rattling off all the mistakes he had seen on the court. "Terry, no spinning!" he yelled. "Spinning is a sign of weakness! Just do what we teach you!" He complained and criticized so insistently that you would have guessed his guys had lost by 20 points. In fact, they had won by 30.

For the younger guys, who were confused by O'Brien's gloomy reaction to a 30-point blowout, Zach stepped up to translate. "If you're not ready to accept coaching, you'll never get better at any-thing in life," the frenzied assistant coach told them. "This is the time when you correct things, after a win."

As he boarded the bus, O'Brien knew that against a better, less intimidated team, the game might have gone the other way. Still, it was good feeling to be starting the season with a win, especially in Salem.

•　•　•

O'BRIEN REFUSED TO LIVE IN THE PAST. Perhaps that, more than anything, explained his string of successes. All those championship banners on the wall were good for intimidating opponents, but banners did not win games. O'Brien used mental tricks to keep him and his guys hungry. The next game was always tougher than the last, even when it really wasn't. He and his players were not allowed to savor the last win.

As the season began to take shape and Charlestown followed up its blowout opener against Peabody with two more easy wins, Ridley and Hood were feeling good. So were the sophomores who were seeing lots of playing time—at the expense of the juniors. Still, despite being 3–0 on the season, O'Brien could tell his team was not clicking. Then, a few days before Christmas, Charlestown's home opener against East Boston High School let everyone else see what he'd been feeling.

For generations, there had been tension between Italian East Boston and Irish Charlestown. Now that the high schools in both neighborhoods were dominated by minority students from other parts of the city, the rivalry had morphed into something different, less about geography and ethnicity, more about pure sports. But that didn't make it any less intense. In recent seasons, Eastie had seethed in resentment; no matter how competitive its squads were, they seemed doomed to watch O'Brien's boys coast to the state finals year after year. Now sitting above Charlestown in the newspaper rankings, the Eastie squad was convinced this would be its dragon-slaying year.

From the tip-off, Eastie embarrassed Charlestown, roaring at one point to a 23-point lead. Eastie's 6-foot-3 forward, who could be either dominant or lumbering, depending on the game, had an explosive day, putting up 24 points and pulling down 10 rebounds. Charlestown managed to close the gap late in the second half, but Eastie walked off the court with a 10-point win. It was Charlestown's first loss on its home court in six seasons.

·When O'Brien was out of earshot in the coming days, the Charlestown players descended into bouts of finger pointing. The blame game got so bad that Hood and Ridley called a players-only meeting to try to shut it down. Meanwhile, O'Brien settled into a funk. He wasn't sleeping well. He knew what was wrong, but he was struggling with how to fix it. Hood, whose fullback-like drives to the hoop could ignite the Charlestown offense, was erratic. Spot, whose outgoing manner and handsome face masked a potent insecurity, was drowning in self-doubt now that his sweet shot had gone south. O'Brien knew enough psychology to understand that's why Spot was suddenly acting up in practice. Still, he wasn't about to take any crap—in one flare-up during practice a few days before Christmas, he kicked Spot out of the gym.

And then there was Ridley. A game the day before New Year's Eve distilled everything that wasn't clicking in O'Brien's relationship with Ridley. It was the Stop & Shop Holiday Classic tournament, and O'Brien had successfully lobbied to get the final game renamed in honor of Richard Jones. Earlier in the evening, he'd picked up Richard's mother and brought her with him to the gym a few miles away from Charlestown, where the tourney was held.

Charlestown blazed out to a 9–0 lead in the game, largely because of Ridley. In one play, he stole the ball and then drew a foul as he put up a layup that was good. Shortly after that, he sank a gorgeous three-pointer.

Yet as the game wore on, O'Brien grew more and more frustrated with Ridley's preference for hanging out in the safety of the top of the key rather than muscling his way toward the boards. When the game ended, Charlestown walked off the court with a 15-point win. Even though he'd been on the bench for much of the final stretch, Ridley left with a game-high 22 points. When a photographer wanted to snap a shot of Richard's mother with a member of the current squad, O'Brien didn't hesitate, motioning for Ridley to step forward.

But as soon as Ridley sat down in the locker room, O'Brien trained his howitzer on him. "Ridley, you're chillin' out there!" O'Brien screamed. "You gotta be strong!" Zach piped up: "I trust you with my own son, but I don't trust you with the ball in the last few minutes of the game!" As usual, the expression on Ridley's face was as blank as a motel wall. But inside he was burning: *I helped us win this game. Why you yelling at me?*

After four years, he was still getting used to O'Brien's counterin-tuitive approach to locker-room speeches. O'Brien yelled loudest when his team had an easy lead or had just coasted to victory. He was measured during close games. After losses, he was supportive and never yelled. Wins offered his guys enough public support, so he tried to bring them back to reality. But defeats were especially cruel in Boston, where the kids you saw in your neighborhood and on the subway were more likely to be from a rival school than your own. O'Brien knew most of his players didn't have strong family support systems ready to buck them up when they were most down. Losses were no time to make things worse.

Emerging from the locker room, O'Brien ran into a shorter man around sixty years old, who had gray-black hair that was mussed, and spots on his thick glasses. "You should have called more time-outs tonight," Michael Fung said.

O'Brien waved him off with a chuckle. "You're the boss, Mr. Fung."

• • •

EIGHT YEARS EARLIER, when O'Brien first heard his new boss would be an Asian with a graduate degree from the Massachusetts In-stitute of Technology, he worried the guy would care only about academics and O'Brien's cherished basketball program might suffer a death of neglect. He'd been right about one thing: Since taking over as headmaster of Charlestown High, Fung had made it his mission to inject academic rigor into the languishing high school. But Fung quickly became the basketball team's biggest booster. He traveled with O'Brien on the bus for road games. At every game, home or away, the man trained as a scientist wore the same gray T-shirt under his dress shirt and sat in the same spot in the bleachers—five rows back, dead center—because he was convinced it brought the players good luck.

O'Brien and Fung spent a lot of time together. O'Brien insisted on holding Sunday practices, but because school department rules prevented him from having a key to the gym, he needed Fung to open up the school. Fung didn't drive, so O'Brien would give him a ride. While O'Brien spent the afternoon putting his players through the paces, Fung toiled away with paperwork in his cluttered office. On the drive home, the two would get into long discussions and often verbally spar, both of them giving each other unsolicited advice on how to do their jobs better. Fung generally ignored most of the veterans on the faculty, preferring to invest his energy in mentoring the young teachers—most of them female—whom he had hired to help him transform the school. O'Brien was one of the few veterans he bonded with, so much so that other older teachers often asked him to talk to Fung on their behalf.

On the surface, the two men could hardly have seemed more dissimilar—O'Brien, the rough-around-the-edges coach and man of humble roots; Fung, the intellectual administrator and man of privilege. Below the surface, though, they were more alike than not. Both were driven, stubborn, somewhat lonely figures who had devoted their lives to being father figures to others, having been denied functioning relationships with their own fathers. And in their own dealings, there was more than a hint of a father-son dynamic.

The fact that Fung had made urban education his life's work was still a bit of a mystery to his family, and even to him. Born into one of the most successful families in Hong Kong commerce, Fung had dreamed as a young man of becoming a writer. As a teenager he began pursuing both his craft and a woman who was five years ahead of him in age and writing experience. Fung's father, a taciturn autocrat, approved of neither ambition; he thought his eldest son had no future as a writer, and the object of his affection came from an unacceptably poor family. So he sent seventeen-year-old Michael to the United States, to live with an uncle who was a professor at Iowa State. Fung showed up to the campus in Ames, Iowa, wearing custom-made three-piece suits. After three years, he received a scholarship to continue his chemistry studies at the Massachusetts Institute of Technology, a Cambridge university notorious for its competitive culture. There, he earned his master's and finished his coursework for his doctorate. But before he completed his dissertation, he got into an argument with his adviser about some research he wanted to do. If he had been less stubborn, Fung would have realized that he risked throwing away years of grueling study and apologized to his adviser, who wielded great power over his academic career. Or he could have found a new adviser, a complicated undertaking that would have consigned Fung to an extra year of study. He wrote his father, detailing his unhappiness and requesting permission to leave MIT. His father wrote back: *No. You'll be considered a failure.* He bolted anyway, with nowhere to go. The experience only deepened Fung's distrust of authority.

Living in Boston's Chinatown in the late 1960s, searching for a post-MIT path, Fung stumbled onto street protests demanding bilingual education for the city's growing population of Chinese students, who had been largely overlooked amid Boston's yawning black-white divide. Fung became an activist, and that work led in 1971 to a high school teaching job. Improbably, this man with his thickly accented Hong Kong English and a background spent mostly in research labs now found himself in front of a homeroom dominated by tough black kids. One day early on, Fung, nervous and overwhelmed, pulled the class's biggest troublemaker out into the hall. Although Fung was wholly unaware of it, there had been a warrant out for the kid's arrest. As Fung tried to talk to him out in the hall, the principal approached them with a couple of cops, who led the kid away in handcuffs. Fung walked back into the classroom, still confused over what had happened, showing his confusion with a nervous smile. The kids in the class, who had seen their brainy teacher apparently send the troublesome student to jail, concluded they were dealing with one brass-balled Chinese guy. For the rest of the year, nobody bothered him.

As the Boston system hemorrhaged during the busing crisis, Fung, who had married, climbed the ladder. He was named principal of a troubled middle school when he was just thirty-four. He and his wife went on to have four children. He certainly could have afforded to send them to private school, but he insisted on putting them through Boston Public Schools. He figured it would be hypocritical to ask parents to entrust their children to Boston schools if he didn't do the same. A decade after becoming a principal, Fung was promoted to be one of the school superintendent's top lieutenants. Early on in his management life, a top administrator told Fung the secret for surviving in the school system's Kremlin-like bureaucracy: *Say nothing, do nothing, and say nothing well.* Candid, anti-authoritarian, and wealthy enough not to have to worry about making the next mortgage payment, Fung never took that message to heart.

For a while, his outspokenness served him well, but inevitably it caught up with him. That at least partly explained how a man once on track to be a potential superintendent ended up being busted down by the bureaucracy and exiled to Charlestown High.

•   •   •

A S THE NEW YEAR DAWNED IN JANUARY 2005, O'Brien slowly emerged from his funk. Despite all his success in Charlestown, he'd never gotten the appreciation he felt he deserved from the school system or the community. But the bonds he forged with his players were his reward. For four years, he had worked closely with Hood and Ridley, as well as the other senior veterans, George and Spot, helping them through troubles at school and home. But he could hear the clock ticking. He told himself: *I've got to start enjoying this more. Before you know it, they'll be gone.*

He began contemplating an almost unthinkable shift in basketball strategy. But he would wait a few weeks before acting on it.

In the meantime, he made a few smaller changes. Going into a big January 4 showdown against undefeated Cambridge Rindge and Latin School, the powerhouse where Patrick Ewing once played, O'Brien took Spot out of the starting lineup. He hoped it would remove some pressure from Spot's shoulders, allowing him to find his groove coming off the bench and shore up his sagging self-confidence. But on some level he realized that no senior likes to begin the game sitting down, especially a senior who had been a starter as a sophomore. What's worse, Cambridge was where Spot was born, where his uncle had been a well-known player and coach. His uncle, brother, grandmother, and cousins had all showed up to cheer him on.

O'Brien knew that when the 6-foot-2 Spot was feeling good about himself, he was the definition of smooth, pairing his words with velvety tilts of his head and shoulders, as though he were gliding across the dance floor. When he lost his confidence, his eyes turned sad and all the grace deserted him.

Sitting on the bench, looking just as sad as Spot, was Lorenzo Jones. A soft-spoken kid with the buzz cut, Lorenzo had been something of a sparkplug during the previous season. But so far this season, he was a non-factor. O'Brien felt Lorenzo's skills had slipped rather than improved since last season, and chalked it up to the kid's off-season work ethic. Lorenzo couldn't understand why O'Brien was denying him the chance to show his stuff. A lot of those minutes going to Terry and the other sophomores should have been his. Off the court, Lorenzo had been taking a lot of ribbing from his friends about how his ass could handle all those splinters from spending so much time on the bench.

During the game, when Spot was called off the bench, he looked stiff. That stiffness never really went away. But the rest of the team came alive, especially the sophomores, who would get top billing in the next day's newspaper coverage. Before an electric Cambridge crowd, the Charlestown guys dove for every loose ball, contested every rebound, and left with a 58–51 win.

In the locker room, O'Brien was beaming. "I feel like we turned the corner today," he said, prompting the team to erupt in applause. Then he walked over to Terry, put his arms out, preacher-style, and yelled, "Do you feel it?"

Lorenzo was uninspired: the veteran junior had never been allowed into the game. The next morning, fed up with a fresh round of benchwarmer jibes, he walked to the office off the gym where O'Brien was sitting, rapped on the door, and handed in his uniform. He had quit the team.

6

A TASTE OF
THE HIGH LIFE

HOOD SAT IN THE JACUZZI AT THE HILTON GARDEN INN, his shoulders leaned way back, his chin tipped up to the ceiling, his face sporting a grin worthy of a Club Med commercial. "This is the life!" he purred.

To his left sat Ridley. The fact that Hood was choosing to spend his free time with Ridley said a lot about how their relationship had evolved with the season. Before they became co-captains, Hood had never bonded with Ridley. He saw him as something of a goody two-shoes—never talking back to Coach, always staying on the good side of his teachers. Ridley just didn't seem to live in the same real world of housing project turf battles that Hood did. Still, for Hood, there was something that didn't add up. If Ridley was as soft and surface as Hood thought he was, how come the other guys on the team spent so much time hanging with him? It was only after Hood started joining them in Ridley's bedroom, watching ESPN and BET, listening to Lil Wayne and Jay-Z, that he began to see what all the other guys saw. First of all, Ridley may not have lived in the projects, but his apartment in a Dorchester three-decker literally bordered one of Boston's toughest projects. So he had to navigate some of the same minefields Hood faced just to get to school every day. More than that, Ridley off the court and out of school seemed a lot more real to Hood. He was funny—and could even be cutting. He was interested in girls and having a good time. He was cool. More and more, Hood relaxed his scowl when he was around Ridley and let him see more of who he was.

While Hood luxuriated in the Jacuzzi, Ridley wore a pained look. He was battling the flu. Ridley didn't know it, but Hood had a lot more to worry about than a fever and some mild nausea. Still, Hood was determined not to let anything stop him from enjoying the weekend getaway.

Hood and Ridley and the rest of the guys were spending two nights in the Hilton, having all their meals covered, because they were participating in a competitive invitational tournament that drew teams from all over the country. It didn't matter to them that their Hilton was in Springfield, a defeated city in western Massachusetts that even the Chamber of Commerce would have had a hard time pitching as a getaway. One study found that Springfield had a violent crime rate nearly twice that of similarly sized American cities. Unemployment ran high, and half the residents in the city's South End lived below the poverty line. A year earlier, Springfield's mob boss, Adolfo "Big Al" Bruno, was shot in the chin, neck, elbow, cheek, and groin as he left the Our Lady of Mount Carmel Society after his regular Sunday night card game. And about eight months before the Charlestown boys made their visit, one of their rapper heroes, 50 Cent, triggered an hour-long melee during his surprise performance at a Springfield club after he dove from the stage into the crowd, allegedly punching one woman and trampling another.

No matter. A trip was a trip, and Hood and the rest of the guys felt like college stars traveling in style. This was their taste of the high life, a mid-season reward for everything O'Brien put them through—the grueling practice schedule that included regular Sunday sessions, the relentless criticism on the court, and the never-ending lectures off it. They knew if they just could hang on and live by O'Brien's rigid rules for a few more months, they had a good shot at getting an even more satisfying serving of that high life, the one that accrued to members of a state championship squad.

Moreover, Springfield wasn't just any depressed city. A visit there was as mandatory for serious students of basketball as Cooperstown was for baseball fans because Springfield was where it all began. In December 1891, James Naismith, a thirty-year-old phys ed teacher at the School for Christian Workers, nailed two half-bushel peach baskets to the edge of an elevated indoor track, divided his eighteen stir-crazy students into two teams of nine, and taught them to bounce a fat ball and toss it at their side's basket. There were no holes at the bottom of the baskets, so Naismith kept a ladder nearby for use after each score.

The Hilton where the Charlestown players rested their heads was just a parking lot away from the domed Basketball Hall of Fame. Still, they didn't get too excited about being on sacred basketball ground. For most of them, hoop history extended no farther than the previous night's monster dunk by LeBron James. What they did get excited about was how the name on their jerseys carried weight in basketball circles across the state. They heard people reach for the same word to describe the Charlestown program: *powerhouse*. They liked hearing that.

•   •   •

O'BRIEN HAD USED THE SPRINGFIELD GETAWAY AS LEVERAGE. The week leading up to the Hall of Fame High School Invitational, he warned the guys daily about the need to get caught up on their schoolwork. The seniors had been through this before and had heeded his warnings. The sophomores may have been contributing on the court, but they were still trying to slide by in school. So while Hood and Ridley sat in the Jacuzzi, the sophomores—big men Terry Carter and Troy Gillenwater, guards Paul Becklens and LeRoyal Hairston—sat doing homework for hours on Friday night in the overheated James Naismith conference room off the Hilton lobby. O'Brien told Troy he was lucky to be there at all. He had suspended him a week earlier for a bad attitude. As the sophomores stared at their algebraic equations, O'Brien and his assistants took turns playing study hall monitor, staring back at them. When the team had checked into the hotel, O'Brien asked for the manager, so he could confirm his reservation for the conference room. The manager had been impressed. Charlestown, the manager told O'Brien, was the first team to request a study room. O'Brien laughed. "Well, don't be too impressed. We need it!"

Over the years, O'Brien and his meticulous attention to detail had created a certain rhythm to the Charlestown program, a reliable calendar of rewards and penalties, expectations and excursions. The players knew what previous squads had been treated to, and they expected nothing less. O'Brien took steps to make sure he could keep the bennies coming. His zero tolerance for the guys being anything but polite in their interactions with everyone from hotel clerks to tournament ticket takers ensured that Charlestown developed a reputation for having a program that turned out good kids. While the organizers of the Springfield tournament rotated teams in and out of their roster every year, Charlestown remained a fixture. And when, going into this year's tournament, organizers had to trim costs by underwriting just one night's stay in the hotel rather than two, O'Brien cajoled them into making an exception for

Charlestown. He knew how much a full weekend stay had meant to his players in the past, and he didn't want to shortchange the current squad. He made sure to be generous in his praise for the organizers and relentless in his reminders to his players about how impeccable their behavior had better be to show their gratitude. "You owe it to the guys who will come after you," he said. "You're all part of the same Charlestown family."

Hood had been on the Springfield trip several times before. So on Saturday morning, as he sat in the hotel lobby watching ESPN, he knew O'Brien would soon appear and then guide the team across the parking lot to the Naismith Memorial Basketball Hall of Fame. O'Brien knew that once his guys got inside, he and his assistant coaches would spend the morning soaking up all the exhibits they could squeeze in while the players would head directly for the basketball court in the center of the complex, under the basketball-shaped dome. There, they would spend the morning shooting baskets and playing two-on-two, while grade school boys from the suburbs looked on in awe.

By the afternoon, the sophomores were back in the hotel study room. Paul, who was Ridley's cousin as well as the gifted starting point guard, had his head bent over a geometry book. But for his bigger eyes, he looked like a shorter version of Ridley. But their attitude toward schoolwork was entirely different. Ridley did what needed to be done and took O'Brien's criticisms head-on. Paul did barely enough to get by and tried to avoid O'Brien whenever possible, once hiding under a giant pile of clothes in his bedroom when his coach made a surprise home visit. Although Paul had finished his algebra the night before, he was still way behind. Like the rest of Charlestown's sophomore class, he was forced to take two math courses. Fung, the headmaster, insisted that sophomores double up to help improve the school's tenth-grade state standardized test scores. But to all those kids who hated math to begin with, this mandate meant only more tedium and fewer opportunities to take elective courses. O'Brien complained repeatedly to Fung that kids needed electives as release valves. Also, the coach had for years been using the good grades his guys received in electives like drama to help them wow college admissions officers on their potential, rather than having them focus on their sub-par performances in all those math classes.

Sitting beside Paul, with his face scrunched up behind a history book, was 6-foot-4 Terry. With high cheekbones, short hair, and a muscular upper body, Terry would have fit right in on the cover of an Abercrombie & Fitch catalog, playfully lounging around with other beautiful people leading charmed lives. In reality, his life had been studded with misfortune. His father was in jail, his mother was dead, and Terry had spent years bouncing around the system. Just when he appeared to be on track, he'd find a way to lose his way. For a couple of years now, he'd had a stable advocate in his corner, Harry Landry, the court clerk who served as his unofficial guardian. Working in a tough city court, Harry was hardly naïve, but he saw something special in Terry. His steadfast support for Terry had strained his marriage, since his wife didn't quite trust the kid. It wasn't an issue of race. Though Harry was white, his wife, like Terry, was black. Harry would sometimes wonder if she was right and he was going to end up feeling burned by Terry. But then something like Terry's stabbing would snap him back and make him realize how much the boy needed him. When Harry had taken him to have the stitches removed, the doctor told him how lucky he'd been: One or two millimeters and he could have lost the use of his right arm.

"Hey, Coach," Terry said, standing up from the Hilton conference room table. "I finished my homework. Now can I please *leave?*"

By the late afternoon, O'Brien was in his hotel room, watching a rebroadcast on local cable of a Longmeadow High School game. In a few hours, O'Brien's boys would be playing the team from Longmeadow, a wealthy suburb of Springfield. The video quality on the community access channel could hardly have been worse. But O'Brien saw what he needed to. "Longmeadow's big man is good, but he's getting tired, huh, Steve?"

Steve Cassidy was standing behind an ironing board, pressing the white dress shirt he would wear under his red Charlestown sweater vest. The assistant coach put the iron down and stepped closer to the TV to get a better look. "Yeah, he's good."

Cassidy and O'Brien were sharing one room, while the other two assistants—Zach and Hugh—were bunking together down the hall. The conversation between Cassidy and O'Brien always alternated easily between athletics and academics, and this afternoon was no different. Lying in his bed, with TV remote in hand and his royal blue sweatshirt lifted up off his gut, O'Brien asked Cassidy if he thought the two study sessions had been enough for the sophomores to get through their homework backlog. Cassidy was skeptical.

"Then we'll make them do it after the game," O'Brien said. "Do you think we should reserve the hotel computer for tonight, like 9:30 to 10:30?"

Just then, Zach came bounding into the room, telling O'Brien he had to switch the channel to the gripping North Carolina college game.

"Nah," O'Brien said, smiling as he pointed to the grainy video of the Longmeadow game. "We're scouting."

At 4:45 PM, the players piled into three vans and headed from the hotel to the Springfield College gym. Five players squeezed into the van Cassidy drove, each one wearing headphones, with the muffled sounds from different songs sneaking out of each pair.

The gymnasium was a round, white structure with blonde-wood bleachers and a gleaming wooden floor. A large sign read, "Springfield College: Birthplace of Basketball." The college was the modern-day incarnation of the School for Christian Workers, where Naismith had first hung his peach baskets. A girls' game was in progress as the Charlestown guys filed into the bleachers. They kept their headphones on, but their arrival had been noticed. Most people in Boston were content to ignore Charlestown's winning ways. But a tournament like this one attracted basketball aficionados, and to them, the boys from Charlestown mattered.

•   •   •

HOOD SAT IN THE BLEACHERS, training one eye on the girls' game and one eye on Terry's game chatting up a girl. She looked fine— a petite white girl from western Massachusetts who wore boots and blush that were the same shade of pink. As Terry spoke, inching closer to her, she twirled her reddish-brown hair around her finger and her cheeks flushed. When he walked away a few minutes later, a klatch of her friends encircled the girl to find out what the good-looking guy from Charlestown had said.

Hood smiled as he watched the scene unfold. For a few weeks now, he'd been trying to enlist his teammates in a pact: No more girlfriends for the rest of the season. They brought too many head-aches, clouding players' concentration levels. He made it clear he wasn't asking anyone to give up girls—just commitments. Ridley initially signed on, but then he met a Cape Verdean girl named Ash-ley, who was cute, with caramel skin and curly hair, and before long Ridley dropped out of the no-girlfriend pact.

Hood thought Ridley would eventually come around. In the meantime, Terry clearly had the right idea in making the most of their getaway. Many of the players were trying to run away from their responsibilities, at least for the weekend, and Hood had more to run away from than most.

Although he still hadn't breathed a word of this to O'Brien, Hood had been going through a rough couple of months with Tia, his longtime girlfriend. It began in October, when she'd dropped a bombshell: She was pregnant.

Hood was furious. He knew that fathering a baby could mess up his path. He knew O'Brien would be even more steamed if he found out. Hood responded by shutting down, refusing to talk to Tia for two weeks. That naturally upset her, and she stayed out of school for all that time because she didn't want to bump into him in the hall. Then one day he called her, and in his own way, sort of apologized for how he'd been behaving. He began giving her rides to school every day in his father's car. Tia resumed her habit of hanging out at Hood's house after school. When Hood was at practice, she just sat with his mother, now on medical disability, following her successful lung surgery. When Hood came home from practice, he and Tia would sit and talk.

A few weeks before the Springfield trip, things began to change again. The word in the corridors was that Hood was seeing other girls. He never came out and told Tia, but she had ears and eyes. She figured he was taking advantage of his status as a sports star rather than taking responsibility for his obligations. She decided she was going to have the baby, with or without him. She held out hope that he'd come to his senses and come back to her.

But Hood was headed in a different direction. It was around the same time that he made his pitch to the other guys to join him in giving up girlfriends.

• • •

WHEN THE GAME BEGAN, the Charlestown players looked groggy. Longmeadow put the first points on the board. Before long, though, Charlestown found its rhythm, and went on a tear, scoring 10 unanswered points.

When Ridley dished off a pass to a teammate who went on to score, Hugh, the assistant coach charged with keeping stats, smiled and put a slash mark next to Ridley's number in the "assists" column. The assist—the basketball term for the last pass leading directly to a score—was one of the more important metrics in O'Brien's world. It showed a player's willingness to put the team's glory ahead of his own.

In the bleachers behind Hugh sat his wife, Emily, a fixture at all the Charlestown games. She was there not only to cheer on her husband, but also her nephews Ridley and Paul.

Besides Emily, only a handful of Charlestown fans had made the ninety-minute drive to get to the game. But what Charlestown's boosters lacked in numbers, they made up for in style, thanks to Hood's father. Willie Barnes showed up wearing an unforgettable orange-beige leather suit, two gold bracelets, a gold watch, a pair of square-tipped shoes, and some nice-smelling cologne. He sat in the front row, on the opposite side of the court from Emily and the rest of the Charlestown contingent. Underneath his jacket, he wore one of his red rally T-shirts with his son's number 3 on it. "You're gonna see some real ball," he told the people in the stands around him, as he lifted the Canon T70 and began snapping.

Longmeadow, led by the muscular 6-foot-3 kid O'Brien had watched earlier on TV, edged back into the game. Besides him, his team was a methodical, slower, all-white throwback squad common in the western part of the state where basketball began. But he alone was dominant enough to keep Longmeadow in the game. At the half, Charlestown was up by five.

In the second half, Charlestown committed enough stupid errors to let Longmeadow's dominant player keep his outmatched team in the game. At one point, Spot knelt down to tie his shoe, in the middle of play, as the Longmeadow forward he was supposed to be defending jubilantly gestured for the point guard to pass him the ball. O'Brien erupted on the sidelines. Spot looked back at him, resting his fingers on the number 1 on his jersey, as if to ask what he'd done wrong. Then, in the fading minutes of the game, when Charlestown should have been running out the clock to protect its narrow lead, Ridley called a timeout.

Hood came to the rescue, making a key steal at the end to put the game away.

When the buzzer sounded, Charlestown, despite its overwhelming advantage on the court, was lucky to escape with a 5-point win. As the players filed off the court, Terry locked eyes with a cheerleader for the other team and slowly mouthed, "You're gorgeous." She blushed, letting her pom-poms fall by her side.

When O'Brien walked into the locker room, the players were lined up on a bench, execution-style. A few of them chewed nervously on their plastic mouth guards. O'Brien was chewing too, on his upper lip, as he leaned against the wall, listening to Zach rant and Hugh read off his depressing tally of stats from the game.

"That big kid wanted it more than us," Zach complained. "That team is not even that good. Where's the will?"

Hugh, waving his clipboard with all the stats he'd collected, jumped in: "We got only *four* defensive rebounds in the second half! I guess he got all the rest of them."

Cassidy reminded the guys of all those basketball aficionados in the stands. "This was your chance to show them what Charlestown is all about!" he said, shaking his head.

Finally, O'Brien joined in, telescoping in on Ridley's brain-freeze late in the game. "We're up by three, and he calls a *timeout*! I've never seen that in the *third grade*!"

The players pulled up their jeans over their shorts, and O'Brien and Zach headed out of the locker room, standing by the door and replaying the low points. Although Spot, who'd sunk a trio of three-pointers, felt he had turned the corner, his coaches were stressing about how much more they needed to see from him.

Just then, a young blond guy in a polo shirt came bounding over. He introduced himself as an assistant coach for Springfield College and said to O'Brien, "I was wondering about number 1?"

O'Brien looked surprised, considering how he felt Spot had played. But he quickly recovered and said, "He's available."

"Great," said the assistant, handing O'Brien a recruitment information packet. "Could you give this to him?"

In the post-game meal, O'Brien sat with his assistants, barely picking at his chicken sandwich. There was some commotion at one of the players' tables across the room. Hugh sat down with his food and explained what had happened. "Terry found a bug in his sandwich."

O'Brien waited a few beats. "Good," he cracked.

Back at the Hilton, the players congregated around the TV in the lobby, watching an NFL playoff game. The mood was downbeat, but not because of their poor performance on the court. Their taste of the high life would end when they headed back to Boston in the morning, back to reality.

After the game, before they climbed into the vans, a few of the guys had been talking to some attractive local girls, and one of them had given up her cell phone number. George, the squared-faced senior, had programmed it into his phone, but when he went to retrieve it in the hotel lobby, he realized he'd accidentally deleted it. Hood and Terry were furious. As a veteran, Hood was much more realistic than Terry about how hard it would have been to arrange a rendezvous while keeping O'Brien in the dark. But George's screw-up with the girl's phone number doomed any hope of trying. "I can't believe you lost the number, nigga!" Terry fumed.

For Terry, it could have been worse. He had finished his homework earlier in the day, so at least he could spend the night relaxing, if not with the female companionship he'd been working all day to arrange. As for the rest of the sophomores, O'Brien herded them back in the overheated conference room for two more hours of late-night study.

7
—
TOWNIES IN
BLACK AND WHITE

THE CHARLESTOWN SCHOOL BUS CHUGGED through South Boston, a congested neighborhood of alphabet-lettered streets lined with three-decker apartment houses overlooking Dorchester Bay. Then it made its climb up a steep hill and arrived at South Boston High School. The school looked like the perfect setting for a historic battle: a brick mountaintop fortress surrounded by a perfectly circular roadway that could have doubled as a moat. In fact, in 1776, George Washington's surprise late-night maneuver of having cannons hauled up that very hill was enough to convince the British Redcoats to leave Boston for good.

Once inside the 100-year-old school, the players found a far less intimidating scene. The gym was tiny, dark, and sweaty. It looked as though it belonged to a vintage elementary school. There were no seats, so the spectators stood rimming the court, in the narrow space between the boundary lines and the exterior walls. If they dared to stretch their arms during a yawn, they ran the risk of interfering with the play on the court.

A few minutes before tip-off, O'Brien watched Hood lead the rest of the guys single-file onto center court. Then Hood began the same pre-game ritual O'Brien's squads had been performing ever since Richard Jones's days on the team. He stood in the middle as Ridley and their teammates formed a circle around him, crouching down and putting their arms on each other's shoulders. As they all began to sway rhythmically, Hood rapped, "When I say Charlestown, y'all say Riders. Charlestown!"

The guys yelled, "RIDERS!"

"Charlestown!"

"RIDERS!"

For as long as anyone in Charlestown could remember, the high school sports teams were known as the Townies. Officially, that was still their name, but none of O'Brien's players called themselves that. It's not that they had a strong objection to the word. They weren't even born when "Townie" became shorthand for "white and angry." To them, Riders just sounded better.

O'Brien, of course, knew how racially loaded the nickname was, and he was glad his guys had found their own substitute. About the only people who still called them Townies were sportswriters and announcers. O'Brien had toyed with getting rid of the name for good. But he knew that would enrage Charlestown's dwindling corps of old-timers, those white-haired souls who spent their days idling in front of the Post Office and Papa Gino's, on the triangle of benches that locals called Jurassic Park.

· Besides, O'Brien realized that sometimes it's better to let matters take their natural course. As he surveyed the South Boston gym on this winter afternoon in 2005, he marveled at how unthinkable the scene would have been thirty years earlier. Back then, Charlestown and Southie were the twin Alamos for the army the white working class had mobilized to defend its way of life from the attack of a federal judge's school desegregation order. Before busing, South Boston High's student body was even whiter than Charlestown's—

99.3 percent, to be exact. But on this afternoon, besides one bench-warmer for Southie, the squads for both schools were entirely black. In fact, besides that kid and the coaches for both teams, there wasn't another white face in the gym.

• • •

ON JUNE 17, 1775, one year before Washington's cannon surprise in South Boston, Colonel William Prescott stationed his ragtag group of militiamen on Breed's Hill in Charlestown. With a sea of Redcoats approaching, his poorly armed men were reputedly told, "Don't fire until you see the whites of their eyes." The Battle of Bunker Hill—it drew its name from the nearby spot where Prescott intended to engage the British—was something of a suicide mission for the colonists. They were vastly outnumbered and their losses were staggering. But the victorious Redcoats' losses were twice as bad. Convinced the upstart colonists were insane in the casualties they were willing to endure in this American Revolution, the British military began to waver in its commitment to putting down the rebellion. The Redcoats had won the battle militarily, but they lost psychologically. They slunk out of Charlestown, but not before the Royal Navy's cannon fire burned down most of the buildings in town. The experience singed onto the Charlestown psyche an outlook on life: There would always be outsiders trying to mess with their "Townie" way of life, but they were strong enough to beat back any challenge, no matter how lopsided the odds might be. They could even win by losing.

In 1843, Charlestown memorialized its famous victory from defeat by dedicating the Bunker Hill Monument on the summit of Breed's Hill. Those who walked up the 294 steps winding inside the monument were treated to an unrestricted view of Charlestown, whose narrow streets spidered across the cozy 1-square-mile town.

Down on the waterfront was the U.S. Navy yard. Established just after the creation of the navy itself, the yard and the businesses that sprang up around it governed Charlestown's boom-or-bust economy. Longshoremen worked the wharves, and laborers packed the produce that was transported through Charlestown on rail and boats. They worked 'round the clock, and between shifts, they headed for the pub. Charlestown, it was said, had more bars per capita than any town in the country. The need for laborers attracted so many Irish-Catholic immigrants that the working-class English Protestants whose ancestors had settled the town soon felt threatened. Vulnerability turned to violence when a mob of them burned down a convent in town, in one of the ugliest incidents of anti-Catholic vigilantism in American history.

Trying to hold on to some power despite their falling numbers, the monied Yankees in town helped push through a plan in 1874 to have Charlestown surrender its independent status and become part of Boston. Many of Charlestown's Irish supported the move, since their people were on their way to wresting control of the capital city's political machine. By the turn of the century, Charlestown was the most Irish neighborhood in the nation's most emerald city this side of Oz. But most people in Charlestown would come to regret the merger. Boston bosses saddled Charlestown with the infrastructure required to support a growing urban center that none of the more powerful neighborhoods wanted in their backyard. There was already a state prison. Then came the ugly green stanchions that held up the highway, and, most painful, the elevated railway called "the El," which shaved off commuting time into Boston for residents of the North Shore but blighted Charlestown, blocking the sunlight and leaving the downtown dirty, empty, and entrapped.

Yet the Townies proved time and again that although they could be screwed with, they could not be beaten. The place became even more tribal, with extended families packed into the same house and the kids never straying far. They looked out for each other and shared a distrust of outsiders and a contempt for climbers in their midst. Let other Boston neighborhoods encourage the aspirations of the "lace curtain" Irish. Charlestown's Irish were content to stay where they were.

No structure in town better embodied this attitude than the old Charlestown High School building, a granite structure that stood directly across the street from the Bunker Hill Monument. It may have been steeped in history, but the school was never a place for academic achievement. The best and brightest generally left town for high school. In the late 1960s, Charlestown High was sending only 15 percent of its graduates on to college—the lowest of any high school in the city. The makeup of the student body hewed closely to that of the town—mostly white Irish Catholics. In 1967, there were only ten nonwhite students, including a few blacks.

For nearly a century, Charlestown proudly stood still. It was Irish, working-class, loyal—and suspicious of anyone who didn't match that description. "Townie" may have been a tag uttered with a sneer in most places, but it was a badge of honor in Charlestown, emblazoned on the jerseys of the high school sports squads, which attracted passionate followings.

Charlestown was a place of low expectations, besides the certainty that things wouldn't change. Then in the 1970s, everything did. The local economy collapsed after hundreds of longshoreman jobs disappeared and the navy closed the Charlestown yard. Police and firefighter jobs, long doled out by the Irish political machine, became harder to get as pressures mounted to get more minorities on the payroll. Finally, in 1974, federal Judge W. Arthur Garrity Jr. decided that Boston Public Schools—the oldest free public system in the country—were hopelessly and maliciously segregated, despite the fact that Massachusetts had outlawed segregated schools even before the Civil War. Faced with intransigence by bigots on the Boston school board, the judge blew up the school system. Court-ordered busing sent thousands of black kids from Boston's blackest neighborhoods of Roxbury, Mattapan, and Dorchester into its whitest wards of Charlestown and South Boston, and thousands of white students in the opposite direction. Boston had more famous white neighborhoods than Charlestown and Southie, such as Beacon Hill and the Back Bay, but they belonged to the upper class, so a war over slots in the city's crumbling public schools touched the lives of residents there about as intimately as famine in Africa.

The Townies railed against busing as the latest assault on their close-knit culture. They also railed against the hypocrisy they saw in educated, affluent liberals backing the busing edicts to assuage their white guilt while stowing away their own children in private or suburban schools. Wouldn't these liberals feel differently, the Townies argued, if they were forced to send their children to schools deep in the ghetto where most white adults dared not tread?

The Townies knew their fight was in many ways a hopeless cause: one tiny working-class neighborhood taking on a federal judge backed by the full power of the city and federal governments. But as Townies, they were used to battles with long odds. Their campaign often turned ugly, attracting helmeted riot police with their white shields and billy clubs, and network news reporters with their blow-dried hair and can-you-believe-this head-shaking. To the outside world, the Townies were largely seen as angry bigots. For sure, there were plenty of racists within their camp. But there were far more people who weren't motivated by racism but rather by a sense of profound powerlessness.

When busing took effect at Charlestown High in September 1975, some 200 Charlestown mothers sat in the middle of a street by the school, reciting the Lord's Prayer, chanting "Here we go, Charlestown!" and ignoring the cops' attempts to get them to leave. Throughout the year, black kids were met with racial slurs and grotesque graffiti, and fistfights between black and white kids broke out regularly in the corridors of the high school. Once, when a white sit-in on the school's main staircase turned violent, the black students were herded into classrooms on the top floor and then squired by police down fire stairs, out of the building, and onto school buses, which Townie kids then pelted with rocks. Busing put Charlestown on the map like nothing in its history since that battle on Breed's Hill. And this time, it was for all the wrong reasons.

On the morning of April 5, 1976, more than 100 white Charlestown High students made the easy walk to Government Center, the barren brick-paved lunarscape surrounding the charmless block of concrete known as Boston City Hall. It was the nation's bicentennial year, and leaders in Boston—a city touted as the "cradle of liberty"—were preparing to strut their democratic bona fides all summer long. The students figured it was the perfect time to test the depth of that commitment. Along with their usual anti-busing placards, they brought along bicentennial banners and American flags. Outside City Hall, they met up with about 150 kids from South Boston High and then headed inside to the City Council chamber at the invitation of Louise Day Hicks. For a decade, the frumpy but cunning middle-aged Mrs. Hicks had been converting white resentment over pressure to desegregate Boston schools into electoral gold, allowing her to take control first of the School Committee and then the City Council. The bigots on the School Committee had for generations managed to starve black schools of resources, refusing to so much as acknowledge the glaring disparities. That cynical path led inevitably to a lawsuit by the NAACP, which in turn led to Judge Garrity's explosive busing order. But by 1976, the anti-busing movement had radicalized to the point of making Hicks look like a moderate. To the students from Charlestown and Southie crowded into the council chamber, she preached perseverance yet patience. They left determined to ratchet up their protest by taking it to the nearby federal courthouse from which Garrity had fired his rocket.

As they crossed the plaza around 10:00 AM, the throngs of students were getting pumped. Near the front of the pack was a junior named Eddie Irvin, who was vice president of his class at Charlestown High. Not far behind was a Southie sophomore named Joe Rakes, who was carrying an American flag on a staff. Just as they were rounding the corner, Theodore Landsmark came bounding up an alley that fed into the plaza. He was hurrying because he was late for a community meeting he was scheduled to chair at City Hall. Landsmark was a twenty-nine-year-old Yale-educated lawyer wearing a three-piece suit. He was also black.

"Get the nigger!" one of the kids yelled. Eddie Irvin was part of the hive that swarmed Landsmark. The first hit came from behind, knocking off Landsmark's glasses. Then came a blow to his face, breaking his nose, and sending him to the ground. The high-schoolers continued to pummel him, with punches and kicks. Just as Landsmark managed to get himself up, Joe Rakes came charging at him, brandishing the flag staff like a spear. Landsmark was able to lean back enough to avoid being impaled, but the staff gashed his face. A fast-fingered photographer for the *Boston Herald American* managed to capture the savage scene just before the point of impact. The photo showed a black man in a three-piece suit stumbling to avoid being speared by a pole holding the very symbol of American freedom. It all looked so willful, so tribal, so hideous. The photo, titled "The Soiling of Old Glory," sailed around the globe en route to winning the Pulitzer Prize. Overnight, the image of Boston as the birthplace of abolitionism was gone, replaced by one that turned it into Birmingham North.

•　•　•

THAT SAME BICENTENNIAL YEAR, Christine Rossell participated in a public forum on busing. The dais was filled with members of the pro-busing brain trust—professors, lawyers, advocates, and experts. Several were black, but most, like Rossell, a young assistant professor from Boston University, were white. The crowd was thick with white working-class parents. After listening to the brain trust extol the importance of busing, a white parent in the audience stood up and cut through the clutter: "Excuse me, how many of you have your children in the Boston Public Schools?" Uncomfortably, not one of them could say yes. Huffs and finger wagging rippled through the crowd. Rossell searched her mind; in the entire constellation of pro-busing experts across the city, she could think of only one who had his kids in Boston schools.

Just one year earlier, Rossell had arrived in Boston with a reputation as a rising-star political scientist whose research proved school desegregation did not cause white flight. Judge Garrity's critics had long complained that all his busing plan was doing was opening up the accelerator on the flight of white students from city schools. Garrity believed smaller family sizes in the age of the birth control pill were more responsible than busing for the shrinking white population. But until Rossell arrived, the judge had no data to back up his hunch. He quickly tapped her as an adviser.

Rossell's findings contradicted those of a more senior academic who had found evidence of significant white flight. With breezy confidence, she dismissed anyone who challenged her conclusions. But, like any good social scientist, she continued collecting data and even widened her sample. That's when, privately, she began to worry that her critics were right. The districts in her original sample had fairly mild desegregation plans. When she looked at those with plans closer to Boston's—it was hard to find any north of the Mason-Dixon Line as disruptive or contested—she had to admit that white flight was real, and quite extensive. But when she brought her new data to Garrity's chief adviser, Boston University School of Education Dean Robert Dentler, she concluded he didn't want to hear it. It was clear to her that Boston parents—black and white— were voting with their feet, and those who couldn't afford to get their kids out felt stranded and embittered. Many white students assigned to black schools simply didn't show up, and eventually dropped out for good.

Dentler had initially found Rossell to be a promising young academic. But as she became more strident in her criticism, he came to see her simply as an obstructionist. He told her he thought her estimates of Boston's white flight were inflated because for years the school system had been padding its student rolls to increase state aid. He accused her of going to the other side. "I was hard at work trying to make the court plan go," he explained later. "And she was busy trying to call it off. What else could we do but stop talking to each other?"

Dentler, who lived in the affluent suburb of Lexington, insisted that his residency was irrelevant. Rossell found that position insulting to all the parents who couldn't afford to get their kids out. She began telling her friends, none of whom had their kids in Boston's crumbling schools, "A liberal is in favor of busing other people's children."

In 1978, the school system attempted a fresh start in Charlestown, opening the new, hulking, brick-walled Charlestown High as a replacement for the old granite one up the hill. But the Townies did not go quietly into the night. During a football game on the new Charlestown High field in 1979, a trio of Townie teens climbed onto the roof of the Bunker Hill housing project across the street. Then one of them used a .22-caliber gun to turn a black football player from the opposing team—a Roxbury kid named Darryl Williams—into a quadriplegic.

Determined to avoid the mess of Boston, many urban districts across the country opted for more voluntary desegregation plans. In 1989, Boston switched to its "controlled choice" plan, where students were allowed to list their top choices for schools, but administrators continued to use the student's race in deciding which choices would be granted. Five years later, Rossell and a city councilor drafted a plan to remove racial considerations from school

assignment by restoring neighborhood schools and creating mag-
net schools, which focused on a particular field of study, such as
science or the performing arts. Neighborhood schools, she said,
would help revive some of the community cohesion in places like
Charlestown and would persuade more white parents to keep their
kids in public schools. The sad fact, she said, is most whites aren't
comfortable being in the minority, and unless they can be guaran-
teed a school where they are in the majority, most of them won't
return to the public schools. City and school officials ignored Rossell's suggestions. It wasn't until the 2000–2001 school year that
Boston school officials, in response to a federal lawsuit filed by a
group of white parents, stopped using race as a factor in deciding
which students would be assigned to which schools. For most
schools, officials began reserving half the seats for kids from the
neighborhood, and half for kids bused in from other parts of the city.

Largely because of busing, Boston was tarred with a national
reputation as a racist city. But Rossell pointed to surveys showing
residents of Boston to be more progressive in terms of racial attitudes than just about anywhere else in the country, with one exception: views on school desegregation. Rossell came to believe
that, for the working class, busing had been a tragedy. "This was
such a mistake," she said. "We should have done it gradually and
voluntarily. Naïve white liberals like myself took these white
working-class people who've been screwed in life and made them
pay the price while we sat it out."

While maintaining that busing was unavoidable, even Dentler
eventually admitted the price had been high. During the early
1980s, he was teaching a course at the University of Massachusetts'
Boston campus when a white student from Dorchester raised her
hand and told him his busing plan had left her with lousy teachers
in her classrooms and chaos in the corridors. "I can't write a paper
worth a damn thanks to what you did," she said. Dentler was taken
aback, but he didn't duck her accusation. "You probably were

harmed," he said. "Do you want to learn how to write now? I'll put in the extra effort." He did, and she learned, but a generation of kids had lost out.

And what did Boston's blacks get out of it? The most decrepit and shamefully undersupplied schools in black neighborhoods were closed down. And for once, the educational needs of black children commanded attention from the city's power brokers. But here, too, the cost was high. These children were forced to withstand a daily barrage of vicious slurs, being told again and again that they were the problem. Black neighborhoods lost a good deal of their cohesion without tight school communities at their center. And all that attention from the powerbrokers turned out to be short-lived.

The real shame of busing is that it was a class war dressed up as a race fight. Michael Fung, who lived through the battles as an administrator, once summed it up this way: "Busing is basically a joke. You move poor white kids into the schools of poor black kids." To Fung, the only fair, effective route to desegregation would have been a "metropolitan plan," extending the busing mandate to include the affluent suburban school districts around Boston. For nearly a decade before Garrity's busing order, a voluntary busing program called METCO had been in effect, sending a select group of Boston kids to some of the white school districts surrounding Boston. It continues to this day, but the numbers have always been too small to have much of an effect in either the suburbs or the city.

Those close to Garrity insist that the judge had intended to mandate a metropolitan plan for Boston but pulled back after the U.S. Supreme Court ruled against a similar plan in Detroit. Garrity was determined that his ruling not be overturned on appeal. By that measure, he succeeded. But in a much more important way, he failed. By refusing to require the involvement of the suburbs, Garrity put the burden of desegregation squarely on the shoulders of the poor, making it, like crime and graffiti, a problem that only the inner city had to worry about.

By the dawn of the twenty-first century, the story in big cities across the nation was largely the same. In Los Angeles, 84 percent of public school students were black or Hispanic; in Chicago, it was 87 percent, and in Washington, D.C., 94 percent. Fatigued education reformer Jonathan Kozol began his crusade for equality in public education with the publication in 1967 of *Death at an Early Age,* his withering indictment of racism in the Boston schools, based on his year teaching in Dorchester. In 2005, he wrote a depressing book cataloging how little had changed in urban education, *The Shame of the Nation: The Restoration of Apartheid Schooling in America.*

While Boston Public Schools were nearly 60 percent white before the busing order of 1974, three decades later that figure had fallen to about 15 percent. Desegregation was dead.

Sadly, the schools were just a reflection of the segregated communities around them. The 2000 Census found whites to be in the minority in Boston for the first time in history. But closer inspection showed how old patterns refused to die. True, many in the white working class had left Charlestown and Southie. But they were replaced largely by white yuppies. Outside the housing projects, the black population of Charlestown and Southie was close to zero. With the suburbs thoroughly white, nearly half the blacks in Massachusetts lived in Boston, with the vast majority of them clustered in the city's three blackest neighborhoods of Roxbury, Dorchester, and Mattapan. Data on big cities across the country found minority populations to be as segregated as they had been ten years earlier. Even income did little to dislodge these patterns. The average black American earning $60,000 a year lived in an area with almost double the poverty rate as the average white American earning less than $30,000.

Yet in the Boston school system, everyone seemed to be sleepwalking through this post-busing world. Because the forces of white flight were not powerful enough to move buildings, many schools remained in white neighborhoods long after the white students decamped for private or suburban classrooms. Still, the public school seats in Boston's white neighborhoods needed to be filled. So black kids like Hood and Ridley—as well as kids all the way down to the elementary level—still spent a big chunk of every day commuting across the city, navigating through gang turf wars, to get to white neighborhoods where the schools were just as dominated by black and Hispanic students as the schools down the street from their apartments. That couldn't possibly be what the social engineers of the 1970s had in mind. Christine Rossell continued to complain, but no one seemed to listen. "What is the point of busing black kids from black schools in black neighborhoods to black schools in white neighborhoods?" she asked. "What is the point of that? I mean, it's *insane.*"

•   •   •

T HE LAST WHITE KID TO PLAY on the Charlestown basketball team graduated in 1997. Ian Urquhart, who was born in 1978, had grown up a Townie in a changing Charlestown.

The Townie families with options chose to exercise them, sending their kids to parochial schools or selling the family house and fleeing to the suburbs. More and more, their Georgian townhouses and colonial revival row houses were snatched up and restored by yuppies, who sent their kids, if they had any, to private schools. Even the old granite Charlestown High building was eventually converted into high-end condos. The Townies' slots in Charlestown's schools were taken over by black and Hispanic kids bused in from elsewhere.

Still, for most of Ian's time growing up, Charlestown retained its Townie vibe—tribal and tough. In 1993, he entered Charlestown High as a freshman and hung out with other Townie kids who were now the minority. Ian took to the Townie culture of low expectations, skipping class, being in a hurry to get nowhere. But everything changed his sophomore year.

Ian tried out for the basketball team, which by then had been all-black for some time, and was surprised when he made the cut. At the time, O'Brien was in his second year as coach, coming off the soul-sapping one-win season. The man was clearly determined to win more this time out. But what struck Ian about O'Brien was what he demanded of him off the court. "I had never worked that hard before," Ian once explained. "You were held accountable. You had study hall; you had to be nice to your teachers." His grades improved, and so did his game.

For some time, Charlestown's basketball fan base had been small, because there was no coherence to it. The Townies who breathed and bled Charlestown had fled or lost interest and weren't about to come back to cheer on a bunch of black kids wearing C-town jerseys. The black kids' families weren't interested in traveling to a part of the city whose mere name conjured memories of people getting pummeled just for being black. And the yuppies, who slept at night in their restored row houses, cleared out of town at the first sight of morning light. They had absolutely no connection to high school sports, which for generations had been indivisible from Townie culture.

But once Ian, a genuine Townie from his green-blue eyes on down, started getting some real playing time, the team began once again to attract the locals. Off the court, Ian remained friends with his fellow Townies, although their culture of low expectations seemed more and more foreign to him. He found he had more in common with the black kids on the team who, thanks to all of O'Brien's prodding, had their eyes set on college. With O'Brien's help, Ian got into Skidmore College, while several of his teammates went to equally selective schools. "Before this program," Ian said, "nobody from Charlestown High was going to Bates, Bowdoin, or Skidmore."

When he returned after graduation four years later, Ian found a Charlestown that had quickened its pace of change to the point where it was becoming unrecognizable. Gone was much of the ugliness of its racially charged past, as well as much of the grime and crime. In its place were trendy restaurants serving up $32 entrees. The old high school wasn't the only familiar building to have gone condo. So too had most of the old Navy Yard. In fact, just about all the fixtures of the Olde Towne were either gone, on their way out, or transforming into something else to stay alive. There were only a few places where the yuppies and the Townies coexisted. At the Warren Tavern, a lovingly restored 1780 Federalist structure, a couple of Townies in work boots and jeans could often be spotted at the bar during the lunch hour, while the tables were occupied by real estate types wearing dark suits and making deals in their cell phone earpieces.

Ian briefly became an assistant coach for O'Brien before enrolling at the New England School of Law. "Charlestown was traditionally a working-class Irish-Catholic neighborhood. It's not that way anymore. Now it's filled with young urban professionals," Ian said. "I can't say that's a bad thing. I've become one of them."

·   ·   ·

HOOD AND RIDLEY LED THE WAY into Northeastern University's Cabot Center on a Saturday night in January. Although the game between Charlestown and Catholic Memorial was being played on a college court, it was listed as a home game on the Charlestown schedule. Despite the snow and slush that blanketed Boston, the game drew the families of Hood and Ridley as well as several hundred Charlestown fans—more than any regular-season game on the team's actual home court. That's because Northeastern University sits in Roxbury, and for most of the players' families, getting there was a lot simpler than getting across the city to Charlestown. So O'Brien made sure the game became a fixture on the annual Charlestown schedule. Because he knew his black players wore jerseys representing a neighborhood that once violently excluded their kind, he was always looking for ways to let them make the Charlestown experience their own.

For generations, the Charlestown team's official colors were red, white, and blue, a tribute to the neighborhood's patriotic past. The uniforms stayed the same, but O'Brien let his seniors vote each year on what color the rest of the gear should be, from sneakers and socks to sweatshirts and team jackets. They almost always opted for black.

All the time O'Brien spent marinating in black culture with his players made him more sensitive to the subtle racism that his guys had to deal with in an age when most overt bigotry had become socially unacceptable. For instance, it was common for white coaches of white-dominated suburban teams to explain away their losses to Charlestown with phrases like, "Their athleticism really hurt us," suggesting the black players' dominance could simply be attributed to their God-given speed rather than the skills and stamina they had developed in hour upon tedious hour of practice.

Still, O'Brien's occasional attempts to speak his players' language could make them wince. In a recurring locker room lament, the middle-aged Irish guy would yell, "You're *chillin'* out there!"—leaning his shoulders way back and putting both hands out, all casual and cool. No matter how often he struck that pose, he never looked casual or cool. In practices, he sometimes tried to mimic the easy way in which his guys discussed matters of race. He was smart enough never to use the word "nigga," which some of the players, like their favorite rappers, used as frequently as prepositions. Instead, O'Brien would try his hand at jokes. Invariably, they were as clumsy as his chillin'. Once when a couple of players were barking commands to a light-skinned black teammate to collect the practice balls, O'Brien cracked, "You can't make him shag the balls; his mamma's white!" As his players groaned and rolled their eyes, O'Brien grinned.

More remarkable, though, was how little race intervened in their relationship. Guys who'd been with O'Brien a while could tell he cared about them, on the court and off. They noticed how he'd think nothing of driving twenty hours in a weekend to visit one of his former players in college.

Charlestown out-hustled the team from Catholic Memorial, which consisted mostly of white, slower players who passed well. In a single possession midway through the half, the Charlestown players grabbed one offensive rebound after another, tossing up seven shots in a row until one finally dropped in. After that, Catholic Memorial had no way back.

In the corner of the gym, just like at every one of Charlestown's home games, a stocky, studious senior named Jerome Allen—who went by the name J-Rome—stood behind huge speakers, spinning hip-hop records. Though he often had to strain to be heard over the music during timeout huddles, O'Brien thought it was worth it, if it helped relieve his guys of some of the race baggage associated with playing for Charlestown. J-Rome blasted the latest release from 50 Cent, "Disco Inferno," a new favorite of the Charlestown cheerleaders. When they heard "Shake sh-sh-shake that ass, girl," the cheerleaders broke free from their formation and did as 50 said.

8

REMATCH

UNLIKE HOOD AND RIDLEY, GEORGE RUSSELL was no star. The stocky, square-faced senior couldn't jump high or run fast or shoot particularly well. But he was tough under the boards, and he was always hustling to get better. O'Brien prized George's loyalty and discipline. After using him as a utility player for three years, he'd finally made him a starter. George was enjoying his new status.

But while he was walking to class on a Friday morning in early February, something popped into George's head that stopped him cold. The regular season was already three-quarters over. Back in December, after the Charlestown guys had been humiliated during their home opener against Eastie and O'Brien responded by dialing up the duration and intensity of the team practices, George had felt the end of the season couldn't come fast enough. But now that George was finally getting a chance to enjoy the celebrity that came with being a starter on the best basketball team in Boston, he was wishing he could slow down time.

So much in his life had improved over the last two months—athletically, academically, and socially—all that really matters in high school. Following that Eastie loss, Charlestown had gone on a tear, winning eleven games in a row. George knew some of those wins had more to do with the weakness of the opposition than the strength of Charlestown. He also knew the hardest stretch of the schedule was the final one, which would begin the following night with a rematch against Eastie. But for the first time he was operating with the confidence of someone who knew he had a key role to play. With his smothering defense and his willingness to throw some elbows under the boards, George had proved his worth in recent weeks. He'd even found a way to earn a few extra bucks in the process. When O'Brien had noticed that too few of his players were taking "charges"—planting their feet under the hoop and bravely drawing an offensive foul from the opponent charging toward them—he decided to offer his guys $5 every time they did. George liked the extra spending money so much that he kept a running accounting. Anytime he drew the call during a game, he would yell over to the bench as he jogged to the other end of the court, "That's five dollahs, Coach."

George also kept a close eye on another incentive program: the "star chart" hanging in the locker room, which O'Brien used to track player achievements like improving their grades. In a few hours, George would find out whether he'd earned a critical five-star bonus when he learned what his grades were for the second quarter. For the first time in his life, George had a real shot at making the honor roll.

Success on court was also doing wonders for George's social life. During a passing period between classes, he positioned himself in the landing of a crowded stairwell that was painted bright green. Then he began his favorite pastime, something he called "playing the hall." He shouted to a girl who was descending the stairs, "La-Toya, I called you last night." He put his hand up to his ear to pantomime a phone. "I wanted some *company*." She smiled and gave him a warm hug.

Despite the way he loved to socialize in school, outside of school George mostly kept to himself. When the rest of the guys on the team hung out together out at Ridley's, George stayed away. "When you gonna come hang out at my place?" Ridley would often ask him. "Someday," George would say. While the other juniors and seniors always got rides home after the games, either from family members or their friends, George rode the team bus home with all the younger guys. He'd sit with his arm resting on the back of the bus's thick green seat cushion, listening to his Sony Discman. His new favorite was The Game, a West Coast disciple of 50 Cent. The Game had used a college basketball scholarship to shake loose the shackles of Compton's street life, but he blew it after he got caught hustling drugs on campus. According to the biography he gave after fame found him, he was shot five times in 2001, and twenty-three hours later, "I woke up from a coma and I had the gift of rap."

Like a lot of the kids around him, George had grown up in a dreary housing project and had a father who was in and out of jail. When he was in middle school, his mother sat him down in front of the TV and made him watch the unsparing HBO prison drama *Oz*, so he'd see where street life got you. "That scared the hell out of me," George once said. "I knew I didn't want that—taking showers and having guys come up to you."

When it came time to pick a high school, George sought advice from an older guy who lived in his project. At 6-foot-5, Cori Boston had a sweet jump shot and was a player to watch. Cori told George to follow him to Charlestown. "Look at the other high school teams in Boston and see how many of those guys end up in college, and then look at Charlestown," Cori said. "It ain't even close." The idea that George—who wasn't a natural athlete and whose test results were low enough to have him tracked into special needs classes— would be thinking about how he could use basketball to get to college was pretty remarkable. O'Brien took immediately to the kid's work ethic, but his lack of gifts meant he had to log a lot of time on the bench before gaining his starting spot.

During his first-period class, called Law and Justice, George sat in the back next to Spot, his smooth-talking teammate with the

Hollywood smile. George told Spot about a new girl he had just begun "talking to," which meant they were somewhere just shy of dating. Until recently, George had been dating a short, talkative, pony-tailed girl named Shay. But he'd grown frustrated by all the reports he was getting about how Shay was flirting with other guys, including Troy, who was George's 6-foot-5 teammate. George refused to confront her about it, so Spot did it for him. After the team's easy win the night before, Spot went up to Shay and cussed her out for two-timing his buddy George with another baller. Shay denied it.

George told Spot that after that exchange, Shay had confronted *him*, saying, "I heard from three people that you heard people are talking about me and Troy!" So George pretended he didn't know anything about it.

"Just tell her you did!" Spot said, waving his San Diego Padres cap with the unbent brim to make his point. "Why won't you?"

"I don't need to," George said. "I got another girl."

"What's her name?"

"Chadry, or sumptin' like that," George said. "I didn't know her name. I called her cell phone and some old lady answered. So I said, 'Is you daughter there?'"

Spot burst out laughing. "Man, you got some serious problems! What if she had another daughter?"

"Nah. The other sister is like nine."

The conversation resumed in Pre-Calculus class. When a Chinese kid sitting in front of them tried to join in, Spot closed him down. "What do you want, *Tiny*?"

"Hey, my girls are satisfied," the Chinese kid shot back, with a nervous smile.

There wasn't much hostility among the Charlestown High's three main minority groups—blacks, Hispanics, and Asians—but there wasn't much cross-pollination either. Blacks held a slim majority, but their dominance transcended numbers. The school had a black culture to it, and the Hispanics, the Chinese, and the few remaining whites had no choice but to accept that. When kids tried to step out of their groupings, racial zingers were the prods used to pen them back in.

The Chinese kid tried his own prod, calling Spot "fried chicken."

Spot laughed and reminded him, "Hey, *you* guys do chicken wings."

The Chinese kid turned away, but Spot wasn't done, perusing the take-out menu in his mind to keep the buffet of slurs coming. "What's the matter, Crab Rangoon? You got a problem, Beef Teriyaki?"

George had no interest in joining in the racial food fight. He had just been given reason to celebrate. His math teacher had told him he'd be getting an A for the quarter. "My first A in math in my life!" George loudly announced, as though volume would make the achievement seem more real.

During his Environmental Science class, George bummed a piece of loose-leaf paper off the girl behind him and wrote down all the grades he knew he was getting for the second term.

Law and Justice: B+

Chemistry: A−

Gym (actually study hall with O'Brien): A

English: B−

Pre-Calculus: A

Environmental Science was still an unknown. If he earned at least a B-minus, George would make the honor roll.

"Hey Mister, what grade I got in this class?" George called to his Environmental Science teacher.

Steve Carroll was a dedicated but tired veteran teacher who had grown up in Charlestown and who was now counting the days until his retirement. He kept a sign in his classroom that read TIME WILL PASS. WILL YOU? He knew this environmental science class wasn't much of a class at all. When he described it as a science class, he bent his fingers to indicate quotation marks around the term.

Classified as an independent study, the course required students to read, at their own pace, chapters from a textbook and then take multiple-choice tests, while Carroll sat behind his desk, staring back at them. At times, the pace George chose was the one that saw his head down on his desk and his eyes closed.

"You're the only thing that's standing between me and the honor roll," George told his teacher.

Carroll wouldn't reveal his hand. "If you didn't sleep so much, you'd be all set," he said.

Thinking about how a C would kill his best chance ever of making the honor roll, George began to regret all those naps. But, damn, the class was boring. What was he supposed to do?

Because it was a Friday, George spent one of his periods in the school's career center, using the computer to research colleges. His guidance counselor, a twenty-six-year-old blonde Boston College grad named Kristyn O'Brien, was no relation to his coach. But she was a big believer in the basketball program and eager to work closely with the coach in helping his players get to college. Kristyn sat at a computer table with George, pumping him for information so she could complete his financial aid application.

"Do you have any dependents?" she asked.

"Huh?"

"Any kids?"

"No way, Miss!" George said, shaking his head furiously. "I'm not having no kids until I'm fifty, and then I'm having only one. No more than that."

When she had completed the form, she encouraged George to go online with his password to find out his latest SAT results

"No, they ain't ready yet," George said, looking away.

"Yes, they're available starting today."

He looked around the room, saw a half dozen of his classmates hunched over computers, and then waved her off. "No, not now. I'm too nervous."

Kristyn understood why. The first time George took the SAT, his combined score in math and English wasn't much over 600, out of a possible 1,600. The second time it jumped, amazingly, to 1,100. George and his guidance counselor were elated. But the elation faded quickly, as there was a notation in the computer system requiring George to call the College Board immediately. As it turned out, a jump that big automatically triggered a College Board investigation. The result was George had to take the test once again. If he came within 100 points of his high score, he would be allowed to keep the 1,100. If he didn't, the score would disappear.

The suggestion behind the automatic investigation was hard to miss: The kid must have cheated. But George's coaches and guidance counselor couldn't believe that for a minute. For starters, how would you even cheat on the SAT? What's more, if the coaches were asked to pick anyone on the team capable of cheating, George would have shown up near the bottom of everybody's list. The kid was as straight as his jaw line. They figured he had just gotten very lucky in his guesses, and they were worried. Luck like that didn't strike twice.

•   •   •

HOOD WAS SITTING WITH SOME FRIENDS at a table in the corner of the cafeteria when he spotted George and Spot walking through the door. George headed for the lunch line, but Spot, wearing loosely laced Timberlands and a wide grin, made his way to Hood's table. It was clear Spot was still beaming from his performance on the court the night before, when he'd been the high scorer. The game before that, Hood had been the high scorer himself. The winning streak seemed to lift everybody's spirits, but they knew it could all end the following night, during the rematch against Eastie.

So they celebrated while they still could. Instead of settling for the cafeteria's cardboard-textured pizza, Hood had conspired with

Spot to order out. Not a minute after he arrived at Hood's table, Spot turned around and headed back out, slyly exiting the cafeteria for his rendezvous with the delivery man. Soon he was back, sitting across the table from Hood, pulling grease-stained paper bags from his pockets. Tawanda Brown, their slender, fast-talking friend with large eyes and long manicured nails, stood in front of Hood to block the view of the cafeteria monitors as he devoured his tasty cheeseburger dripping with ketchup and mayo.

As far as rebellion goes, it was pretty mild stuff, particularly for Hood, who had been the reigning suspension champ of his middle school. Somehow for Hood, acting out to the point of getting suspended no longer held the same appeal. It wasn't worth the endless lectures from O'Brien he'd be forced to endure. Besides, a lot of what O'Brien had stressed during all his lectures in the past seemed to have seeped into Hood's brain.

During his freshman year, when O'Brien would take him to Burger King to try to get to know him, Hood would sit across the table and stare back coolly at the coach or down at his French fries. Back then, he thought the coach was just somebody else trying to use him for his own advantage. But across their years together, Hood realized O'Brien was different. Why else would he check in regularly with Hood during the off-season? Or ask after Hood's mother and give pep talks to his younger brother? Or spend so much energy trying to get Hood on track to get to college?

Over the years, Hood had let his coach into his world, past the icy looks and clipped responses that he used to keep most other adults at a distance. Hood could tell O'Brien treasured the access. Still, Hood was determined not to leave himself vulnerable, so he kept up some of his defenses. He simply couldn't count on how O'Brien would react if he revealed that Tia was pregnant. So when it came to the matter that was weighing most heavily on his mind, he told his coach nothing.

When the year began, O'Brien let Hood know he was determined to see him get an acceptance letter and a good financial-aid package from a solid Division III college. But as the season went on, and Hood's game improved and the bond between them appeared to grow tighter, O'Brien raised the stakes. He told Hood he thought he could earn an athletic scholarship. Those were harder to come by and available only from the bigger college programs in Divisions I and II. That would mean a lot more work for both of them.

Hood had come to see college as both something he wanted and something that wasn't a given. As a star tailback on the football team, he was used to hearing people in Boston tell him he was destined to play Division I ball. He assumed the offers would pour in, as everyone predicted. When they didn't, he grudgingly came to accept what O'Brien had told him: "It's great if those come. But in the meantime, I want to make sure you have realistic options." O'Brien was all about realism. He said he had seen too many guys hanging around gyms in Boston, talking about all the scouts who had once banged on their door. O'Brien told his guys he wanted them to leave Charlestown with more than just stories.

With Hood, O'Brien had made it clear: His wildly inconsistent transcript of B's and D's, depending on the class and his mood, wouldn't cut it this year. He also had to improve his SAT scores. Hood needed a combined 820 on his SAT to meet NCAA requirements for scholarship athletes. Hood had met that mark, but not by much, and most schools wanted to see it higher. At O'Brien's instruction, he had retaken the test a few weeks ago and told his coach he thought he'd done better. Today he would find out for sure.

After lunch, when Hood walked into Kristyn O'Brien's office, George was already sitting there. Her office, on the fourth floor, in the section of the building where all the walls were painted orange, was one of the guys' favorite hangouts during the school day, partly because meeting with their guidance counselor gave them an excuse to slip out of class, partly because they found her so easy to talk to, and partly because they found the young blonde counselor and track coach so easy on the eyes. She logged onto the College Board website to check Hood's score. It wasn't there.

She dialed the 800 number. The voice on the other end asked to speak with Hood.

Sitting beneath a sign that read ATTITUDE IS UP TO YOU, Hood held the phone up to his ear and listened for several minutes, without saying a thing. "Aww-right," he said, finally, before hanging up the phone.

"What's the deal?" Kristyn asked.

"She said I had to call back next Friday."

"What does that mean?" she asked nervously.

George shook his head. "That's exactly how it started with me."

When Kristyn logged on to check George's latest scores, the news was as bad as everyone had feared. His combined score hadn't gotten out of the 600s. That 1,100 was writing on sand, and the latest score had washed it away.

Still, George wasn't going to let that ruin his day. In the hall, he had bumped into Mr. Carroll, who finally relented and told George his grade in Environmental Science: B. For the first time in his life, George Russell was on the honor roll.

•   •   •

SWEAT WAS EVERYWHERE. On the face of the point guard. On the back of O'Brien's neck. On the court, in invisible, slick puddles. The same white Gatorade towel was used to wipe away the moisture in all three places. High school basketball is seldom pretty. But, at its best, it's intense, riveting, and gritty.

It was one of those nights.

Towering banks of dirty snow crowded the parking lot of East Boston High School, which sat overlooking the water, not far from Logan International Airport. The snow banks were reminders of the blizzard that had hit Boston a week earlier, but on this first Saturday in February, the temperature had climbed into the upper 40s. The thaw had begun—everywhere but inside the Eastie gym.

The place was thumping. Yellow DO NOT CROSS police tape was stretched along the perimeter of the court, to keep spectators off it. Eastie, whose state-title dreams had been repeatedly shot down by Charlestown, was dying to be the gunner this time. Both teams came into the rematch flying high. Since the Eastie players had dismantled O'Brien's squad two months earlier, they were sure they had the edge, especially on their home court.

In contrast to O'Brien in his tired red sweater vest and black slacks, David Siggers, Eastie's forty-one-year-old head coach, appeared to have stepped right out of a fashion spread, modeling a sharp charcoal suit with a pink-and-white striped dress shirt, open at the collar.

Charlestown showed up short one big man. A few days earlier, Terry Carter, the stabbing victim, had disappeared, and nobody had been able to find him. Yet a familiar face had returned to the starting lineup. O'Brien's gamble at yanking Spot from the starting five a month earlier appeared to have paid off in helping the senior regain his confidence. Fresh from the 20-point, 10-rebound performance off the bench two nights earlier, Spot couldn't mask his excitement at being on the floor for the opening tip-off. But Charlestown's biggest change really caught Eastie by surprise. Jack O'Brien, who had ridden his defensive strategy of a full-game, full-court press to four straight state titles, was switching to man-to-man.

Siggers and his players looked confused when the Charlestown guys didn't pressure the ball for the full length of the court and instead set up in a conventional half-court defense. Confusion was exactly what O'Brien was aiming for. The two teams had faced each other so often over the past few years that O'Brien figured Eastie had gotten too good at breaking down the vaulted Charlestown press. And as much as the change to man-to-man defense had rattled the Eastie guys, the Charlestown players seemed excited to be doing something different.

Seventeen seconds into the game, Ridley muffled the Eastie crowd by sinking a 3-pointer, the type of clutch play that proved him worthy of the Division I scholarship he'd received. Spot quickly began hitting shots and pulling down rebounds. Charlestown raced out to a 12–2 lead.

Eastie's imposing 6-foot-3 forward took to the foul line and swished a free throw. That free throw stopped the bleeding and sparked an Eastie run. Before long, Charlestown's lead had shrunk to 2 points.

An argument erupted when Charlestown assistant coach Steve Cassidy charged up to a referee and accused East Boston's official scorer of deliberately undercounting the number of fouls called against one of Eastie's stars. Charlestown's scorer, a black honor roll student named Bie Aweh who alternated with her twin sister in doing the books, had pointed out the discrepancy to Cassidy. "And it's not the first time!" the usually reserved Cassidy yelled to the refs.

Eastie's scorer was no school kid. Jessie Stokes had white curly hair and a generous stomach, and looked distinguished in his suit and tie. He was left-handed and held his score book at an odd 180-degree angle as he made his notations. When he heard Cassidy hurl the accusation against him, he smacked his red pen down on the table and stood up to stare him down. "Don't you *ever* accuse me of cheating," he thundered.

Stokes was close to sixty years old and black. Cassidy was thirty years old and white. The standoff had obvious overtones. Commotion rippled through the crowd. A few minutes later, a black man in his thirties sitting a few rows behind the scorers' table called over to Stokes and said, "He shouldn't be disrespecting you! If it happens again, you just give me the code and I'm in." But mostly the standoff was a reflection of how charged everything about the game was.

When play resumed, the whipped-up Charlestown team widened its lead. With less than a second left in the half, sophomore LeRoyal Hairston drove to the hoop, laying the ball in and drawing a foul. Sinking the foul shot turned it into a three-point—or "and one"— play. When the buzzer sounded, Charlestown was up 41–29.

Midway through the second half, Eastie came back, cutting a 10-point Charlestown lead to 4 in just over a minute of play. LeRoyal's hot hand from the first half cooled some, and when he was pulled out of the game for a rest, he thought he was being penalized. He exploded on the bench. That got Zach, the always excitable assistant coach, fired up even more. "Don't be selfish!" he yelled, insistently tapping on LeRoyal's arm.

O'Brien had long struggled with how to handle LeRoyal, a melancholy 6-footer. His jump shot was nearly as reliable as Ridley's, and just as gorgeous in its form. But while O'Brien had always stressed the importance of players being even-keeled, LeRoyal was the definition of up and down. When he drained a 3-pointer, he had the showy habit of punching his chest three times. But when he was involved in a turnover, he often tried to blame someone else, tossing a scowl at a teammate. Still, O'Brien had seen at least one encouraging sign. LeRoyal had gotten closer to Hood, despite the fact that he lived in a project called Orchard Park and Hood lived in Academy Homes, and the rules of the street dictated that OP and Academy guys were enemies. Somehow, the Charlestown basketball program had allowed them both to rise above that divide, without sparking trouble between their project gangs. O'Brien hoped Hood would be able to get through to LeRoyal in a way that he and Zach couldn't.

As the clock wound down, every play and call seemed weighted with the intensity of a championship game. The competing chants of "Let's Go, Charlestown!" and "Let's Go, Eastie!" clashed from opposite sides of the court. Nestled in the middle of the Charlestown contingent, in his lucky seat five rows back, sat Michael Fung. As the volume climbed around him, the headmaster remained perfectly silent, his chin resting on the palm of his hand.

The humidity from the warm weather melting the snow outside became a factor inside. Several times, the game had to be stopped so Eastie's coach could kneel down in his smart slacks—he had discarded his suit jacket just minutes into the game—and wipe dry a slippery patch of moisture on the court.

Hood repeatedly powered to the hoop. Back in the game, LeRoyal drained a couple of key shots. From the bench, Zach pumped his fist in the air. Down the stretch, LeRoyal made it to the foul line eight times, hitting seven. As the final buzzer sounded, an Eastie player tossed up a 3-pointer. It sailed through the net. Too little, too late. Charlestown walked off with an 89–76 win.

The Charlestown players rushed into the blue-and-yellow locker room, screaming and jumping to bump their chests in the air. O'Brien strode in a few minutes later. "Great job, guys," he said, "but I've got to get this out of the way." He walked over to LeRoyal, who was savoring his dazzling performance in the final minutes. But O'Brien was still smarting over the tantrum he had pulled earlier in the game, when Zach had subbed him out.

"You should never, *ever* act that way in your life!" O'Brien yelled, just inches from his face. "Understand something. We *don't* substitute for missed shots!"

LeRoyal stared straight at the floor.

"Look at me!" O'Brien demanded. "You could go 0-for-40, and I wouldn't care, as long as you were playing as hard as you can."

O'Brien took a few steps back and lowered his voice: "We're in a battle here. You have to be thinking, 'I've got to protect my *family!*'"

9

—

FATHERS, SONS, AND SURROGATES

BEFORE BREAKING THEIR HUDDLES, the Charlestown players yelled, "One, two, three—FAMILY!" O'Brien tried to compensate for his players' often chaotic lives by building a rigid team structure that offered the trappings of home. Each December, he sent out Christmas cards featuring a team photo. Every spring, he invited his former players back to the Charlestown gym to play against the current team in an event he called the Alumni Game. All season long, he turned the locker room into the equivalent of the family kitchen, posting newspaper articles about his players alongside his gold-star chart on one of the walls, as though it were a refrigerator door. But what made the experience most like a family was O'Brien's nagging, supportive, smothering, abiding involvement in his players' lives.

No one knew that better than Olivia Dubose, a short woman with a voice that sounded authoritative when she spoke and glorious when she sang. Until her retirement the previous fall, Dubose had served as Charlestown High's assistant headmaster for as long as

O'Brien had been at the school. Time and again, she had watched the evolution of the relationship between O'Brien and his players. Early on, they'd bristle at how overbearing he could be. They'd walk into Dubose's office and complain, "Who's this white man who's trying to be my daddy?"

Give him a chance, she'd tell the boys. In her own heart, she knew the score. "A lot of them have been yelled at their whole lives. But they haven't seen the difference between someone scolding them and someone molding them." As a black woman whose husband was the pastor of a prominent black church, Dubose became a guide and a confidante to O'Brien. She'd never seen anybody like him. To others, she described his devotion in the language she used in her church life. "It's a calling, a ministry for him."

When O'Brien was growing up, his mother, Teddy, thought her quiet, altar-boy son would eventually become a priest. A devout Catholic, she had grown up in a day when many Irish-Catholic mothers viewed the priesthood as the noblest of paths for their sons to take. In a way, O'Brien had become a priest without a collar. But he was no saint. A saint gives without expecting anything in return. O'Brien needed his players and their problems as much as they needed him.

He was a middle-aged man whose only real family commitment was caring for his seventy-five-year-old mother in the Medford home they shared. Many years back, his younger brother had convinced their mother to let him add a second floor onto the family's white ranch-style home, where he could live with his wife and kids. Jack O'Brien was cordial but not close with his brother's family, even though they lived right above him and Teddy. He and his siblings each had to find their own way of dealing with the turmoil from their father's severe depression. Some families get closer in the face of adversity. Others, like O'Brien's, drift apart.

But he was genuinely close to Teddy. She'd be sure to buy him the cashews and Gatorade he liked. He bought her a new dishwasher and stove and would continually ask, "Ma, what else do you need?" Around her neck she wore a necklace he had given her; inscribed on the back of the pendant was the familiar Irish blessing, "May the wind be always at your back." Yet mother and son were careful to respect each other's privacy. He told her next to nothing about his coaching success; she had to read about it in the papers. She only learned of the impact he had on his players' lives when their mothers would call the house looking for O'Brien and end up telling Teddy all that her boy had done for theirs.

Olivia Dubose knew he was devoted to his mother, which made his silence on the subject of his father all the more surprising.

About eight years back, O'Brien began worshipping with Dubose and her husband at their New Hope Baptist Church in the South End of Boston, bringing along the players he had become closest to. He figured they would be more comfortable in a black church near their neighborhood than in a white church in his. The experience brought him closer to Olivia Dubose. He eventually opened up to her, telling her he'd lost a girlfriend. "She passed out of his life, somebody he really loved," Dubose said. "I don't know if he's gotten over it."

O'Brien would say later that he hadn't, though he refused to talk about the relationship in any detail. Although he was sometimes accused by players' families of being too prying with his interest in his guys' home lives, O'Brien kept his own personal life walled off, even from the people at his side, like Hugh and Zach. In their many years with O'Brien, they had met his mother only a few times and had only the haziest recollections of meeting a girlfriend.

Dubose would occasionally overhear his players saying things like, "The reason he can deal with black people so well is because his girlfriend was black." That dovetailed with memories recounted by reporters from his Salem days of a woman with caramel skin occasionally coming to games to cheer O'Brien on. But she remained largely a mystery even to those who were closest to him. A few inferences about the relationship were clear, though: It had never led to marriage or produced any children. And it had never gotten serious enough to interfere with his relentless devotion to his basketball players and program.

In later years, Dubose saw O'Brien gingerly return to the dating scene, including a brief courtship with Charlestown High's Spanish teacher. But he admitted it never got too serious. "It's almost that you don't want to have a relationship that deep again," he once explained. People told him all the time that he'd be a good father. He didn't disagree but mused that he had chosen "a different route."

Dubose always felt O'Brien was doing the Lord's work by, as she put it, "filling the space in these boys' lives." They, in turn, filled the space in his. But she prayed he would find a wife someday. "Sometimes," she said, "I feel he's forfeiting a lot in his life because of what he does."

O'Brien was careful not to refer to himself as a father to his players. If an absentee father made efforts to get back into the picture, O'Brien usually encouraged the son to accept him. "Sports can do that," he said. "Maybe it provides an opening, a chance for them to have a relationship with their fathers."

It was a chance that never came to Jack O'Brien.

•   •   •

RIDLEY MCCLARY JOHNSON SHARED HIS NAME and good looks with his father, but, until recently, not much else. Because everyone called his father McClary, there were no name mix-ups. When a few of Ridley's friends found out his middle name and began calling him Mac, he tried to put a stop to it.

As he stood in the warm-up line for the final home game of the regular season, Ridley watched his father walk through the blue doors to the Charlestown gym and take a seat in the bleachers.

McClary was an articulate, bearded, forty-five-year-old Honduran who worked as a technician for a medical equipment company. He spoke with a mild accent whose flavor was both British and Spanish, a byproduct of his parents having come from an island off the coast of Honduras once controlled by the Brits. In recent years, Ridley had seen less and less of his father. There was no animosity in their relationship. There just wasn't much of a relationship.

Most of Ridley's teammates had, at best, distant relationships with their dads. Hood was pretty much the only veteran on the team who was living with both his mother and father in the same home. But McClary had none of the typical excuses other fathers used for their lack of involvement: Ridley was McClary's only child, he lived just a few miles away from him, and the boy had never been in any kind of trouble.

During the season McClary had begun to take the first steps toward reestablishing closer ties with his son. He often gave Ridley a ride home from the games he attended. He explained his regular attendance this way: "I've never really come before this year. But he was doing well in school, in basketball, so I thought it would be good to come show my support."

Ridley wondered why the support was only coming now. "I don't really pay attention to it," he said. "I just see that he's there." And, clearly, when he wasn't. "He's only missed, like, three games all year."

Ridley glanced over at the bleachers on the other side of the court. He knew part of the reason his father had come to so many games had to do with the twenty-five-year-old with the small glasses and long hair who was waving at him. Emily Coleman, Ridley's aunt, his mother's youngest sister, wasn't much older than Ridley, but she had a maturity about her and functioned as a sort of surrogate father for him. Personable and blunt, she was fearless in advocating for herself and her family. Ridley even kept a picture of her on his bedroom wall.

Before the season began, Emily had pulled McClary aside and laid it all out to him. With Ridley headed to the University of Toledo next fall, she told him, this year might be his last chance to connect. As the regular season came to a close, she could see how McClary and Ridley were still stiff around one another. Given the distance between them, that was to be expected. But she remained hopeful that the relationship would blossom and that Ridley would benefit. "He needs to learn how to be a man."

Charlestown's opponent from Lawrence, a former mill city northwest of Boston, featured some Hispanic players who were so fast that they made O'Brien's lightning-quick squad look slow. In the locker room, O'Brien warned, "This is the fastest team in America. They fly!" Lawrence came into the game having won sixteen in a row. If the streak continued, for once O'Brien could have been the one to excuse the loss with a veiled reference to the opposing team's "athleticism." But O'Brien wasn't interested in excuses. He wanted a win.

During the game, Emily used her cell phone to check in with McClary from across the court, as Rebecca, Ridley's mother and McClary's former wife, sat beside her. Ridley had used a rubber band to gather his braids into a ponytail. Rebecca didn't like the look. In the second half, he looked lackluster on the floor, as Lawrence scored 10 unanswered points to close Charlestown's lead to 2. Zach pulled him out of the game. "You gotta give us something, Ridley!" he shouted. Rebecca knew what was wrong. She yelled over to her son as he sat on the bench. "Ridley, take that ponytail out!" When he returned to the court without the ponytail, he pulled down a key rebound and began draining shots, helping put the game away for Charlestown. Rebecca tapped Emily on the leg. "See, I told you that ponytail was messing him up!"

Emily pointed to a pretty girl with long curly hair who was sitting a few rows away from McClary—Ridley's new girlfriend, Ashley. Not much happened in his life without Emily knowing about it.

"She's cute," Emily told Rebecca. "And light. He like 'em light!" Ashley's caramel complexion was common among Cape Verdean people, who traced their heritage to an archipelago off the African coast that was colonized by Portugal and used as a slave-trading center. Emily asked, laughing, "How come she hasn't come over to introduce herself to me yet?"

Emily was used to being a constant in Ridley's life. She and her husband, assistant coach Hugh Coleman, filled that same role for the entire Charlestown program.

The Coleman family's deep history with O'Brien and Charlestown all began with Hugh, and Ridley would have never come to Charlestown had it not been for him. Warm and energetic, Hugh had a smile for everyone he saw, except perhaps the older man sitting behind Emily, trying to make funny faces with Hugh and Emily's effervescent two-year-old daughter, Jordyn. "That's Hugh's father," Emily whispered.

Hugh didn't see it that way. He had forgiven his mother for her faults, but he felt his dad had been AWOL from his life for too long. Now that the man had been back some, Hugh saw him more as a distant uncle. When Hugh was in college in Maine and O'Brien would drive up to see him, he would introduce his coach as the man who had done the most to help him get to college. "*This*," Hugh would tell friends, "is my father."

•   •   •

A FEW DAYS AFTER THE WIN over Lawrence, O'Brien stood in the Charlestown gym and began practice the way he usually did, locking elbows with the players in a circle at center court, reviewing the stats from the last game, and trying to motivate them for what lay ahead. But since it was George Russell's birthday, O'Brien ended his comments by handing the senior a T-shirt. Three months earlier, when he'd gathered all the players for the rules-of-the-road meeting, O'Brien had them fill out a 3×5 card with their contact information. "And write your date of birth there as well," he'd told them. He used the info to make sure every player got a T-shirt on his birthday.

O'Brien's thoughtfulness off the court seemed almost maternal. He gave his guys tips on how to wash their uniforms, compulsively checked to make sure the locker rooms were safely locked when they were playing on the road, and regularly doused their home locker room with watermelon-scented Glade to mask the stench of all that cotton and nylon soaked in sweat. But on the court, he fell easily into the stereotypical role of father from generations past—stern, demanding, and stingy with praise. So it only took a few minutes for the tenderness of the locked-arms huddle and the birthday-gift presentation to fade.

By the time Hugh walked into the gym around four o'clock, O'Brien was wearing a face as grim as his gray hooded sweatshirt. Running the players through a defensive drill, he blew into his whistle repeatedly and furiously, shouting, "No! No! No!" In contrast, Hugh, who had a goatee and a permanent grin, looked the picture of contentment. He didn't seem the least bit self-conscious, despite having a little girl's hot-pink backpack slung over his shoulder. Holding his hand was the backpack's owner, Jordyn, whom he had just picked up from day care. O'Brien yelled for the players to get on the line for some suicides. "You gotta sprint!" Then he spied Jordyn out of the corner of his eye. He walked over, scooped her up, kissed her, and then put her back down before huffing three times into his whistle. "Everyone sprint, or get *out!*" Hugh led Jordyn to the bleachers to take a seat.

Hugh grew up the second oldest of nine kids. His mother had her first son when she was just fourteen. That boy eventually went to live with an aunt in Baltimore. A promising musician, he became ensnared in the street life and was gunned down. His body was re-turned to Boston and laid to rest in Oak Lawn Cemetery.

Because Hugh's mother had missed out on her teenage years, by the time she had three or four kids, she decided to make up for lost time. Hugh would recall how she got caught up in the partying scene, as did his father. When Hugh was only about seven years old, he assumed the role of guardian for his sisters and particularly his brother Derek, who was six years younger and utterly devoted to Hugh. "I learned to sense danger," Hugh once explained. "We were around a lot of drugs. We'd go to people's houses and I'd say to him, 'Do *not* move!'" He learned to discipline. Sometimes, he had to spank his brother.

One day, his house was raided and both his mother and father were sent away. Hugh and Derek and two sisters had the same fa-ther, but their other siblings had different dads. For a time, the family was broken up. Then his Aunt Marlene—actually the aunt of the father of Hugh's youngest brother—agreed to take the kids in and keep them together. When it came time to choose a high school, Hugh's mother, who'd been out of jail for some time, was dating a guy who lived in Charlestown. She suggested her son se-lect Charlestown High. Hugh didn't think so—the only thing he knew about Charlestown was it was all white, and none of his friends were going there. Reluctantly, he listed it as his last choice.

He tried out for the basketball team in O'Brien's first year as coach. Hugh was small and his ball-handling skills weren't great, but O'Brien loved his upbeat attitude. He got the last slot on the JV team. Hugh still had a lot on his mind, though. Aunt Marlene pulled him aside and told him, "You worry about doing well in school. I'll worry about taking care of the kids." With that, Hugh finally felt he had permission to focus on his own development. He blossomed as a student, making the honor roll through lots of hard work and a whole lot of schmoozing. And he blossomed as a basketball player, helping O'Brien transform the team from its disastrous first season into a squad that advanced several rounds in the state tournament. Hugh was exactly the kind of kid O'Brien had traditionally had the most success with: someone with heart and grit, willing to work hard and listen up; someone who had overcome a crazy home life and wanted better for himself. By his senior year, Hugh was president of his class and captain of both the basketball and football teams. It was hard to find anybody on the staff or in the student body who didn't like him.

O'Brien knew all those credentials would make Hugh's college application a compelling one, especially if admissions officers granted him an interview and got a feel for his infectious enthusiasm. There was only one gaping hole in the package: his SAT scores. It didn't take O'Brien long at Charlestown to realize how crippling the SAT could be to inner-city kids with dreams of getting to college. None of the tricks he taught his guys on how to get ahead in class—asking teachers for extra help or extra-credit assignments—worked with standardized tests. After doing some research, O'Brien found a solution: colleges that did not require SAT scores for admission. Hugh was admitted to both Bates and Bowdoin, two top-ranked Maine colleges whose SAT-optional policies had succeeded in making them only more selective. Eventually, he settled on Bowdoin.

Before Hugh left for Maine, his Aunt Marlene, whose health was beginning to fail, told him, "I'm going to watch you graduate." Getting to commencement turned out to be harder than Hugh imagined.

For him, freshman year was a foreign land. When it came time to select his first courses, he took suggestions from older students, who clearly had come from more rigorous high schools: Computer Science 101, Environmental Science, Government 150, African American Art History. He quickly found himself in over his head. Computer science sounded like a Slavic language he couldn't even begin to decipher. The environmental science class was taught by a rotating cast of professors, all of whom seemed to Hugh to contradict one another. His government professor looked like Colonel Sanders and sounded like John Houseman. During exams, Hugh would often wear an expression as blank as the blue book he'd just been handed. Yet when he looked around the classroom, he felt like the only one who didn't get it. When he tried asking his professors to explain things again after class or requesting extra-credit assignments, he found them unreceptive. Only his art history teacher seemed willing to work with him. As he neared the end of the first semester, he was in deep academic trouble, with three F's. His C in art history was all that stood between him and academic suspension.

Only on the basketball court, playing for a Division III college team that lacked the intensity of his high school program, did Hugh feel complete. One night late in the semester, returning from an away game, he found O'Brien waiting for him outside his dorm. His coach had made the two-and-a-half-hour drive after having received an urgent call from a Bowdoin dean.

"Why didn't you tell me what was going on?" O'Brien asked.

Hugh didn't know what to say. He was embarrassed to be in such a bind. More than that, he was surprised to see his high school coach standing in front of him at nine o'clock at night.

"I thought you'd be mad," Hugh stammered. "I thought you'd say, 'Forget it. I'm not going to deal with this anymore.'"

"How could you think that?"

"Hey, that's just how it's been all my life."

In this moment of crisis, their relationship entered a new, deeper phase. O'Brien helped Hugh break down his second-semester coursework like an opponent's defense. "At the beginning of the semester, get a tutor—don't wait until you get into trouble. Mark up your syllabus. If you have a paper due in a few weeks, do a rough draft and show it to your teacher and ask him if you're going in the right direction."

Hugh wasn't so sure. "Isn't that like cheating? Won't they say, 'C'mon, do it yourself. You're in college now.'"

O'Brien waved that off. "Hughie, it's their job to teach you."

He finished the second semester with all C's.

By then, he had become much more acclimated to college. Used to being just one of many contributors on the Charlestown court, he was immediately a star on the Bowdoin team. He was named the state's Rookie of the Year. On campus, he was known for his warm personality and his stylish dress. Unlike most freshmen, he refused to drink. He was sure addiction ran in his blood and worried that if he ever even dabbled in booze or drugs, he might get hooked. He used his talents as a DJ to become the life of the party without having to get high.

During spring break of his freshman year, Hugh returned home to his family who, for several years, had been living in Lynn, a small, gritty, coastal city north of Boston. One afternoon his sister brought her friend Emily over to try on their prom gowns. Hugh's mother called him into the room. "Doesn't Emily look nice?"

Hugh looked her up and down and smiled. "Oh, you look *very* nice."

Emily, a junior at Lynn English High School, had the tall build of the basketball player she was. She was smart and funny, attractive and easy to talk to. They hit it off. The next day, Emily found an excuse to come by the house again, where she found Hugh in the bathroom cutting his brother's hair. As she walked by and said hi, he turned around and impulsively planted a kiss on her.

Emily's voice said, *What'd you do that for?* but her smile said, *God, I loved that.* They continued their conversation the next night, and the night after that. At that point, Hugh was heading out for a weekend in New Hampshire with O'Brien. Ever since Hugh's first-semester crisis, O'Brien had been taking him on periodic weekend retreats, going snowshoeing or hiking or jet skiing. He found the long car rides were the perfect setting for heart-to-hearts about school, basketball, and life. O'Brien preached discipline, remorselessly: "No sex until you're married."

When Hugh got back, he called up Emily and asked her to the movies. She found him to be so much more of a gentleman than the guys she was used to seeing around the neighborhood. She couldn't really compare him to previous boyfriends, because she'd only had one. Hugh opened doors for her, held her hand. She learned later that most of that training had come from O'Brien. The dating continued, long distance, all through Hugh's time at Bowdoin, even after Emily herself went off to college. O'Brien counseled homespun caution: "Take your time. Don't put all your eggs in one basket."

At the end of his junior year came another crisis. In addition to A's and B's, Hugh had gotten a D. Normally, that wouldn't have been fatal, but those three F's freshman year turned this latest D into a noose. O'Brien drove up and advocated for him in a meeting with the dean. In the end, Hugh was given two choices: either return for his senior year without being able to be on the basketball team, or take a year off and earn some credits at another college before returning for senior year. Hugh broke down in tears. He couldn't imagine life without basketball—whenever he was feeling beaten down by his coursework, he could always find release by walking into the gym and shooting basket after basket for hours. And after all the sweat he'd put into staying in the academic game at Bowdoin, being ejected even just for one year would be admitting defeat. Privately, O'Brien worried that if Hugh left campus and headed home for a year, he would never return to earn his degree. He'd seen that happen with players before. Eventually, O'Brien hatched a deal with the dean. Hugh, who had been majoring in English and education, would spend a year as a teaching intern and assistant basketball coach at Bridgton Academy, a college preparatory school in Maine, while also taking courses at a college nearby.

Hugh returned to Bowdoin the following year, feeling rejuvenated. Then, second semester, came another complication. Emily, who was in college at Salem State, was pregnant. Hugh was worried about what it would mean. And he was scared as hell to tell O'Brien.

As the semester wore on, Hugh realized he couldn't delay the inevitable anymore. He told O'Brien. Instead of blowing up at him, O'Brien played it cool. He looked disappointed, but he just calmly asked a few questions and then moved on.

A few days later, Hugh was having breakfast with O'Brien when the coach's tone turned angry. "Why'd you do this?" he blurted out. "We talked about this!"

Hugh hung his head down. He felt so bad to have disappointed O'Brien. Then it hit him. "This is what a father does. You don't let that stuff go. You don't just not address it." And so he told O'Brien, "Thank you."

O'Brien then asked him, "Do you love her?"

"Well, yeah. Emily's unbelievable. She's going somewhere in life. She's a wonderful girl all around."

"Then why don't you marry her?"

Hugh fumbled around for a reason. "We don't have any money."

"It doesn't take much money to get married," O'Brien shot back. "Being married is what you do. Having a wedding takes money, but you don't need that."

Early on in her pregnancy, Emily had begun telling Hugh, "We need to be married by the time this baby is born." Hugh kept trying to brush that off. "Why do we have to rush into it?"

But now, after talking about it more with O'Brien, his mind began to change. He thought to himself: *I want to always be able to tell my child, "Look, we tried to do it the right way, and that's all we ask of you."*

In May 2002, Hugh Coleman, in cap and gown, stepped forward to collect his bachelor's degree from Bowdoin College, one of the relatively few black students in his graduating class. Beaming from her wheelchair in the audience was Aunt Marlene. "I told you, baby! I told you!" she said, hugging him. A year later, she would be gone.

On August 9, three months after graduation, Hugh and Emily were married.

Ten days later, Hugh stood in the delivery room, using his video camera to capture every moment of Jordyn's arrival into the world.

•   •   •

ZACH ZEGAROWSKI PACED the sidelines, frantically rubbing his balding head. "I can't take this anymore! This is the most disgusting thing I've seen in my life!" Charlestown had just missed its eighth layup. The assistant coach sat down and then just as quickly popped back up. The Comcast Tournament, held on the spanking new court of Boston College High School, a parochial school in Dorchester, was a two-round tournament that marked the end of the regular season for Charlestown. The results would decide Charlestown's place going into the state playoffs. There was even more on the line. The boys from Charlestown were facing Salem for the first time since last March, when the Witches sent them packing early in the playoffs and put an end to their four-year state-championship reign. For Zach, the Salem connections ran incredibly deep. Not only did he grow up in Salem and play for the Witches before O'Brien was forced out of his coaching job there, but one of his friends and former high school teammates was now the Salem head coach. Zach could easily have been a head coach on his own. He had the passion and the talent. But he also had a wife and four young children. He knew that to lead a team the right way, the way he'd seen O'Brien—his teacher, friend, and, in many ways, father figure—do it, you needed to put your whole life into it. He wasn't ready for that.

Nor was he ready to see history repeated. The loss to Salem last year had ruined his whole summer. Charlestown was not going to give this one away. In the locker room at halftime, with Charlestown up by just one point, Zach yelled, "You're acting like it's a *friggin'* YMCA game!"

As the second half began, among those watching courtside was Bill Loughnane, the new BC High coach. For twenty years he had led the team from South Boston High School, winning three state titles. He was friendly with O'Brien—for a while the two were the only white head coaches in the city league—and they had somewhat similar coaching styles. But as the father of three young boys, Loughnane lived in a different world. "I like those boys," he would say, pointing to his high school players. "But I *love* my boys at home." For O'Brien, there was no such distinction.

The big difference in the second half was that O'Brien had turned to an old friend: Charlestown's smothering full-court press. It simply wore Salem down. Charlestown won by 18 points. Offensively, only Ridley had a good night, scoring 24. Hood had a more lackluster 12 points. Unfortunately for Hood, it happened to be a game when a few college scouts had come to look at him.

Still, that didn't take away from the joy of a big win. After the buzzer, Hood called his teammates into a huddle in the corner of the court. "Yo, this one is for the Charlestown guys who lost last year."

Hood didn't have to wait long for an opportunity to improve on his performance. Twenty-four hours later, Charlestown faced Newton North in the final game of the regular season. Newton was the number-one-ranked team in the state, but Hood was not intimidated. Repeatedly and fearlessly, he drove to the hoop, and he ended the game with 27 points. Spot started strong but twisted his ankle and had to come out early in the game. Charlestown shot a dazzling 92 percent from the foul line, and walked away with an 81–70 upset.

In just two weeks, O'Brien's team had beaten Eastie, Lawrence, Salem, and Newton North—their strongest rivals in the state. No one would have predicted that after Charlestown's brutal home opener. But now everyone on the team was smiling. Everyone, that is, except Troy. Walking off the court, the 6-foot-5 player complained that he hadn't gotten enough opportunities to score.

The guys had yet to hear from another big man on the team, the muscular 6-foot-4 Terry Carter, who had disappeared before the Eastie rematch. But Terry's guardian, Harry Landry, was in the crowd. He knew what had happened, and the news wasn't good. Terry, who had come out of the Department of Youth Services system, had gotten mixed up in the street life again. He was temporarily sent back to a DYS lockup, officially because of truancy. Harry's face told the story: "I had to put him out," he said regretfully. "I gave him three chances. If it was my own flesh and blood, I would have done the same thing."

During the post-game award ceremony, O'Brien beamed as Hood was named most valuable player of the tournament, Ridley was named to the tournament all-star team, and George, who just found out he'd been accepted to Salem State College, received a $300 scholarship.

In the locker room, O'Brien told the guys, "Winners get this far." He mentioned that he had just been invited to be a coach for the Michael Jordan Classic, a national game for high school all-stars that would take place at Madison Square Garden. He also said that in a few weeks the regional referees' association would be giving him its annual coach's award for good sportsmanship. "That's because of you guys," O'Brien said. "You act good during games, especially you seniors." He threw one arm around Hood's shoulder and lifted the other to point to his head, telling the rest of the team, "You wouldn't have gotten this far if it wasn't for him. He's had the best year of anybody here. Sometimes he tries to do too much. But when I coach, I try to do too much. I'd rather have a guy who's an attacker rather than a guy who's not sure of himself."

O'Brien then turned to Ricardo "Robby" Robinson, the final senior on the squad. "I want you to have this," he said, handing over
the team's massive tournament trophy. "Ricardo comes to every
practice, works hard, doesn't say anything, isn't concerned about
playing time." He surveyed the seniors standing around him, and
pointed to each one. "You got MVP, you got All-Star, you got the
championship trophy, you got money." When he got to Spot, he
stopped before adding, "And you got injured." O'Brien laughed, and
Spot did too, but there was hurt in his laugh.

Robby, on the other hand, couldn't have been more pumped.
The kid was a study in contrasts, with the "Fear No One" and
python tattoos that he'd had inked into his arms and the collection of nineteen Teenage Mutant Ninja Turtle action figures that
he kept in his bedroom in their original boxes, next to the stack of
utility bills he paid every month. Robby shared an apartment in
Mattapan with his older brother, a rapper hoping to make it big,
but they led largely separate lives. Robby paid his share of the
bills with the government benefit check he had been splitting
with his younger sister since his mother's death during his freshman year. He had learned how to stretch the money, which he
would stop receiving after high school. After paying the gas heating bill, half the cable bill, and his car insurance, he usually had
about fifty bucks left over each month for food. Like George, Robby
had just received an acceptance letter from Salem State, but he was
more excited about Radford University, a Virginia school he had
stumbled across while surfing the Internet. Robby walked out of
the locker room, clutching his new hardware, grinning. "I leave
trophied up. Coach says I play hard and I never complain."

•   •   •

A FEW DAYS LATER, SPOT SAT IN HIS BEDROOM playing NBA Live on his PlayStation 2. He split his time between his mother's house in Dorchester and his uncle and grandmother's new two-family place in Brockton, a faded factory city south of Boston. On moving day, before they carried the first box inside the house, he and his uncle had backed the U-Haul into the driveway and stood on its hood to hang the basketball hoop. First things first. Spot had a bedroom and a PlayStation in each place. Nobody on the team was better at NBA Live than Spot. If only mastering real-life basketball could come as easily. As Spot sat on the edge of his bed, nimbly guiding the PlayStation control pad, Mark Brathwaite, his thirty-seven-year-old uncle, walked into his room. With his father in and out of jail for much of his life, Spot was happy to have his uncle to fill the void. "I consider him like my father," he once explained. "He's tough on me, wants the best for me. I can talk to him about anything—girls, whatever."

His uncle played high school ball for Cambridge but had two kids by the time he was a senior. He often told Spot about how he had to push his oldest in a baby carriage to day care before he could get to school. So he never held back in telling Spot and his own kids about the hard realities of sex. "Don't come home with no babies," he would say. "I talk to them about condoms and all that stuff because no one ever really sat down and talked to me about it."

By now, Mark had gotten used to attending his nephew's games at Charlestown High, but he often reminded Spot about an incident that happened to him in the 1980s at the Charlestown Boys and Girls Club, when he was a teenager playing on an all-black traveling basketball team. A fistfight broke out, and then it turned into a melee as older white Townies came roaring in. The cops had to escort Mark and his teammates out to their van. "When I was growing up," he told Spot, "Charlestown and Southie, those were two places you didn't go as blacks, after dark anyway."

Spot's cell phone chirped. "What's up, Coach?"

O'Brien was calling to check in and let Spot know he'd made an appointment for him with a physical therapist to help him heal his ankle. Spot liked the way coach never began a phone call talking about basketball. O'Brien liked the way Spot never finished one without first saying, "Thanks, Coach."

They'd come a long way since sophomore year, when O'Brien threw Spot off the team. This past fall, O'Brien had taken him to visit colleges and prep schools. Now, even though some college coaches were still showing mild interest, O'Brien was recommending that Spot do a postgraduate year at a prep school. A transitional year studying and playing basketball at a private high school would allow Spot to boost his grades and improve his game, and hopefully position him for a Division II athletic scholarship.

Spot trusted O'Brien implicitly and followed his lead. But he still hadn't figured out why his own father, who had recently been released from jail, was suddenly coming to his games. O'Brien had his doubts about the guy. During one game, Spot's father, sitting in the front row, starting yelling at one of the referees so aggressively that a cop came over and escorted him out of his seat. O'Brien could only look on and wince, wondering how Spot would handle the embarrassment. But O'Brien didn't share those concerns with Spot, for fear of interfering with the small chance the kid might have in forging a bond with his father. Instead, O'Brien remained upbeat, trying to boost Spot's confidence, telling him that by doing better in school and basketball, he was helping bring his father back into the fold and his family closer together.

"I guess you can say that," Spot said. "But I look at it in a negative way sometimes." He figured if his father really cared, he would be there when he needed him most, rather than showing up only to bathe in some of his son's glory.

•   •   •

A T THE HEART OF JACK O'BRIEN'S DEDICATION to his players was a piece of his family history that few people knew and he never spoke of. As a coach, O'Brien used just about every psychological tool at his disposal—encouragement and anger, sympathy and scorn. His mother even saw him reading psychology books from time to time, trying to find new ways to get through to the team. He wouldn't deny the enormous gulf in experience that stood between him, a middle-aged white guy from the suburbs, and black teenagers from the highest-crime corners of the inner city. But he maintained that all it took to begin closing that gap was becoming invested in these kids' lives, learning about the dreariness that held them back and the dreams that kept them going. Still, it was remarkable that in all his counseling to get his guys to deal with their troubled relationships at home, particularly with their fathers, he never opened up about his own.

Jack's sister said their father, John O'Brien, was a good man who worked hard, a guy who tried to be the best provider and father he could be. When the kids were young, he loved to take them away on weekend trips, to ice skate in New Hampshire or swim on Cape Cod. But as the years went on, the combination of his old-school ways and the demons his depression had invited into his mind made for a tumultuous home life. When Jack was a teenager, things came to a head, and his father moved out of the house and moved in with his own mother, the Nana whom Jack O'Brien treasured. Things improved once his father was diagnosed with bipolar disorder at the Veterans Administration hospital. He was put on medication. Gradually, relations improved between his parents. His father would come by the house in the morning or afternoon and then return to his mother's house for supper and to sleep. Still, Jack continued to avoid his father, retreating more into his own world, with basketball an increasingly important outlet.

When he was younger and needed an escape from the tension at home, Jack found it at his Nana's house in the neighboring city of

Malden. She was nurturing, in her old-fashioned way. She would feed him, give him money. There was never any doubt that he was her favorite grandchild. When his father moved in, Jack cut down the time he spent at his grandmother's, going mostly when his father wasn't around. After being stabilized on medication, his father resumed work as a grave-digger at the local cemetery. But during a bout of kidney problems, a doctor took him off his meds, cold turkey.

In the fall of 1986, Jack was preparing to begin his second season as Salem High coach. At 7:50 AM on the morning of Thursday, October 23, John O'Brien, then fifty-seven years old, called the Malden Police Department. There'd been an accident, he said, and they should come quickly. Police arrived to find Florence O'Brien, his eighty-nine-year-old mother and Jack's Nana, on the floor of her kitchen. John O'Brien was in a bedroom on the first floor. He did not resist when the cops handcuffed him and led him out of the house. Florence O'Brien had been stabbed to death by her son.

Two years after Jack O'Brien and his controversial bid to get the Medford High coaching job dominated the headlines of the local newspaper, there was a new flurry of front-page headlines involving his family. His father was eventually tried for murder and found not guilty by reason of insanity. Jack found out what happened from his mother; he could not face the trial. His father spent a year and a half in a state mental hospital before being sent to live at a local VA hospital. In time, he was allowed to return home for dinner on weekends, though his oldest son never showed much interest in trying to repair their relationship. He died in 1993, at the age of sixty-four.

Teddy remained devoted to her husband throughout his life, and she continued her devotion in his death, regularly bringing flowers to his grave. When people asked her about another kind of devotion—how her son could be so completely committed to his basketball players—she would smile and say, "I don't know how he does it." But deep down, she thought she did. "You know what I think?" she said one day, sitting in her living room as the Little River Band song "Reminiscing" played on a muffled, cube-shaped AM radio. She paused, with the shadow of disloyalty crossing her brow. But then she continued her explanation of her son's commitment to his players, allowing herself only the mildest criticism of her deceased husband. "He likes helping them because his father got very sick, and he really didn't have a father."

III

THE POST-SEASON

10

THE CITIES

DURING THE WEEK between the end of the regular season and the start of the post-season state tournament came something called the Boston City League Championship, which the guys called simply "the cities." The city title had no significance beyond bragging rights, and no effect on the multi-round state tournament whose winner walked away with the title that mattered. But bragging rights for winning the cities meant a lot to Boston kids. Few Boston fans ever made the journey to western Massachusetts for the state final, but they always packed the stands for the city final.

Wearing a dark tailored suit, David Siggers strode into Roxbury's Shelburne Community Center to watch Charlestown compete in the semifinal round. In a few hours, Siggers's squad from Eastie would play its own semifinal game. The winners of both games would face off in the finals the following night. The odds were good that Eastie and Charlestown would resume the rivalry over the city title.

As Charlestown's semifinal wound down, Siggers fixed his eyes on O'Brien, watching him stalk the sidelines, shouting to guys as though they were down by 2, even though they were up by 30.

Siggers shook his head. "Before Jack, there was *parity* in Boston."

Although O'Brien was friendly with many coaches—black and white—outside Boston, around the city it was a different story. Siggers was just one of the many Boston coaches who looked at O'Brien's impossible record and assumed all he cared about was winning.

Part of O'Brien's popularity problems had to do with race. Here was a white guy from the suburbs who'd come into an urban school a decade earlier and managed to build a program that repeatedly overwhelmed other city teams coached by black men who were of and from the community.

But there was more to it than that. O'Brien's string of successes had triggered suspicion. How had he managed to get so many good players year after year? Abner Logan, one of the longest-serving high school coaches in Boston, summed up the assumption within the city's coaching fraternity: "You hear around the city how players are being directed to Charlestown."

O'Brien dismissed the criticism as nothing but jealousy. Although coaches were prohibited from recruiting players from other communities, they were allowed to talk up their programs to Boston middle-schoolers and their parents—who were allowed to list their top choices for high school—as long as they did it responsibly. Despite the whispered charges that O'Brien was engaged in illegal recruiting, there was no evidence that he was doing anything different from most other coaches in the city. Except, of course, he spent all his time doing it.

O'Brien did his homework, attending middle school games and tournaments, shaking hands and handing out Charlestown calendars, making it his business to know the talent coming up the ranks. But ever since his teams had begun winning state championships, the middle-schoolers had sought him out. That was true of four of his current starting five. Hood was the only starter

O'Brien "recruited" as an eighth-grader, and he ended up at Charlestown only because his mother decided to send him there. When Hood's middle school transcript had crossed Michael Fung's desk, the Charlestown headmaster asked O'Brien, "Jack, what on earth are you trying to do?" Fung figured that Hood, with all his suspensions, was going to be more trouble than he was worth. Hell, he wasn't even tall. But Fung had seen O'Brien work his championship magic with the most improbable raw materials in the past. He knew that the most bankable middle school basketball talent— the kids who had height and skills, decent grades, and on-the-ball parents—were getting snatched up by coaches outside the city, whether by suburban schools participating in the voluntary METCO busing program or private high schools looking to upgrade their teams. So Fung had to laugh when he heard the accusations about O'Brien. "If people accuse Jack of recruiting, I would say he is not a very good recruiter."

Other factors conspired against O'Brien. Like all true believers in a cause, he could be tiresome. He sometimes went too far in fostering in his players an "us versus them" attitude toward the outside world. And his courtside dramatics during games, when he paced and pouted and threw up his arms every time one of his guys made a mistake, gave the impression that the final score was the only thing that mattered to him.

But if all he cared about was winning, he would have done things differently. He would have steered his best players to the easiest classes rather than the more challenging ones. He would have forgotten about his former players rather than root himself in their lives. He would have cut his tallest player a lot of slack rather than toss him off the team on the eve of the playoffs.

On the Charlestown bench, 6-foot-5 Troy Gillenwater was nowhere to be found. At practice two days earlier, O'Brien had pulled him aside. The sophomore had a lot more going for him than just height—he was funny, a great rapper, a good ball player. But O'Brien felt he played in a self-centered style that was dragging the team down. He'd been warned and suspended, but nothing changed. When Troy had complained about not getting the ball enough in the exhilarating Newton game, it convinced O'Brien to kick him off the team for the rest of the season.

.   .   .

O'BRIEN LED HIS TEAM into the big, bright athletic center at the University of Massachusetts–Boston. As the clock ran down on the girls' city championship game, the Charlestown boys sat in one section of the bleachers, staring straight ahead, listening to rap on their headphones, while O'Brien and his assistants sat in the next section over.

Ridley, who had Jay-Z playing in his ears, was wearing jeans that were freshly pressed. A few hours earlier, he had stood at the ironing board in his kitchen, which looked out onto one of Boston's diciest projects, and worked to get all the wrinkles out. He was also wearing the Charlestown team jacket from last year, the one whose lettering boasted, "City League Champions." It was the first year in a while that O'Brien couldn't have "State Champions" printed on the outerwear, but at least he had the city title to fall back on. Charlestown had won the cities four years in a row. No one wanted to think about what the jackets would say at the end of this post-season if, as most people were predicting, Charlestown lost in tonight's city finals and again in the state tournament.

O'Brien watched as Ridley's father began scaling the bleachers, making his way over to his son. Wearing loafers with his jeans, Mc-Clary extended his hand to Ridley. "Good luck tonight," he said with the cheery stiffness of an insurance salesman making a cold call.

"Thanks," Ridley replied.

Not far from Ridley, Robby sat waving around a piece of paper for Spot to see. The paper was an acceptance letter he had received earlier in the day from Radford University, the Virginia school he still knew very little about.

"Division *One*, man!" Robby purred.

Spot, whose own post-high school plans were still shaky, grabbed the letter out of Robby's hands and looked it over before saying, "It's not like you're gonna play ball there, nigga!"

When they started out with O'Brien, most guys viewed college as somebody else's dream, and their only concept of what it took to get to college came from watching the NCAA's *Road to the Final Four* on TV during March Madness. For the seniors, four years of O'Brien's nagging had helped change their attitudes and their conversations. But actually getting to college was still far from a sure thing for most of them.

That was particularly true of Hood. His goal of earning an athletic scholarship would face a critical test when the game began. An assistant coach from Adelphi University was traveling from New York to watch him play. The head coach at Adelphi, a Division II school on a leafy Long Island campus, was a friend of O'Brien's. He'd be more likely than most to trust O'Brien's word and to take a chance on a kid like Hood whose talents weren't always obvious. Still, Hood had to show Adelphi something.

O'Brien needed him to have a great game, both because Adelphi would be watching closely and because the Charlestown squad's performance often hinged on how well Hood played. If Ridley had an off-night, the team could usually find offensive production from other players. But since Hood was more the soul of the team, when he was off, it tended to sap the squad's drive.

Although O'Brien told people all the time that his record of getting kids to college meant more to him than all the state and city titles, he also knew that his whole program was built on winning. For his boys, nothing succeeded like success—an experience mostly absent from their lives before O'Brien's arrival. Many guys chose to come to Charlestown, and put up with his impossible demands on the court and in the classroom, because they knew they had a good shot of leaving with a championship ring or two. If the wins stopped coming, O'Brien worried, so would players willing to put up with his rigorous expectations.

In the L-shaped college locker room, the lockers were so wide the guys could sit inside them as they listened to O'Brien give his pre-game talk. "This is like a new season," he said. "You've done a great job to put yourself in this position. If someone watched us during the first Eastie game, they would have said, 'That team's not very good. They're gonna have a rough year.' But you know what, we came back strong. We've played tough teams, we've been down, we've been up. We've faced it all." He led the team prayer and then sent them out.

After tip-off, Eastie quickly set the tone for the game, blazing out to a 7–0 lead. O'Brien paced the sidelines, screaming. Then Ridley found his hot hand, scoring Charlestown's first 6 points. Determined to prove he was more than just a finesse player, he charged the boards, pulling down one rebound after another. But besides him, the rest of the team was flat, especially Hood.

The assistant coach from Adelphi University, a thirty-four-year-old with a goatee, looked puzzled as he sat in the stands, a spiral notebook on his lap, and watched Hood miss shot after shot. Was this the player he had driven four hours to see? Adelphi had also been interested in the star of the Eastie squad, a lithe 6-foot-2 guard who drained a trio of 3-pointers as the first half wore on. After getting a peek at his transcript, though, the Adelphi coaches realized he would never pass academic muster. Hood was in better shape academically. But if he played in the second half as poorly as he had in the first, he could be valedictorian and it wouldn't matter.

At halftime, Eastie was up by 6. It would have been a lot worse if Ridley had been as cold as the rest of the team. Overall, Charlestown had shot 13-for-40. Hood walked into the locker room having scored just 6.

In his halftime talk, O'Brien was more measured than usual, speaking in a voice raspy from all his first-half screaming. He exhorted his guys not to be out-hustled, telling them, "It's gonna be a war." But the second half began like the first, as Eastie widened its lead to 12 points. Ridley, on his way to a game total of 23 on the night, couldn't hold them off alone. Then, more than midway through the second half, Hood came alive, driving to the basket with one powerful layup after another. With four minutes to go, he powered up to the basket to tie the game. O'Brien was going crazy on the bench, yelling "Rebound!" and "Rotate!" and flapping his arms. Thirty seconds later, Ridley converted a rebound into a basket that gave Charlestown its first lead of the game.

Fearing a repeat of years past, when promising Eastie starts were snuffed out by powerful Charlestown finishes down the stretch, David Siggers began howling at his guys to keep it together and not let this one get away.

The lead seesawed for the next few minutes. Then, with fifty-nine seconds left in the game, Ridley's cousin Paul unleashed a beautiful 3-pointer from the baseline, giving Charlestown its biggest lead of the night: 72–69.

Eastie's shooting guard got fouled and nailed both shots from the paint, bringing his team to within 1 point. With sixteen seconds left, Charlestown coughed up the ball. Eastie's sophomore point guard, who hadn't scored the entire game and who had transferred from Charlestown earlier in the school year, threw up an off-balance jumper from left of the foul line.

Just then, a heavily jeweled girl walked into the stands, talking on her cell phone, oblivious to her poor timing in obstructing everyone else's view. "KAMESHA!" a friend yelled from a few rows back. "SIT DOWN!" a chorus of fans sitting behind Kamesha yelled. She did, just as the ball, which had been dancing around the rim for an eternity, bounced in. Eastie was up 73–72.

Charlestown pushed the ball up the court. With the final buzzer about to sound, Hood tossed up a jump shot from the foul line. The entire crowd was standing now—including Kamesha—watching the ball bounce around the rim. On the sidelines, O'Brien stood frozen, his arms extended in flight, a piece of green spearmint gum resting on the tip of his tongue, dry from lack of attention.

The ball bobbled on the rim, refusing to commit, as though following some movie script designed to tease out all the available drama. Finally, it tumbled out.

Siggers and the entire Eastie squad charged onto the center of the court, hurling into the air the point guard whose last-minute dramatics had put them over the top. The Eastie players screamed and danced and pulled their jerseys from their chests in a center-court explosion of joy.

Hood drifted to the Charlestown bench, but seemed unwilling or unable to move any farther. O'Brien, his collar dampened with sweat, remained frozen, refusing to believe it was over.

A few minutes later, Siggers made his way over to O'Brien and gave him a bear hug. "That was a great high school game!" he said. O'Brien was polite, but all the color was drained from his face.

When O'Brien walked into the locker room, he was met with silence.

"Hey. Look at me now," he told his players. "Great, great job. Great, great effort getting back into a game we probably had no business being in." He knew how hard the loss would be for his guys. They would hear taunts the moment they stepped onto the subway. So he reminded them to keep their heads high when they walked out the door. "Don't listen to no hate."

After the last player left the locker room, O'Brien leaned against the wall, flipping through the green score book, replaying the final seconds. Eastie's last shot had looked short to him. Hood's had looked promising. He slapped the score book shut. "Damn!"

The next day, a Saturday, O'Brien kept his phone turned off the whole day. He barely got out of bed. On Sunday, he called Hood to see how he was doing. "What'd you do yesterday?" the coach asked.

Hood said, "I stayed in bed all day."

By Monday afternoon, the mourning was over. O'Brien led his team into a cramped storage room off the Charlestown gym. There, determined to pump them up, he told his players something he'd resisted saying to any of his title-grabbing teams in the past. He knew it was a risk, but he did it anyway, convinced it would help convey just how much faith he had in them. "Listen guys," he told them, "we're going to win the state championship."

11

SURVIVE AND ADVANCE

M ICHAEL FUNG SCANNED a spreadsheet tracking his school's standardized test scores and tapped his index finger on the column for 1999–2000. "This," he said, "is the year basketball saved Charlestown High."

Exactly one week after Charlestown had lost in the 2005 cities, Fung was sitting in his windowless office. On top of his computer table were stacks of reports, wrappers from various items of consumed junk food, and layers of dust; underneath it all, a pair of slippers. In a few hours, the basketball team would play its first game in the state tournament. Fung loved days like this.

People drew certain conclusions when they looked at Fung, with his somewhat disheveled appearance, his accented, imperfect grammar, and the distracted look he wore on his face as he ambled about the school. It took most people a while to figure out that he was tough to the point of stubbornness, clued in as to who was doing what in the chaotic corridors around him, and independent enough to say whatever he felt without worrying about losing his job.

The Charlestown High Fung found on his arrival in 1997 was ailing academically. It was also the victim of perceptions that had been frozen in time a quarter-century earlier. When he would attend fairs trying to drum up interest in the school among Boston parents, many black parents told him things like, "I don't want to send my kid there. It's a white school." Fung could only scrunch up his face and chuckle. "Some of our classes don't even have one white kid in them."

Fung arrived at Charlestown with a plan: force out the clock-watching burnouts on the faculty and replace them with eager recent graduates of elite colleges, young people willing to work hard and stay late. But by the fall of 1999, his campaign was in deep trouble. He had alienated most of the veterans on the faculty. The school's standardized test scores were awful. And a pulled fire alarm one day had escalated into a racially charged clash between the mostly white Boston police contingent that showed up and the mostly black and Hispanic students who had poured out of the school.

Fung was foundering.

Then, in March 2000, O'Brien led the Charlestown team to the first state title in school history. "That takes everybody's mind off the problems," Fung said. "After that, the whole culture changes. Kids considered themselves winners." The next year, Charlestown's standardized test scores improved so dramatically that the school earned a $10,000 award. Fung directed a chunk of that money to support the basketball program.

O'Brien and his boys then made history, stretching their state championship win to a four-year streak. All the while, Fung was remaking Charlestown High. Now, staring at the spreadsheets on his dusty computer table, Fung could take pride in the fact that Charlestown's standardized test scores were the best among Boston's district high schools. The average age of the teachers had dropped from fifty-six to thirty-four. The faculty was awash in graduates from the nation's top colleges.

None of that suggested that Charlestown High was a center of academic distinction. Its test scores may have been better than those at other Boston high schools, but they still weren't very good. Too often, the main demand the school made of students was time served, rather than true learning. And, as O'Brien, a phys ed teacher with a state college degree, liked to remind Fung, some of his young Ivy League hires got crushed in their classrooms and quit after just a year or two.

Fung and O'Brien enjoyed sparring. On bus rides after games, the headmaster would critique the coach's performance in his preferred language of science, saying things like, "Your players shot an incredible 92 percent from the foul line" or "You did not call enough timeouts." The coach would fire back, "Your hiring isn't very good." But on the big points, they couldn't agree more: No one ever helped a disadvantaged kid by feeling sorry for him and letting him make excuses. Hard work beats natural ability every time. The most reliable route out of poverty is college.

In the last decade, O'Brien had helped more than thirty of his players get to college—some to prestigious places like Bowdoin and Bates, some to big-time basketball programs like the University of Florida, and many others to more modest local schools whose names end in "State." Once Fung began seeing how basketball could change lives, the wealthy headmaster got hooked and couldn't wait to see more. "Without basketball," he once said, "I probably would have quit by now. It really gives me something to look forward to."

As the day's second lunch period was about to end, Fung fished two white Styrofoam trays out of the trash barrel in the cafeteria, and began his daily ritual. Unaffected by the din of a hundred conversations or the smell of a thousand tater tots, Fung stopped in front of each table and used one of the trays to rake up the crumpled Fritos bags, half-empty milk bottles, and rubbery pizza crusts. He slid all the detritus onto the other tray, and then emptied it into the barrel. With swift, practiced movements, he had cleared every tabletop in about ten minutes.

At most other high schools, this duty would fall to a lowly staff member, not the headmaster. When Fung started the routine years earlier, he hoped it would set an example for the students, inspiring them to take pride in their surroundings. Instead, it only seemed to inspire mild taunts like, "Hey Mr. Fung, you missed a few wrappers!" No matter. In his three decades working in public schools, Fung had come to believe that the educators who waxed enthusiastic about the goodness of teenagers were either fools or phonies.

"Kids are no damn good!" Fung would tell all the wide-eyed recent college grads he hired to rejuvenate his faculty. "They leave the school a mess. They don't listen. They swear." Then he would pause for effect. "That's why we have to work hard to make them good."

Later that same afternoon, Hood sat in his Law and Justice class. The room was swarming with Harvard graduate students decked out in their Banana Republic best, clutching grande lattes from Starbucks. They came once a week to help Hood and his classmates with college applications. Some of them connected easily with the Charlestown kids. Others did not.

A Harvard volunteer with wire-rimmed glasses and a dirty-blond ponytail sat on top of a desk near Hood and made small talk about the big game that would be played that night. "One assumes one is going to win tonight," she said. "Then what happens next?" Hood ignored her, but she didn't seem to mind. She had more to say. "There's a Chinese saying for this: 'A journey of a thousand miles begins with a single step.'"

Hood, who was wearing an Oakland A's baseball cap, turned his head away from her and started talking to Ridley. The young Law and Justice teacher, Neal Teague, asked Hood how come he hadn't seen Terry Carter around school lately. By now, the players had heard Terry was in the Department of Youth Services lockup. "Um, he went on a *vacation*," Hood said, drawing out the last word as Ridley dissolved in laughter.

Teague rolled his eyes but decided to move on. "You never turned in your essay," he told Hood. "Why don't you do it now." The assigned topic was the current state of school desegregation. Hood tapped the shoulder of the gum-chewing girl seated in front of him, and held out his hand. She dutifully tore out a piece of lined paper from her notebook and handed it to him. Ten minutes later, Hood had produced his essay. Like so much about Hood, it was rough and imperfect, but thought-provoking and powerful just the same.

I think segregation still occurs in schools today. I think it occurs mainly because students don't feel comfortable if they aren't surrounded by people whom they deal with on an everyday basis. I think students hear things about certain cultures and that plays an important role in the choosing of schools. Many students also go to certain schools because it's either closer to their house or because their friends go there. I understand why kids like to be surrounded by their friends because an unhappy society is a dangerous society. You can't expect kids to have fun and learn in an environment in which they are not comfortable.

I don't think that suburban schools are any better than public schools. Suburban schools are just given more money than public schools. Public school teachers work harder than suburban school teachers in my opinion. It's not their fault if the students aren't working hard or wanting to learn. The teachers try their best to see that all students are given the chance to learn and get a good education. The suburban school students just focus more and apply themselves to get a good education. In the end, we are all human and no race is more superior than another.

Hood's educational journey was about to hit a snag. Kristyn O'Brien pulled him out of class. After the problems with his SAT scores in early February, the guidance counselor had arranged for him to take the test again. But when she went to find his score on-line, it wasn't there. So she called the College Board. Standing in the hall, she reported her findings to Hood: "They're saying you never showed up to take the test."

A little while later, Hood ran into Cassidy who, in addition to being his assistant coach, had been his history teacher for two years. The seniors on the team got along well with Cassidy, but if they needed to confide in an assistant coach and wanted to make sure it didn't get back to O'Brien, they went to Zach or Hugh. Cassidy had heard from another teacher that Hood was faltering in his school-work. He knew how bright Hood was, knew he could perform well academically whenever he set his mind to it. During his sophomore year, Hood had earned an award for being the top student in Cassidy's class. But Cassidy also knew Hood often chose to set his mind to anything but his class work. He growled at him, "You're slipping."

In his sixth year at Charlestown, Cassidy was Fung's longest-serving hire. He had come to realize that the teachers who chose to work at an urban high school purely out of white liberal guilt never lasted. He'd grown up in a mixed neighborhood in Bridge-port, Connecticut, the son of a college professor, and went on to earn his master's degree from Boston College. He spent his first year teaching middle-schoolers in inner-city Chicago. The kids walked all over him. He bounced back with a new resolve and a vow never to smile in his classrooms until Thanksgiving.

Over the years, he had become a dependable performer on the Charlestown faculty, a young teacher who brought energy to the classroom but who, unlike a lot of the other young teachers, knew how to keep his classes under control. "I believe in urban educa-tion," he said. "These kids often get a raw deal. But you need to be tough, or they'll eat you alive."

Fung always stressed that when he recruited from the top colleges, he never had to worry about his teachers knowing their material. All these smart people helped him boost the school's test scores. But he admitted that if a teacher couldn't manage the classroom, little else mattered. He often told the story of one hire whom he had liked a lot. One day, he passed her classroom and noticed a student sitting in the teacher's chair. Fung advised the teacher not to let that happen—students must be taught to respect boundaries. No, the teacher replied, she wanted to teach them that they are respected and trusted. Not long after that, her students stole her lunch. Then her credit card. Then her $300 jacket, which they set on fire.

She no longer worked at Charlestown High.

•   •   •

SURVIVE AND ADVANCE. That's how it worked in the state tournament. Charlestown's 20-win regular-season record was now history. To win the state title, the boys of Charlestown would have to navigate through a grueling schedule of six rounds of games held in the span of three weeks in March. One loss at any point, and they were out. Their impressive record for the season was worth one benefit going into the tournament: a bye that automatically advanced them to the second round. But that wasn't much of a gift, since competition was usually weak in the first round.

To fill the long gap between the end of the school day and the start of the 7:00 PM second-round game, O'Brien arranged for the guys to eat dinner and watch a movie in Room 319, where they held study hall after school each day. O'Brien had run out to the Foodmaster to pick up pounds of deli meat, loaves of bread, bags of chips, and bottles of soda. He was in his minivan when he realized he'd forgotten bottled water, and he didn't want Derrick Bowman to go thirsty. The slight, polite sophomore guard, whose dark complexion had led to his nickname D-Black, didn't drink soda. His teammates, who guzzled the stuff like a Winnebago at a Mobil on the interstate, found that beverage stance endlessly fascinating. O'Brien headed back into the store, marveling at the fact that people now paid $1.29 for a little bottle of something that used to be free. He used the second trip to stock up on the plastic produce bags he gave the guys to ice their joints.

In Room 319, as Spot carefully arranged a layer of Lay's potato chips between the ham and cheese slices in his sub, Ridley walked up to the TV that O'Brien had wheeled in, and he slid his favorite Michael Jordan DVD into the player. It consisted of interviews with Jordan talking about his approach to the game, interspersed with footage of his on-the-court heroics that had done so much to change it. Every time one of his soaring monster dunks filled the screen, the guys howled.

Because it was the postseason, the Charlestown bench was heavier by four. Dean "Shoddy" Lambright, Dashawn "Day-Day" Matthews and two other freshmen who hadn't gotten nicknames yet had been called up from the JV team. When the game finally started, against a team from the affluent west-of-Boston suburb of Belmont, Spot found his groove, scoring the team's first 8 points. Aside from one dazzling player, the Belmont team was no competition for Charlestown. The Charlestown guys actually knew Belmont's star pretty well, since he was a black kid from Boston who went to school in the suburbs as part of the METCO program.

Because Charlestown had so much more talent than Belmont and because the crowd was thicker than usual, O'Brien's guys tried to put on a show. There were a few dunks and no-look passes, but also a whole lot of sloppiness, which enraged O'Brien from the sidelines with each passing minute. At halftime, he stormed into the locker room and slammed his white magnetic clipboard against the red lockers. *Thwaaaap!* "Who the *hell* are you guys to waste time out there?" he screamed, the closest he had come to swearing all season. "You're not that good!"

He replayed an instance in which a Belmont player had made it by the Charlestown defenders who'd been double-teaming him. "How can you let a *sophomore* split you?" O'Brien moaned. "Where the hell is the pride? Nobody *splits* us!"

"I, I, I don't see that get-after-it," he stammered, looking as though he literally might cry. "We're so cool out there. I *hate* it!"

Charlestown had gone into halftime with a 25-point lead. The boys went on to win by 43.

As the team walked off the court, Hood's father approached him to see if he needed a ride home. Willie Barnes had driven to the game in the Mitsubishi that he often let his son use. Hood said he was all set. The last few Charlestown games, Willie had noticed Hood's cousin, Eric Barnes, whom everybody called Pookie, sitting there in the bleachers with his friends. Willie thought Pookie—his sister's son—was a nice enough kid. But he also knew Pookie ran with a street crowd. Willie had spent enough time on the street to know that crowd was not good company for a son on track to getting a college scholarship. "Be careful," he'd told Hood more than once, "of these guys coming around now that you're doing well, trying to soak up your glory."

In the locker room this time, O'Brien was the model of calm. "Guys, listen, I thought it was a much better second half." He brought up the Michael Jordan DVD they'd watched before the game. He sensed the players had been trying to channel Jordan's electric play in putting on a show for the crowd, but he reminded them that they had missed the star's central message. "I'd never seen the Jordan film before," O'Brien said. "You guys have seen it a million times. What I got out of it was: hard work, doesn't settle, wants to be perfect. I don't know what you got out of it: 'Look at that dunk!' But he didn't talk about *that*!"

After the last player had left the locker room, O'Brien told one of his assistant coaches why he had come down so hard on the guys at the half. It was tough to explain, but he wanted desperately to send this year's team off with a state title, even more than previous years. These guys didn't have as much raw talent as his championship teams, but they made up for it in heart. He'd grown especially fond of the seniors. Still, he didn't want them to get cocky. Confidence was good. Cockiness got you sent home early.

·   ·   ·

AS O'BRIEN RAN HIS PLAYERS through practice drills the Sunday morning after the Belmont win, the head coach from Adelphi University sat in a black chair at the edge of the Charlestown court. Jamie Cosgrove, who had dispatched his assistants to scout Hood in earlier games, had come to see him for himself. When Cosgrove coached at Division III Endicott College on Boston's North Shore, O'Brien had steered some of his players there. But the stakes were a division higher at Adelphi. Cosgrove had scholarships to offer.

For months, O'Brien had made it his goal to help Hood score one of those. Over the years, he'd seen Hood go from angry troublemaker to loyal leader. He recalled how Hood's mother, who by now had recovered well from surgery, had asked him to help give her son direction. He wanted to be able to tell her that her boy had secured his next four years with a scholarship.

Even in the relatively pressure-free environment of practice, Hood performed with the nervousness of someone being watched. His jump shot, never the best feature of his game, was off. Cosgrove, who had a wiry build and thinning hair, wore a serious expression the whole time. But based on earlier conversations he'd had with Cosgrove, O'Brien was confident it was going to work out.

As he watched the college coach lead Hood into a small office off the gym, O'Brien grinned and said, "He's going to offer him."

Twenty minutes later, Hood and Cosgrove emerged from the office and shook hands. Hood headed for the locker room. A little while later, he strutted back into the gym.

A few of his teammates gathered around him. *How did it go?* "Good."

Did he get his offer?

"Nah. He said I'm going to take a visit after the season's over." He was parroting what Cosgrove had told him in trying to soften the blow for not giving him a commitment. But it sounded less convincing coming from Hood's lips, and his voice trailed off.

•   •   •

GOOD NEWS ARRIVED before the next playoff game. Spot learned he'd been admitted to Westminster School, a $35,000-a-year prep school in Connecticut, halfway between Boston and New York. He'd have to wait to see what kind of financial aid he got from Westminster for a postgraduate year there. But Spot's smile was unmistakable as he walked into the gym on March 10 for the third round of the state tournament. With Ridley headed to Toledo, George to Salem State, Robby to Salem or Radford, and now Spot safely taken care of, four of the five seniors seemed to have a road to their futures. Hood's fate—still very much up in the air—weighed heavily on O'Brien. So did pretty much everything about postseason play, which is why O'Brien never smiled much in March.

The game would be played in a house of many memories for O'Brien: the Salem High School gym, forty minutes up the Atlantic coast from Charlestown. When the players arrived at the gym, the ticket-takers were handing out programs that said "Charlestown vs. Lynn Classical." But the boys of Charlestown still had East Boston on their minds. They were convinced they'd be facing their bitter rivals after tonight's game, and the sting from losing to them in the City League championship two weeks earlier had yet to subside.

So, despite O'Brien's warnings, they committed the cardinal sin of postseason play. They looked past the game in front of them. The scrappy team from Lynn Classical made them pay, forcing the game into overtime, before Charlestown pulled out a win.

In the locker room afterward, a familiar face was back.

Terry Carter, whose tumultuous season had begun with his stabbing and had been interrupted by his spell in the DYS lockup, had grown an inch, to 6-foot-5, since his teammates had last seen him. They welcomed him back easily. O'Brien, however, was polite but unforgiving. He'd allow Terry to try to earn back his spot on the team next season, but that was about it.

Outside the locker room, Terry admitted he had messed up. He said he'd been hanging around with the wrong people. He'd begun using drugs. He said he deceived the people who cared about him most—his guardian, his coach, his teammates. "I got in trouble a lot before. But this is the final straw, because I let the team down. This is my first high school team."

Terry said it didn't dawn on him what a great opportunity he had blown until he was in the lockup. "When I'm in there, I'm different from the rest of them. Like, all of those kids, they're arrested for like shooting at somebody. And I was a basketball player. Even the staff, they're like, 'I just seen your name in the paper, and then you're *here*.'"

•   •   •

EFORE THE REMATCH came the retake. On the snowy Saturday morning of March 12, just hours before Charlestown would face East Boston one last time, O'Brien picked Hood up at eight o'clock in Roxbury and drove him to take his SAT again. The College Board had insisted that Hood had missed the previous SAT session. Hood assured everyone he had shown up for the test. But with only one more opportunity to boost his scores, O'Brien wasn't about to take any chances.

The SAT was supposed to be over by 12:30 PM, giving Hood enough time to get to Charlestown High by 1:00 PM to leave on the team bus. But at nearly 1:30 PM, O'Brien was still nervously looking at his watch, wondering where Hood was.

Fifteen minutes later, Hood was sitting with his teammates in the back of a yellow school bus as the block-faced driver tried to navigate the interstate through whiteout conditions. Most of the guys sat with their hoods up, eyes closed, and headphones on. There were also a few cheerleaders aboard. Charlestown's cheering squad was never reliable; even though this was the biggest game of the season, only three of the cheerleaders had decided to show up. Since there was plenty of room, one of the girls brought along her cousin, a tiny girl named Samantha Rivas, who had a pretty face and long tight curls. A straight-A student in middle school, Samantha had been rewarded with one of those life-changing opportunities: A nonprofit called A Better Chance gave her a full scholarship to an elite private high school in the Berkshires of western Massachusetts. She lasted until February of her freshman year, when she left her dorm room in a former mansion and returned to Boston. "I missed my friends," she explained, "even though they aren't my friends no more." She was now in her second year at Charlestown High. "The work is *so* much easier. But I don't do well. Too many distractions."

By 2:45 PM, Hood and Ridley were leading their teammates into the 6,500-seat Tsongas Arena in Lowell. For the first time all season, there would be a real live soloist singing the national anthem, rather than a tinny recording. Whoever won this fourth-round game would still have to survive two more rounds before getting the state title. But Eastie coach David Siggers knew better. Sitting in the stands with his assistants, watching the girls' game wind down, and nervously tapping his foot, Siggers said, "This is the state championship game—right here. This is the real one."

In the first three meetings between Eastie and Charlestown, the team that started the strongest was the team that won. Twice, that had been Eastie. The fourth game followed an ominous pattern, as Eastie surged to a 21–8 lead. But Spot scored to spark a Charlestown comeback. Ridley followed by hitting a 3-pointer. George, his face layered with sweat, succeeded in shutting down Eastie's dynamic big man.

At halftime, the game was tied at 40.

In the second half, LeRoyal, Charlestown's mercurial sophomore, came alive, sinking jumper after jumper. Hood tossed up an air ball, squinting at the rim. O'Brien wondered if Hood had his contact lenses in. Ever since getting Hood and Spot fitted with lenses the season before, O'Brien had been continually battling with them to make sure they put the damned things in their eyes.

Tony Lee, Charlestown's captain from the previous year, now playing for Robert Morris University, had used his spring break to come home and cheer on his former teammates. As the clock ticked under the ten-minute mark, Tony, the bulldog with the puppy eyes, knelt on the floor in front of the bench, jutting his head out and smacking his hand on the edge of the court every time Charlestown scored. He wanted this win as much as they did.

Then, as he had done so many times before, Hood took over late in the game. Senior Westly Perryman did the same for Eastie, hitting clutch 3-pointers down the stretch. The game turned into a big one-on-one.

With forty seconds left, Charlestown took the lead, 72–70. After Eastie called a timeout, O'Brien knelt in front of the bench, moving circular magnets around his white clipboard to show his players how to set up their defense. Their season on the line, the crowd pulsating, O'Brien and his clipboard offered a Zen-like calm. "We need a stop," he said.

They didn't get one. Eastie tied the game. Hood pushed the ball up the length of the court and scored a short jumper with about ten seconds left, giving him 22 points in the game and his team a 74–72 lead. After a timeout, Eastie point guard Tyrone Hughes, the kid who had transferred from Charlestown and had sunk the shot that gave Eastie the city title, moved the ball up the court and dished it to red-hot Perryman. With three seconds left on the clock, Perryman tried to rise above Hood's outstretched arms to release a fade-away jumper from the baseline. Unlike the final-stretch heroics of Eastie's win in the cities, this shot missed. Ridley pulled down the rebound. The buzzer sounded.

This time, the huge pile-on at center court belonged to Charlestown.

In the locker room, O'Brien fought back tears. "In all my years of coaching, at Charlestown, Salem, I don't know if I've ever been as proud." He surveyed the ecstatic faces around the room. "People say, 'Hey, why don't you coach in college?' I don't think I could ever be as happy as this."

Outside the locker room, Terry was sobbing. He could have been part of it.

Hood sported a grin as he walked out of the locker room. It only expanded when he saw who was waiting for him. Jamie Cosgrove, the Adelphi coach, had come back to see Hood play. He'd picked a good night.

"Great game," he told Hood. "We're going to make this happen."

•   •   •

AT 8:30 THE NEXT MORNING, O'Brien sat in his minivan outside Hood's place in Roxbury, beeping the horn. He'd already picked up George, and he would be going next to Ridley's apartment in Dorchester to collect the other three seniors. Then they would all head to a suburban American Legion hall, where O'Brien would receive his award for good sportsmanship from the regional referees' association.

As O'Brien drove, George talked about how Terry had been crying after last night's game.

"Of course he was," O'Brien said. "A big party, and he's not invited. But would he have been there if we were 0 and 18?"

George's cell phone rang. It was his cousin, calling for information about Charlestown's round-five game—the semifinals—which would be played the following night.

"Eddie, we play at 6 o'clock, but get there at 5:30," George said, "and tell my father. Make sure he there." Neither of George's parents had made it to a game all season. Eddie had another question. George looked up at O'Brien. "Coach, how much the tickets?"

O'Brien waved his hand in disgust. "Just tell 'em to be there! Do they ask that when they go to the movies?"

The coach drove past the Church of God of Prophecy as Elvis crooned "Bridge over Troubled Water" on the minivan radio, past the seagulls feasting on the overstuffed dumpsters around the Franklin Field housing project, and stopped in front of Ridley's apartment in a gray three-family house. He beeped, and out came Ridley, Spot, and Robby.

A few minutes later, Spot made an announcement. "Coach, I didn't put my contacts in, on purpose."

O'Brien looked at him in the rearview mirror. "Why?"

"'Cause I *want* you to yell at me. It's gonna be over soon, and you're not gonna be there yelling at me."

O'Brien laughed. "Put 'em in, and I'll yell at you anyway."

As the minivan neared the American Legion hall, Spot squirted a few drops of saline into his palm and popped the lenses in his eyes.

O'Brien was wearing a blue blazer, gray slacks, and a blue-and-red tie. His five players were wearing either sweatpants or jeans. In the parking lot, he told them, "Guys, I think you should leave the do-rags in the car." They complied.

The first major award went to a longtime referee. The man thanked his wife, his children, and his brother, who were all seated at his table.

When it was O'Brien's turn, he thanked the five guys seated at his.

12

PLAYOFFS
AND PAYOFFS

THERE WASN'T MUCH TIME to savor their triumph. Just two days after their win over Eastie, the boys of Charlestown gathered in the gym for their next challenge, pulsating with excitement. In a few hours, they would be playing on the parquet home court of the Boston Celtics, the most storied franchise in NBA history. As they shot baskets on their more humble court, two of their former teammates stood in the lobby, peering through the small windows in the royal blue doors with the vertical block letters that spelled GYM. Terry and Troy, the two tallest players, were on the outside now.

A few minutes later, the team poured out of the gym and began striding up Elm Street. Troy peeled off and headed in the other direction, but Terry tried to blend into the pack. O'Brien pulled him aside and whispered something to him. Terry's face sank. "Oh, OK, Coach," he said, standing in place as O'Brien headed off with the team.

A classmate who had been watching tapped Terry on the shoulder. "What'd he say?"

"He don't want me going to Papa Gino's with the team."

It was a tradition O'Brien had begun during Charlestown's first championship season. Walk to Papa Gino's for a late lunch of pizza and then stroll over to the Boston Garden. When the lovably decrepit old Garden was replaced in 1995, Shawmut Bank paid millions to have the soulless new box named after the bank. But then the bank was bought out and the place became the FleetCenter, before that bank was bought out by the Bank of America, which already had enough things named after it. So a new outfit, TD Banknorth, paid millions to have the arena take on its clunky name. The deal had been announced just a week earlier, so the signs were still being made. But people in Boston were excited to hear that the new bank would be ditching "Center" in the arena's name and resurrecting "Garden," meaning everyone could go back to calling it simply "the Garden" no matter how many more banks were bought and sold.

The Charlestown players flooded into Papa Gino's, the pizza joint next to the post office and the Foodmaster supermarket, passing a trio of old-timers idling on the Jurassic Park benches out front. Fung, who had called ahead, approached the counter to pick up the towering stack of pizza boxes as the players headed for the booths. A stylish real estate agent in her fifties looked on from the takeout line. "This is good to see," she whispered to an out-of-towner behind her in line. "Years back, these kids could have *never* walked here." For two decades after desegregation descended on Charlestown High, you still seldom saw any black faces in the supermarket. It took the gradual desegregation of the housing project next to the high school throughout the 1980s and 1990s for the changes to be felt in the aisles of the Foodmaster. Yet that shift just accentuated the division that had always existed between the two Charlestowns: the projects and everything else.

The guys devoured all the pizzas, except those Fung had ordered with "everything" on them. He thought the "everything" option would be an easy way to please a bunch of boys with big appetites, but they were particular about the type of junk food they ate: yes to pepperoni, no to peppers. Once outside the restaurant, the players began their walk to the Garden.

After four years, the seniors were still strangers in Charlestown. They stuck to their haunts—the Spanish market on Bunker Hill Street where they got their breakfast meat patties, the takeout place behind the school where they got their $3 lunch plates. Although it was once unsafe for blacks to walk around Charlestown, there was nothing preventing them from exploring now. But they had no interest. When Hood drove Willie's car from Roxbury to the high school every morning, he kept his eyes straight ahead. "I don't even look at Charlestown," Hood once said. "I just look at the stoplights and how long it takes me to get to school."

But on this day, the boys took the scenic route, the whole pack of them rolling along the brick sidewalks of Main Street. They walked past faux gas streetlamps and restored townhouses, past the listings hanging in the windows of realty offices for $849,000 condos. The irony of Charlestown is that busing created the boom. Before the early 1980s, houses in this 1-square-mile neighborhood were generally kept in the family, so there wasn't much of a real estate market. The race battles persuaded many Townies to sell, opening up a trove of historic housing located minutes from downtown Boston and triggering a boom that had yet to abate. Busing claimed many victims, but real estate agents like the woman waiting in line at Papa Gino's were not among them.

In truth, all the change produced a lot of good. Property that had been languishing for decades was spruced up. Crime went down, and new businesses moved in. Most significant, bigotry—xenophobia, really—began to recede. Yet something very important was lost in the process.

In the mid-1970s, Patricia Kelly was part of the first group of black teachers assigned to Charlestown after busing began. She experienced its undiluted racism firsthand, being forced to endure angry mobs and ugly slurs. But as she drove around Charlestown, she couldn't help but feel sorry for the Townies. They lived in tight quarters, often with three generations of a family crammed into the same multilevel house, and seemed to function as though the world ended at the town line. Kelly, who was raised in New York and New Jersey and would go on to earn her doctorate, thought to herself, "How insular! They never leave." On one particularly icy afternoon, she offered a ride to an older Townie teacher she'd grown to respect. As Kelly pulled her brown Audi Fox out in front of the school, some Townie kids blasted her car with snowballs. Kelly made no fuss; her car had been hit with rocks and snowballs too many times to count. But her Townie colleague went running after them. They fled, but as she climbed back into the car, she told Kelly, "I know those kids. I taught their parents. I went to school with their grandparents. This needs to stop." From that day forward, Kelly's car never got hit again. "That," said Kelly three decades later, her sense of grudging admiration still strong, "is how tight the bonds of Charlestown were back then."

Now with the Townies gone, the yuppies using it as a bedroom community, and the young black and Hispanic students viewing it as just a place to get in and out of with as little interaction as possible, Charlestown had lost its coherence. The high school, to which Townie culture had been tethered for generations, was now so detached from the neighborhood around it that it might as well have been a barge floating in Boston Harbor. The experience showed how people of different classes and races could easily live adjacent to one another, but seldom side by side. Perhaps coexistence, rather than integration, was as good as it was going to get.

As the boys arrived in Charlestown's City Square, a once squalid patch now shimmering with expensive restaurants, they could see the Boston Garden just across the highway. Spot looked up and smiled. "Man, I never knew it was this close."

When they reached the Garden, they passed a local TV satellite truck idling out front, further evidence that the team had hit the big time. O'Brien guided them away from the main spectator entrance and to a door around back reserved for players and members of the media. They were issued adhesive badges, and a security guard in a powder blue blazer led them through the bowels of the Garden, into a freight elevator, and then down a long corridor leading to the locker room.

Once inside, the players began to strut like Celtics. "Listen, in two years, I'll be here for good," Hood said. Ridley tapped his chest three times. "I'm going to be Paul Pierce tonight." The locker room had TVs hanging from the ceiling and a digital clock that reported the minutes remaining in the girls' game currently being played on the court.

O'Brien stood next to the locker room door, holding his white clipboard and moving around the magnets to review plays, as the guys sat on the carpeted floor in front of him. After offering instructions like "Watch out for number 33 tonight," he said, "Let's bring it in."

With the players' arms meeting his in a huddle at the center of the locker room, O'Brien began the customary pre-game prayer. "Lord, please bless us tonight. Please help us to play with confidence." He ended, as always, by invoking the memories of the players who were with them only in spirit. "Please watch over Paris, watch over Richard. In Jesus' name we pray."

Then Ridley led his teammates in breaking their locker room huddle. "Family on three. One, two, three. FAMILY!" After that, they clapped as they paced nervously around the locker room, waiting for the signal to head out to the court.

Charlestown faced Catholic Memorial, a nearby parochial high school. As the Charlestown players stepped onto the court, about to compete under the bright lights of a real-life NBA arena, lanky sophomore Lance Greene stared up at the Jumbotron scoreboard. "I am speechless," he said, his braces-filled mouth agape.

After tip-off, just as O'Brien had anticipated, number 33, a blond kid who didn't have much height, used his devastating jump shot to get his team going. The Charlestown players looked sloppy, and Spot appeared to be intimidated. After several missed shots, he began nervously passing the ball as soon as he received it, for fear of making any more mistakes. Catholic Memorial raced out to a 20–12 lead.

A woman sitting a few rows behind the Charlestown bench started screaming, "DEFENSE! DEFENSE! Get a man!" Hugh Coleman rolled his eyes. The assistant coach didn't have to turn around to recognize his mother's unmistakable voice coursing through the Garden. She wore her hair in long braids, and a gold chain with a large crucifix rested on her maroon sweater. "Get a man! Stay with him!" The spectators sitting around her no doubt assumed the boisterousness came from a diehard fan whose enthusiasm had been building all season. They would have never guessed this was the first game she'd attended all year. Sitting a few rows behind her, also making their first appearance, were George's mother and father.

O'Brien called a timeout. Huddled in front of the bench, Zach yanked on Spot's jersey. "Are you gonna give us anything? No rebounds, no steals, no foul shots, no layups, NOTHING! It's like we're going four-on-five out there!"

O'Brien, sensing that the dressing-down might make Spot feel more exposed, said soothingly, "It's OK. We need you."

In fact, they didn't.

With Spot and Hood off their game, Ridley came to the rescue. Midway through the second half, he converted a steal into a monster dunk that brought the crowd to its feet and put Charlestown up by 1. In the final frame, he pulled down key rebounds and sank one 3-pointer after another. He finished the game with 23 points, including five 3-pointers, powering his team to a 63–52 win. They were going to the state finals.

After the game, O'Brien guided Ridley and Hood into the media room. The co-captains stood by the soda machine, watching their coach comfortably handle the first round of TV interviews. By now, the bond between them was so strong that Hood didn't seem to mind when, after the reporters finished with O'Brien, they wanted to talk only to Ridley.

When the TV lights went off, the co-captains left the Garden with their teammates, hopping on the subway to continue the celebration at Ridley's house. O'Brien, who had just scored his fifth trip to the state championship game in six years, decided to stick around to watch the state semifinal game between teams in a different division. But mostly he wanted to savor his own win. In the hallway outside the locker room, he picked up the red canvas Charlestown bag containing the team's six practice balls and slung it over his shoulder. He bent down to retrieve the plastic carrier holding the team's six Gatorade water bottles. And then he headed out into the stands to grab a seat.

•   •   •

FIVE DAYS LATER, the players sat in the Charlestown gym, munching on their $3 takeout lunch plates of chicken and rice as they waited for the bus that would take them to western Massachusetts for the state finals. Spot was sporting a new pair of $60 rose-gold cubic zirconia earrings, bought for the occasion.

Meanwhile, O'Brien was in the locker room, showing off the wall of achievement—his "refrigerator door" of clipped articles and gold stars—to the four eighth-graders he had picked up earlier in the morning. All four had already selected Charlestown High as their school for next year. He was bringing them along for the big game today, so they'd see where hard work could get them.

The team rode in style. At first Fung had resisted O'Brien's push for an upgrade to a coach bus. He liked the image of the scrappy city team arriving at the University of Massachusetts–Amherst in an old yellow school bus. But as usual, O'Brien's relentlessness had won out. It helped that Zach's wife had found a bus company willing to charge half the going rate.

The UMass campus, home to nearly 20,000 undergraduates, featured a dreary mix of 1960s Soviet-style architecture. Lots of concrete-and-brick buildings surrounded the curious W. E. B. Du Bois Library, a skinny, twenty-six-story tower that advertised itself as the tallest library in the country. In contrast, the Mullins Center, the basketball arena built after the UMass men's team started its winning ways, was smartly designed, offering nearly 10,000 seats and yet an intimate setting.

Still, for the boys of Charlestown, who had been playing on NBA parquet a few nights earlier, everything about the Amherst experience suggested a step down. They didn't even get to use the UMass basketball team's locker room. Instead, they were assigned a narrow women's room that was a ten-minute walk from the court.

Once inside the locker room, O'Brien pulled his crumpled 3×5 index card from his pocket and reviewed hand signals for some new plays. He used the remainder of his pre-game talk to reflect on the year. He surprised even himself at how quickly the emotion of the moment overtook him. "We've had our ups and downs. Some other people are not here. But you know what?" he said, choking back tears. "I could always count on you guys."

He reminded Ridley that he came in as a shaky ninth-grader, "and you're leaving as one of the best basketball players in the state." He thanked Spot, George, and Robby for being tireless and true.

"And Hood," O'Brien said, putting his arm around his co-captain. "Tough beginning, man. But I don't have to tell you, the basketball stuff's been awesome. And as a person, you've been even better.

"This is hard for me, because it's the last time I'm going to have a chance to coach you seniors," he continued, his voice cracking. "But what better way to go out than to win a state championship and walk out of here feeling like a million bucks. That's what you deserve."

All that stood in their way was the team from Oakmont, a regional school in Central Massachusetts that boasted a 6-foot-6 center.

Charlestown began the game stone cold, missing shot after shot. For the first four minutes of the game, nobody—not Hood, not Spot, not even Ridley—could buy 2 points. Nine attempts, nine misses. Oakmont put up the first points on the board.

The Oakmont fans, who had heard plenty of talk about the unbeatable dynasty from Charlestown, began to wonder what all the hype had been about. Their cheering section was several thousand thick, and they had painted their faces and worn green wigs to match the school colors. Charlestown had lured no more than 200 fans. And most of them looked worried, including Fung. The headmaster couldn't understand it. He was sitting in his lucky spot, wearing his lucky gray T-shirt.

The saving grace for Charlestown, as so often before, was its full-court press. Teams like Eastie had battled it often enough to find some success at breaking through. But it completely stymied the beefy boys on the slow-tempo Oakmont team, who were used to other slow-tempo teams. They wore confused looks, as though they had shown up for a basketball game, only to be told to play Gaelic football for the first time in their lives. Because they kept bobbling easy passes and coughing up the ball, they were unable to capitalize on Charlestown's poor shooting.

Finally, LeRoyal sank a jumper to end Charlestown's dry spell, and Hood followed with a layup. That's all the guys needed to find their groove, and they quickly built a big lead. But Oakmont fought back, closing the gap to 6 points with a few minutes left in the first half and giving hope to the great green masses.

Offensively, Hood's performance was uneven. At the beginning of the second half, he tried to jumpstart his scoring by going in for a dramatic dunk. He missed. Sitting in the stands, Ashley Sena, Ridley's girl, wondered why it was taking her boyfriend so long to grab control of the game.

Depending on the game, Ridley could either be the tentative, soft player that O'Brien had been railing at for much of the season, or the overpowering, electric game-maker who had shown up for the semifinals at the Garden. Not long into the second half of the championship game, the dazzling Ridley emerged. He channeled Michael Jordan, soaring above defenders with dunks and making 3-pointers look as easy as 5-foot bank shots. He also turned into a force defensively, picking off passes and pulling down rebounds. He even had a 4-point play, getting fouled as he tossed up a sweet 3-pointer. After that move, the clock said there was still 3:52 left in the game. But Ridley's dominating performance had sucked the fight out of the Oakmont boys. Even the green masses that filled the Oakmont cheering section seemed to give up down the stretch. Charlestown cruised to a 68–48 win.

When the buzzer blared, the Charlestown players charged onto the court and piled on top of one another. Spot wound up crushed on the bottom, Hood in the middle, and Ridley on top. But they all wore the same unbounded grin of elation. Then Hood pulled them together to do their "rock the boat" huddle chant one last time. He yelled, "Charlestown!" They screamed, "Riders!"

After the media interviews, O'Brien walked into the narrow locker room. Terry Carter, wearing street clothes, was sitting next to his former teammates, exchanging back slaps and soaking up the joy.

"Hey, guys," O'Brien said stern-faced, before the door had even closed behind him. "If you're not a member of the team, would you please leave?"

Terry looked up, said, "Arright," and walked out of the room.

O'Brien told his players, "You should feel good about yourselves, you seniors especially. All five of you are going to college." Ridley had his Division I scholarship at the University of Toledo. A Division II scholarship at Adelphi appeared to be Hood's if he wanted it. Spot had his postgraduate year ahead of him at Westminster, which had just awarded him a fat aid package requiring him to pay less than $500. George and Robby had their acceptance letters from Salem State, and Robby also had one from Virginia's Radford University. "We're proud of you," O'Brien said.

He continued, fighting back tears. "As hard as it is to say goodbye, we'll always be there for you."

They brought it in for one last huddle. Ridley told his teammates, "I want it real loud, y'all. Family on three. One. Two. Three." The guys yelled, "FAMILY!"

Ridley turned to George, who was the only player who had yet to hang at his house. "Georgie, you coming tonight?"

"Yeah, think so."

"You need a ride?"

"Nah, thanks."

Ridley walked into the lobby. Toledo head coach Stan Joplin was waiting to congratulate him. He had returned to see his prospect play. He had no regrets.

As Ridley chatted with Joplin, he spotted his father, McClary, out of the corner of his eye. He waved him over. "Coach, this is my father," he said warmly.

McClary said later that the season gave him new insight into Ridley. "Everyone says he is a great kid, and I got to see that for myself."

Ridley made his way over to the concession stand to talk with Ashley. Then he walked over to his Aunt Emily and told her, "She wants to meet you, but she's afraid you don't like her." Emily, who had stressed that she wanted Ridley to go off to college focused only on his future, and not on some girl back home, gave in to the moment. She strode over to Ashley and gave her a hug. "If he loves you," Emily told her, "I love you."

Fung treated the players to whatever they wanted from the concession stand, but he struggled to pay the $128 tab when the clerk told him credit cards weren't accepted. O'Brien chuckled at the sight of a member of Hong Kong merchant royalty fumbling to cover a bill. The headmaster eventually found a stray $100 bill in his pocket.

Fung and O'Brien boarded the bus. There was a lot more room for the return trip, since most of the players were going home with their families. It was just George, the underclassmen, the coaching staff, and the four eighth-graders O'Brien had brought along for the ride. Two hours later, after the bus pulled up in front of Charlestown High, O'Brien grabbed the canvas bag containing the six practice balls and the plastic carrier holding the six Gatorade water bottles. He bounded off the bus and climbed into his white minivan. The eighth-graders followed closely behind.

•　　•　　•

RIDLEY'S MOTHER had to attend a funeral in Florida, but she knew her son's friends would be coming over after the big game. So before she left, she told him what she had stockpiled: trays of deli meat, rolls, salads, chips, cookies, soda, and even a few Spanish dishes she had whipped up. Win or lose, Ridley and his crew would be well fed. Anything that could last without refrigeration, she had already laid out in the dining room, whose plaque-covered walls served as Ridley's hall of achievement. When she returned home, she would have to make room for his newest state championship plaque.

There were a few adults around—Hugh and Emily, of course, and even McClary stopped by. But, basically, Ridley's crew had the apartment to themselves. Still, they did not depart from their usual routine: crowding into his bedroom to hang out. The normal gang was there: Spot, Robby, Hugh's brother Bernard, Ridley's cousin Paul, their slender, no-nonsense friend Tawanda from the girl's basketball team, and a couple of other guys and girls. Lorenzo Jones, the soft-spoken junior who had quit over playing time at the start of the season, was in the crowd, saying he was happy for them and talking about his plans to transfer to Eastie next year. "You my boys. I don't want to go against you, but I gotta look out for myself. I gotta play."

For hours, they talked, laughed, ate, horsed around, played on the computer, and kept the TV on a loop, going from ESPN to BET to MTV. Hood showed up late. George never did. When the video for "Is That Your Chick" by rapper Memphis Bleek, along with Ridley's favorite, Jay-Z, came on the screen, Spot shrieked and started delivering each line rapid-fire. The rest of the room danced around him. The song's lyrics, partially but coyly bleeped by MTV, were about bitches awed by dicks—exactly the kind of obscene, misogynistic, oversexed lines that got Christian conservative groups so worked up about how the urban rap culture was ruining our youth.

The members of the Charlestown basketball team were hardly choirboys. But too many of them had seen booze and drugs and guns ruin the lives of people around them. On some level, many of them understood that basketball was their chance at a better life. Unlike all those high school kids from the suburban land of second and third chances, where weekends were often built around parties with binge drinking and drugs, the Charlestown guys knew they didn't have much room for screwing up. That's why Ridley's room was such an oasis. Nothing bad could happen there.

So on the night when they'd won the state championship, the star jocks of Charlestown—inner-city black kids from the most fearsome basketball program around—were squeezed into a 12×12 room, drinking soda, singing, and dancing. Even Christian conservatives would have to admit it was a pretty wholesome scene.

When the Memphis Bleek song ended, Spot flashed his Hollywood smile and shouted, "I'm going to repeat! I don't wanna leave Charlestown!"

Jack O'Brien, the most dominant high school basketball coach in Massachusetts, still began each practice mopping the gym floor.

O'Brien did his work in the corridors of Charlestown High as much as on its basketball court. As Ridley looked on, O'Brien gave instructions on college applications to Jason "Hood" White.

Ridley Johnson and Bernard Coleman waiting for a city bus on Blue Hill Avenue. Ridley's commute to Charlestown took an hour and twenty minutes each way.

Ridley ironing his own clothes as his mother, Rebecca, looked on. The view out the kitchen window was of one of Boston's diciest housing projects.

Ridley's dazzling vertical leap and his perfect shooting form put him on the radar of college recruiters.

Hood's new earring.

Hood and his father, Willie Barnes, grew closer as Hood's high school years wore on. Willie was a fixture in the stands for Charlestown games, and even had his own rally T-shirts made.

Hood found his guidance counselor Kristyn O'Brien easy to talk to, as did his teammates; from left, Lamar "Spot" Brathwaite, George Russell, and Ricardo "Robby" Robinson.

Hood was the player opponents tended to fear most. His fullback-like drives to the hoop could turn around a game for Charlestown.

O'Brien's goal for his program was to turn strangers into brothers, wayward boys into successful young men. Every year he was able to see the fruits of his labor return for the annual Alumni Game. PHOTO BY PAT GREENHOUSE OF THE BOSTON GLOBE.

O'Brien held up assistant coach and former player Hugh Coleman as an example for his younger guys. Hugh had graduated from Bowdoin College and returned to teach at Charlestown High. Two of his younger brothers had followed him onto O'Brien's team, as had two of his nephews, Paul Becklens (standing immediately behind O'Brien) and Ridley.

O'Brien came down hardest on his guys when he felt they were coasting. Here, he was flanked by his assistant coaches; from left, Steve Cassidy, Hugh Coleman, and Zach Zegarowski.

In the locker room before every game, O'Brien led his players in prayer.

Headmaster Michael Fung and Coach Jack O'Brien formed an unlikely bond.

In the hall before an early season game, O'Brien reviewed plays with Lamar "Spot" Brathwaite, whose confidence tended to sink when his jump shots didn't.

13

MIND OVER MATTER

THERE WAS NO SIGNING CEREMONY when Hood's scholarship offer finally came in, partly because there was always less pomp with Division II offers than with the Division I variety, and partly because even after it came in—against the odds—Hood refused to sign. O'Brien couldn't figure it out. He had sweated out the roller-coaster of Hood's SAT mystery, finally seeing the kid produce scores that were acceptable, or at least not bad enough to stand in the way of a free ride to college. He had grown hoarse making the tough-as-nails coach from Adelphi University look beneath Hood's uneven play and awkward jump shot to see the gamer and leader that O'Brien saw, and then to pony up one of his coveted four-year scholarships. And now Hood was going to turn it down?

He understood Hood's disappointment that his offer wasn't wrapped up in an all-inclusive package like Ridley's was. It was a mix of financial aid and grants, with no D-I perks like dough for travel, books, and clothes. And he understood Hood was still hearing a lot of unsolicited advice from hangers-on in his neighborhood, who were telling him he was so good at football and basketball that he should hold out for a D-I offer to play both sports. O'Brien tried explaining that offers like that almost never happened. College basketball coaches kept their jobs only if they won, so what coach is going to risk seeing one of his hoop stars break a leg during a football game?

"If you had other offers, that would be one thing," O'Brien told him. "But this is it. Are you going to walk away from $100,000?"

The coach brought up another sore spot between the two of them. Ever since Hood's girlfriend, Tia, had told him she was pregnant, he had avoided passing on the news to O'Brien. He didn't want to deal with the looks of disappointment and lengthy lectures that were sure to come. Since Tia went to Charlestown High, it would have seemed impossible for him to keep this secret for long. But Hood caught a break when Tia transferred to a special program for pregnant mothers at a high school across town. Still, as spring rolled around and Tia's belly grew big, word inevitably got back.

O'Brien was worried. But for a while he didn't say anything. O'Brien's whole focus with his guys was being pro-active, nagging and badgering them to be smart and avoid missteps before they happened. Before long, Tia would be in a hospital room delivering Hood's baby. There was nothing he could do about it now.

Yet O'Brien had spent more than a decade coaching kids from the inner city, where pregnancy was almost as familiar a part of the teenage landscape as acne, and to his knowledge no one had ever fathered a baby while still on his roster. Now, one of his guys had sullied that record, and not just any guy but the soul of his squad, the impenetrable kid O'Brien prided himself on having gotten through to. Not only had Hood failed to heed his warnings, he had failed to confide for months. All season long, O'Brien had taken comfort in how close he felt he and Hood had become. But how close had they really been?

With Hood threatening to blow his best shot at rising above all the forces that tethered him to the streets of Boston, O'Brien broke his silence and brought up the subject of the baby. "The best way you can help a child," he stressed, "is to go to college. Get your degree so you can get a good job and support your kid, become a role model."

Eventually, O'Brien called in for some reinforcement from Hood's father. One night in their Roxbury townhouse, Willie took his son aside. "You know I ain't got no 100 grand, so what you gonna do?"

Hood told him he wanted to play football. Willie couldn't argue with that. He'd always thought his son was a better running back than a shooting guard. But even if Hood wanted to play football as well as basketball, he reminded his son, he only had the one offer. So he should take it. After a year, he could always transfer. "You ain't got a whole list, where you're Kobe Bryant and everybody wants you," he said. "If you're baking a cake and you need two eggs and you only got one, you gotta bake that cake with just the one egg. Your next cake you can go to Stop & Shop and get a dozen eggs."

Hood told his father he thought there were other missing ingredients. He suspected that more coaches had called O'Brien to express interest in him, but that since they weren't friends of his like Jamie Cosgrove of Adelphi, O'Brien chose not to pass on the information. "I don't think so," Willie told him plainly.

Willie thought there was something else at play in all his son's hemming and hawing: He seemed afraid to leave home. He had gotten so used to being a star at Charlestown High and one of the cool kids around Washington Park, his favorite haunt in Roxbury, that he didn't want to lose all that to become some low man at a white school on Long Island. "Leave these friends of yours leaning on the fence," Willie told him. "When you come back from school, you're gonna see them. But if you don't go, you're gonna be standing by the fence with them."

Willie had seen Hood hanging around with his cousin Pookie and
other kids who had no shot of getting away from Boston's streets.
He knew there was a dangerous appeal in their lifestyle of no pressures, new girls, and familiar faces. So when Hood started making
noise about maybe taking a year off, Willie shot it down.

"You ain't got time for no pauses," he told his son. "You just
don't. Because life is short. It can be snuffed out anytime."

·   ·   ·

GOOD TIME EMPORIUM, a cavernous mega-arcade in Somerville,
just over the Charlestown line, looked like an eleven-year-old
boy's vision of heaven. Billed as New England's largest indoor
amusement center, it offered batting cages, go-karts, pool tables,
bumper cars, a bowling alley, a basketball court, a laser tag arena,
and enough video games to make the place its own profit center for
the electric company. Attached to the main game hall was a high-
ceilinged banquet hall, separated by thick walls that muffled the
whiz-bangs and hollering next door. On an afternoon in late April,
one month after the state championship, O'Brien whirled around
the banquet room handling last-minute logistics as the players and
their families took their seats. Dressed in a navy suit, the coach
checked to make sure there were utensils at the end of the buffet
line, which was teeming with warming trays of meatballs, pasta,
chicken parmesan, and string beans. He made sure each table had
several 2-liter bottles of soda—the managers of the facility had allowed him to bring in his own beverages to keep costs down. Finally, he made sure the piles of booty he would be handing out to
his players were in order.

When the end-of-the-season banquet began in earnest and
O'Brien called up the players one by one to collect their rewards, an

assistant coach first handed them each a large black trash bag. They needed the bag to carry their haul of sweatshirts, T-shirts, sweatpants, jackets, gym bags, framed photographs, and lacquered championship plaques.

It bugged O'Brien that the association overseeing high school athletics in the state was so cheap that all it gave the players on the championship basketball team was a lousy ribbon and medallion. After all their hustle, O'Brien's guys deserved more than that. He made sure they received it when the banquet rolled around.

He knew the promise of this end-of-the-season extravaganza had been a powerful motivator for his guys when they were slogging through January snow to get to his mandatory weekend practices. So each year, he tried to top himself in the scope of the swag he handed out. He cajoled the people who ran Good Time Emporium to give him a good rate. But even with the discount, the bill for the banquet and all the goodies he handed out approached $10,000, equal to his and Zach's combined annual coaching salaries.

O'Brien covered the tab through a variety of sources. Before the season had begun, he set up his players several times outside the Foodmaster to collect quarters and dollar bills from shoppers as they made their way into the store. Even if Charlestown residents had no connection to their winning high school basketball program, O'Brien was impressed with their generosity outside the supermarket. The effort pulled in a couple of thousand. But the biggest contributions came from two of his former players, who both attended the banquet.

Rick Brunson showed up in a suit that showed off his 6-foot-4, 190-pound frame. He'd won a state title with O'Brien in Salem, but his loyalty to his coach made him part of the Charlestown family. The thirty-two-year-old told the crowd that despite being married with two kids and despite having just finished up his eighth year in the NBA, "I still think of my state championship every day of my life." Brunson was a journeyman player, fighting each year to make one NBA squad or another, and thanks in part to the perseverance he learned from O'Brien, he always managed to earn a slot.

Harry Dixon, an intense, fit forty-one-year-old, had played on the Medford High School freshman basketball team when O'Brien coached there. Years later, when he and his fiancée went over the invitation list for their wedding, Dixon had a revelation. One of the people he wanted there most was O'Brien, a guy who had been in his life for just three months. O'Brien had managed to teach him lessons about discipline, sacrifice, and teamwork that had lasted a lifetime. The lessons sure had paid off. Dixon had been a wildly successful executive at computer storage giant EMC and then founded two high-tech companies. People familiar with his roots—he was raised in a Medford housing project by a single mother in a family with five kids—often asked him how he'd done it. Dixon would open his blue eyes extra-wide, smile, and say simply, "I met this guy." People had trouble seeing how a freshman basketball coach could have changed the course of his life, but Dixon didn't. In the late 1990s, after he'd been out of contact with his freshman coach for years, Dixon read an article about O'Brien and his work at Charlestown. He saw those same words: discipline, sacrifice, teamwork. He dialed up his old coach and had been finding ways to help out ever since.

Seated at a table across the room, Fung turned to the person next to him and pointed to Dixon. "That guy is a billionaire—with a *b*," Fung said. Dixon had made the *Forbes* list of the 400-richest Americans, and in 2000 ranked fifteenth on the list of the forty-richest Americans under age forty. Asked if that made him wealthier than Fung, the headmaster chuckled, "One hundred times richer—maybe 1,000 times!"

Other members of the extended Charlestown family were also at the banquet. O'Brien had created a pair of scholarships and named them after the two players whose memory he invoked during every team prayer: Richard Jones and Paris Booker. Both of their mothers were on hand to present scholarships. Ridley received one and Robby the other. Robby could use the dough. He'd been accepted into a competitive one-year program at Brandeis University aimed at helping disadvantaged kids bridge the gap between spotty high school educations and the rigorous demands of college. His coach and his guidance counselor both thought he'd hit a home run, since only about twenty students were admitted each year, and it would cost him nothing. But Robby was still insisting he wanted to go to his first choice of Radford University, despite the lousy aid package the Virginia school offered him; it was loaded up with loans that could bury most kids of limited means, never mind Robby, who had no parents.

The former Charlestown players congregated over by the bar. Ian Urquhart, the Townie-turned-yuppie, chatted with his former teammate Nick Souffrant, who had graduated from Bentley College and was now working in finance. Both Ian and Nick had found their college basketball experiences to be something of a letdown after Charlestown. Next to Nick and Ian stood Basil Wajd, whose Charlestown connections ran deep. He played for O'Brien and his stepbrother, Rashid Al-Kaleem, had been the most heavily recruited player during the whole of O'Brien's Charlestown tenure. Rashid had left the Division I University of Florida over frustrations with lack of playing time and ended up at the Division II American International College in Springfield. Basil said Rashid was planning to transfer again to another school: "I think he wishes he never left Florida." Most of the guys who left O'Brien's exhausting, loving, combative, exhilarating Charlestown family found themselves in search of that same experience in college. They never could find it. Basil was about to graduate from Merrimack College, a well-regarded Division II school north of Boston, and had only good things to say about the basketball program there. Still, he said, "You can never really match the intensity of what Coach has built here."

After O'Brien handed out the haul, he turned things over to Zach, who bounded to the podium. Zach was dressed about as formally as he ever did, in a button-down shirt and khaki pants. Gesturing strenuously with his arms, he cracked a few jokes about some of the players and then got serious, talking about how O'Brien had spent the last month going here, there, and everywhere to get the gifts just right. "Boston may not understand and appreciate him, but he gives so much of himself," Zach said. "Don't take it for granted." As he began to relate what O'Brien had meant in his own life, Zach broke down. Unable to finish the thought, he put his head down on the podium and sobbed. Instinctively, the seniors began to applaud. Someone yelled, "That's arrright, Z! We're with you!"

That pattern—a speaker delivering a series of upbeat comments before dissolving, suddenly, into sobs—would be repeated all afternoon. Robby did it when he talked about Ridley taking him in when he needed a place to live. Ridley did it when he talked about how much strength he drew from Robby. Spot did it when he talked about how lucky he felt to have been part of the program. George, who received the basketball clock for finishing first in O'Brien's star-chart competition, did it when he talked about Spot. As George rested his head on the podium, Spot stood up, walked to the dais, and threw his arms around George. Their hug lasted for more than a minute, as the crowd thundered its applause.

Still, no one was quite prepared for Hood's performance. Even though all the previous speeches were heartfelt, they contained the um's and repetition to be expected from high-schoolers inexperienced at public speaking. But Hood's—which he delivered extemporaneously, without so much as a note—had rhythm and range as well as raw emotional power. His habit of swaying behind the podium was the only clue that he, too, was a novice at addressing large crowds and was battling some nerves.

With his parents looking on from separate tables, Hood used his talk to thank the people who had helped him succeed, grouping them into categories. In academics, there was math teacher Diane Raimondi. "Before this year, I was a terrible math student, not because I didn't do the work, but because I didn't think the teachers was trying as hard as they could to help me," he said. "Miss Raimondi was the first math teacher in my life who actually helped me understand the work." There was history teacher and assistant coach Steve Cassidy. "History was always one of my favorite subjects, but he made us work. I remember being in a race with a Chinese kid in our class for the best average. That was important to me, because not many people can sit here and say that they actually beat out a *Chinese* kid for an award." And there was guidance counselor Kristyn O'Brien. "She wasn't looking at the fact that I walk around and look mean. She sat down with me, talked to me; she got to know who I was. She helped me along the way."

Then Hood moved on to his fellow players. Here he was by turns funny and poignant. He singled out Spot, whose girlfriend worked at a local sporting goods store. "Everybody in here should thank him for getting us a discount at FootAction." He got more serious as he moved down the list. "My man Ridley. Before this year, we never really hung out. But the more I got to know him, I saw what everybody else saw. He's a good person. I'm happy because I don't think I'd ever meet someone like that again." He told the crowd that he was able to get close to LeRoyal, the talented sophomore who lived in the Orchard Park project, solely because of the Charlestown basketball program. Under any other circumstances, Hood would have hated LeRoyal, and vice versa, simply because they came from rival projects. "But we could become friends because of the team. I could go to OP because I was with him."

He moved on to Tony Lee, the captain of the previous season's squad who was now a freshman in college, a former rival with whom he had once stood on top of a car in Mission Hill throwing punches: "He was the first person I ever met in life that was exactly like me," Hood said. "We both come from rough backgrounds. We both changed our lives. There was a time when we were ready to beat people up together, when we ran from the PO-lice together." That line drew a big laugh from the crowd, but Hood started to cry. Applause wafted over the room, steadying him.

When Hood started talking about his father, Willie smiled broadly. "Growing up, I used to like to hang outside, hang with the crowd," Hood said. "Everything that my father tried to tell me used to never go in my head. Now that I've grown up, I realize that a lot of that stuff he was telling me, if I'd used it, I'd probably be in better shape." He said he was just grateful he learned his lesson in time, unlike his cousins and older friends who never got the chance to turn their lives around. "I watched people die. That's what made me want to change." Now he was trying to be a role model for his younger brother and the other kids who were struggling in his neighborhood. "I know where the life of people who don't listen can lead to."

Hood looked out into the crowd and locked eyes with his mother. Since the cancer surgery on her lungs, she was easily winded, but today she looked buoyant, dressed in fashionable clothes, her face full of smiling pride. "Sometimes I wake up, and the first thing I hear is my mother swearing," Hood said, drawing laughs. "Sometimes I be sitting alone, and could never imagine going through life without her. She brought me into the world, and she taught me a lot. The courage she shows every day going through life teaches me the same courage. One of the main reasons that I want to go to college is a lot of people believe I can't do it. Doing it could be one of the greatest gifts I can give back to my mom."

He wasn't about to let that opportunity go by. He had signed with Adelphi.

He closed his talk by focusing on his coaches. He'd already thanked Cassidy during his remarks about his teachers, which was fitting since he'd always associated Cassidy more with the classroom than the court. Zach, he said, had taught him how to be trusting and unselfish. Of all the coaches, Hugh could relate best to what players like him were going through, because he'd been through it before. "Hughie gave us a lot of speeches. Those speeches be *long*," he said, as the rest of the guys erupted in laughter. "Sometimes he talks straightforward; sometimes he talks the other way and you just gotta shake your head like you know what he's talking about. But believe it or not, a lot of us think that what he told us saved a lot of lives."

Finally, he got to O'Brien. "Freshman and sophomore year, I thought Coach was, like, a pain. He talked to us a lot, called us a lot. But junior year, I started to respect Coach as a person and a coach. Not many people call you during vacations, want to know how things went, try as hard as Coach did to make sure we're doing the right things in school, make sure we're becoming good people. Senior year," he said, welling up with tears but steadied once more by applause, "Coach didn't want to kick people off the team. But he understood that if everybody's goal is not the same, there's no way the team can focus. So during the year, some people quit or got kicked off." He didn't have to rattle off the names—Terry, Troy, Lorenzo—since most of the people in the crowd knew the score. "But we can't complain because we won the championship, and the people that were on the team, we worked together, helped each other, and all of that was because all of us bought into his system."

He finished by addressing the younger guys whose team it would be next year. "Don't stop now," Hood said. "Keep pushing, keep working hard. Become better students, basketball players, and people. Keep walking that straight line." To anyone who would try to get them off track by questioning what they're doing, Hood said, "You gotta remember, those who mind don't matter, those who matter don't mind."

IV

THE OFF-SEASON

14

CRIME'S CALL

EXACTLY ONE WEEK AFTER THE BANQUET, one of the school cops stationed at Charlestown High tracked down O'Brien. The cop received a regular report listing arrests involving high school kids, and that morning's fax contained a name he was sure would pique the coach's interest. "You gotta see this," he said.

O'Brien's eyes froze on the name: Jason White. *What was Hood doing getting arrested?* He knew the cop was one of the many adults at the high school who didn't think much of Hood. They didn't like the way he stared at them with those piercing eyes under that stiff-brimmed baseball cap, or the way he shot back smart-ass comments when they told him to move along. They had long ago decided Hood was nothing but a thug.

The coach sensed the cop was trying to rattle him with this notice that one of his favorite players had been pinched. He didn't want to give the guy the satisfaction, so he shrugged and moved on. Part of him didn't want to believe it. How could someone who had matured so much, who had mesmerized the banquet crowd with his talk about personal growth under O'Brien—how could this kid have gotten arrested? If O'Brien knew anything, it was that

Hood was not the thug so many people made him out to be. At the banquet, hundreds of people had seen for the first time the special side of Hood that O'Brien had first glimpsed years earlier. So what the hell was he doing a week later, giving his critics the chance to strut?

O'Brien went to the office off the gym and called Hood's father. Willie was fuming at his son's stupidity, but he told O'Brien the whole thing was mostly his nephew's fault. Hood and Pookie were both nineteen, but their lives were headed in different directions. Willie had warned his son that hanging out with Pookie could only lead to trouble.

According to Willie's account of what happened, just after ten o'clock the night before, he'd been watching the news in the second-floor bedroom of their Academy townhouse in Roxbury. He heard some car doors slam shut and looked out the window to see Pookie walking from his car, which had all its tires flattened, and heading toward Willie's Mitsubishi. Hood and Pookie had just come back from dropping Tia with her bulging belly off at her home in Columbia Point. Willie said he saw Pookie holding a cell phone in one hand and a gun in the other. Hood was in the driver's seat of the Mitsubishi. As Pookie approached the passenger-side door of the Mitsubishi, Willie yelled at him, "Tell Jason not to move my fucking car!" He would explain later, "I knew something was going to be bad if Pookie got a gun, so I figured I'd put a stop to it by taking my car back."

By the time Willie got down the stairs and out the front door, the pair was gone. Hood and Pookie stopped at a Walgreens, bought a Coke and a Sprite, and headed out to Bowdoin Street in a rough section of Dorchester. The apparent purpose of the trip was for Pookie to get back at Lei Briggs, his nineteen-year-old erstwhile girlfriend—who was carrying his child and who, he was sure, had slashed his tires—and her cousin's boyfriend, with whom Pookie had a previous beef. Around 10:35 PM, Hood pulled the Mitsubishi down a side street, a dead end called Bowdoin Park, and Pookie grabbed one of the melon-sized chunks of asphalt they had put on the floor of the back seat a little while earlier. He got out of the car and walked toward a Pontiac Bonneville that belonged to Lei's cousin's boyfriend, and hurled the asphalt rock at the windshield. A few minutes later, in response to a 911 call, a Boston cop pulled up in his cruiser, threw on his takedown lights, and called for backup. He saw Pookie throw a rock to the ground and hop back in the Mitsubishi.

The cops' initial search of the car for guns turned up empty. All it took was one look at the shards of glass and chunks of asphalt to realize that two nineteen-year-olds were up to no good. But in a city where murders were piling up at an alarming rate, there were a lot more serious problems for Boston cops to be worried about than a busted windshield. In another day and another place, the cops might have forced the offenders to clean up their mess, apologize, and pay for a new windshield, chalking it all up to teenage foolishness and sparing a clogged court system of a trivial case. Yet that seldom happened in 2005 in the inner city. Besides, any hope of leniency disappeared as soon as one of the cops flipped open the armrest console between the front bucket seats. Inside, he found a Smith & Wesson, .38 special, fully loaded.

Lei's cousin told police that, standing beside the Pontiac, Pookie had called her and threatened her boyfriend, saying: "I already busted his window. Now have him come outside so we can put him in a body bag."

Hood and Pookie were each charged with the misdemeanor of making threats to kill, and the felonies of gun possession, ammunition possession, and malicious destruction of property over $250.

Still, Willie told O'Brien, he thought it would all work out eventually. He said it was obviously Pookie's gun, and that should be clear to any cop or prosecutor who compared Pookie's criminal record with Hood's. Pookie's was lengthy. Hood didn't have one. Yet.

•   •   •

O'BRIEN HAD ALWAYS FEARED the off-season. Without the ability to fill his guys' days with practices and study halls, they were exposed to the elements: slacking off in school and getting caught up in nonsense in their neighborhoods. But as this school year wound down, O'Brien was feeling almost helpless, because the problems seemed so much more dangerous than normal.

In the cafeteria in April, a kid who was part of the Columbia Point gang pulled a knife on one of the most promising freshmen in O'Brien's program, Dashawn Matthews. "Day-Day" was one of the freshmen that O'Brien had called up from the JV squad to play varsity in the postseason. Day-Day had grown up in Orchard Park, the same tough project LeRoyal came from. In the eighth grade, he witnessed a fifteen-year-old friend get stabbed to death at a bus station, simply for answering truthfully when a couple of thugs from a rival housing project asked if he was from OP.

O'Brien liked Day-Day a lot and loved the fact that he had a strong mother at home. Over the years, the coach had found that his players' mothers—since the fathers were typically out of the picture—fell into one of three categories. There were the non-factors: mothers so fatigued at trying to hold things together that they were content to let O'Brien run the show when it came to their sons' lives. There were the blamers: mothers who weren't interested in the grind of holding their sons accountable and instead were quick to scapegoat their teachers and coaches when things inevitably went wrong. And finally there were the partners: mothers willing to hold their sons to high standards, accept no excuses, and have O'Brien's back if their sons tried to blame him for something they failed to do. O'Brien could deal with the non-factors, though doing so always made him sad. He had trouble with the blamers, and their sons seldom lasted in his program. But he cherished his relationships with the partners, who unfortunately were all too rare.

After the cafeteria incident, O'Brien went straight to Fung and told him to expel the kid who pulled the knife on Day-Day. While he was at it, O'Brien said, get rid of the dozen or so hard-core trouble-makers who roamed the corridors every day, making everyone's life miserable but never getting caught. Fung replied that because Day-Day wouldn't tell him the kid's name, he couldn't take any action. O'Brien was furious. He reminded Fung that the identity was hardly a secret. But kids who grew up in Boston's high-crime neighbor-hoods had learned never to name names, especially when those names were attached to gang members. They felt the risk of retri-bution for them or their families was too high. The "Stop Snitchin'" T-shirt was one of the most popular in inner-city Boston in 2005. Some gang members had infamously worn the shirts the year be-fore, as they stood at the back of a courtroom, intimidating wit-nesses during the trial of their friends who were accused of killing a ten-year-old girl.

Whether or not the fear was justified was a matter of some de-bate. There were no recent cases in Boston of witnesses being mur-dered. But there was no denying that the fear was real to people who lived their lives surrounded by crime, in a city where police were failing, appallingly, to solve two out of every three murders and a whopping 96 percent of all nonfatal shootings. How, O'Brien asked Fung, are we supposed to ask kids to name names when the adults around them won't? Fung said he understood where O'Brien was coming from, but he had to justify every expulsion to the school department. And saying "the basketball coach told me to" just wouldn't cut it.

Around the same time, D-Black, the polite sophomore with the dark skin to match his nickname, abruptly left not only Charles-town High, but Boston altogether. He'd been threatened by some kids, so he moved out of state to live with an aunt in the South. O'Brien was upset that D-Black hadn't given him any warning, hadn't allowed him to try to improve the situation. But something the boy said made him wonder if he would have been able to offer much help. D-Black lived in perhaps the most dangerous neighborhood in

Boston, a trio of streets on the Mattapan/Dorchester border that even some cops referred to privately, and hopelessly, as "the Bermuda Triangle." There was a district police station right there, but that did little to deter all the brazen shootings. D-Black told O'Brien one of his friends from the neighborhood had also fled. That kid's father, he said, had advised him to leave town; it was just too dangerous. The father ought to know. He was a Boston police detective.

A few weeks later, Paul Becklens, the wide-eyed sophomore point guard who was Ridley's cousin, got caught with a knife in school. He claimed he was just holding it for a friend, but he was suspended. O'Brien came down hard on Paul, barring him from playing in the annual Alumni Game in June, a highly anticipated event on the Charlestown calendar. "A knife is *not* going to protect you!" O'Brien railed. "Just be smart, and do what we tell you." But deep down, for the first time in his coaching career, he began to wonder if that would be enough. His doubts intensified a few weeks later when Kevin Walsh, a sixteen-year-old Charlestown High sophomore and linebacker on the football team, got caught up in a fight between white and Hispanic kids in the project next door to the school. Walsh, who fought alongside his fellow white Townies, ended up stabbed to death.

•　•　•

TWO WEEKS AFTER HOOD'S ARREST, he and his teammates were invited to lunch with the mayor.

Hood sat on an elegant sofa in the sitting room of one of the most gracious mansions on Boston's ever-gracious Beacon Hill, as Spot and George stood behind him, chatting. Their Law and Justice teacher had taken the class on a field trip to Superior Court earlier that day, but George had decided not to go.

"Was it boring?" he asked Spot.

"Nah, man, it was a murder trial!" Spot replied.

"Black dude?"

"Yep."

"Did they show the gun?"

"No," Spot said. "It was a knife."

"Did you hear the judge say 'not guilty'?"

"No, we weren't there for the—what do you call it?—the verdict."

Although they didn't know it, the four-story brick-and-granite mansion that Spot and George were standing in was connected to one of the most famous homicide victims in Boston history. In 1849, a Harvard-trained doctor named George Parkman had been murdered by a Harvard Medical School professor named John Webster, who buried the remains in a vault under the medical school. Webster had owed Parkman a lot of money and decided to fashion his own repayment schedule. Parkman's son left a $5 million estate, including the family mansion overlooking the Boston Common, to the city for the maintenance of Boston's historic parks. Ever since the Parkman House was refurbished in the early 1970s, Boston mayors had used it for official receptions and unofficial wining and dining.

The Charlestown guys listened as Boston mayor Tom Menino began the afternoon explaining that he had a tradition of rewarding the championship teams from Boston high schools with a luncheon. O'Brien smiled appreciatively, but he couldn't help but wonder why it was the first time he'd been invited, even though it was the fifth time in six years that he had led his team to a state title. Maybe it had something to do with all the preppy white kids standing on the other side of the room, wearing blazers and ties and too much gel in their hair. They were members of the Boston Latin School hockey team, which had also just won a state championship—the first boys hockey title in school history. The parents of students at Boston Latin, which often seemed to operate more like an exclusive private school than an urban public school, had the kind of political juice that ensured their kids were never overlooked by the city's power brokers.

Of the Charlestown team, Ridley was the only one wearing a tie, and his was loosely knotted. Most of the guys were wearing jeans or Dickies pants—Hood's latest preferred brand—along with their new Charlestown team jackets advertising the latest title. Twice a young female mayoral aide asked them, "Would you be more comfortable putting your jackets in the coatroom?" Both times, the guys declined. They were led up a majestic curved staircase and down a long marbled hallway, leading to the home's informal luncheon room. There the guys saw an enormous sub sandwich, stacked ridiculously high with layer upon layer of Italian cold cuts, and wondered how they were supposed to open their mouths wide enough to take a bite without making fools of themselves. Robby shook his head and silently mouthed, "White people food."

O'Brien was feeling good. After the championship, the Boston newspapers had written extensively about him and the team. He'd been fielding calls from acquaintances all over the state. He hoped this luncheon was another signal that a new era of appreciation had begun.

The superintendent of schools, a soft-spoken man named Tom Payzant who had done a lot to improve public education in Boston, arrived late and took a seat between O'Brien and Fung. Payzant mentioned that after he was hired a decade ago, Menino let him live temporarily in the very mansion where they now sat. The Parkman House boasted sixteen rooms and a maid. Then Payzant turned to O'Brien and said he'd enjoyed reading about the coach, particularly a three-part series that had recently run in one of the papers. "Three weeks in a row! I wish I could get that kind of attention," the superintendent said. Realizing how that may have sounded, he added, "I mean, not for *myself*, but for the work we're doing."

The mayor stood at the front of the room and held up a plaque that had been made for each team. When Menino had been first elected, critics discounted him as a low-vision apparatchik. Now preparing to breeze into his fourth term, he had proven himself to be one of the most effective big-city mayors in the country. Yet eloquence eluded him. All the Charlestown players knew about the guy was that he sure must have liked his name, because he had it plastered on signs and buildings all over the city. On the bus ride to the luncheon, Rashaud Skeens, a junior whom O'Brien had just named co-captain for next year's squad, told his teammates, "Yo, I saw the mayor on Channel 24. What is he, a *special needs* mayor? He can't talk! He mumbles."

Now Rashaud and the rest of the team looked on as Menino proceeded to read every word of the boiler-plate message about good sportsmanship that had been printed on the plaque. "And then," the mayor told the gathering, still holding up the plaque, "it's signed by myself, Thomas M. Menino, the chairperson of the School Committee, Dr. Elizabeth Reilinger, and the superintendent of Boston Public Schools, Dr. Thomas W. Payzant."

After all the plaque-reading and sub-chewing was done, the players were led into a chandeliered room to be photographed with the mayor. On his way out of the luncheon room, O'Brien nodded to an older guy with blue eyes behind a pair of rectangular glasses. Michael Contompasis was the sixty-five-year-old chief operating officer for Boston Public Schools—the superintendent's right-hand man—and a friend of the mayor's. Bright and no-nonsense, he had previously served as headmaster of the elite Boston Latin School, and during his luncheon remarks, Menino had reminded the Latin hockey players that Contompasis's portrait was hanging in their school. Contompasis waved O'Brien over. He told the coach that he, too, had read the newspaper coverage of him, but that he had some serious concerns, and he wanted O'Brien to make an appointment to see him. When they met a few days later, Contompasis mentioned that one of the articles described how O'Brien had brought along four eighth-graders on the team bus as it traveled out to UMass-Amherst for the championship game. The eighth-graders had already decided to enroll in Charlestown High that fall. But Contompasis told O'Brien he believed giving them the ride-along violated rules. He warned O'Brien that the bus ride incident fit into a wider perception about the coach being a rule breaker. "You need to be very careful about what the hell you are doing," he said. He thought of it as friendly advice. To O'Brien, it felt anything but.

The new era of appreciation seemed to have ended almost before it had begun.

•   •   •

ON JUNE 3, exactly one month after Hood was arrested on gun charges, Tia went into labor with his baby. Twenty-six hours later, Janijah was born. Labor had been grueling, but Tia, who was eighteen, was glad the baby had come in early June. She wanted to walk with Hood and the rest of her Charlestown class to collect her diploma. The baby's arrival would give her two weeks to recuperate before she needed to don her cap and gown.

Hood had been with Tia and her mother all through the delivery at Brigham and Women's Hospital. Tia let him choose the little girl's name. For much of the year, Hood had been distant with her, and during that same time, she'd seen how the street was calling him more and, to her disappointment, how he'd begun to answer it. But as her delivery date loomed, he'd become more attentive to her again. She hoped his foolishness in getting arrested had woken him up. Maybe now she'd see the reemergence of that tender, thoughtful boy who had first made her laugh and had won her heart. She didn't press Hood on where he'd gotten the name Janijah from. She figured he chose it because it sounded both African and like his real name,

Jason. But she didn't give it too much thought. When she cradled the baby in her arms, she called her "Mamma."

Willie refused to call the baby Janijah. "All these kids giving their babies African names when they know nothing about Africa— Taneeka, Tashanda! Whatever happened to Brenda?" He laughed. "I like simple names, like mine, Willie Harvey Barnes Jr." That name had been passed down through six generations, the youngest being one of Willie's grandsons. Willie decided on his own version of his new granddaughter's name: Jay.

15

NO ORDINARY SUMMER

ONLY IN CHARLESTOWN did the high school winter basketball season end in June. Before Hood and Ridley and the rest of the seniors left for college, O'Brien gave them one more chance to suit up as a member of the state-champion Charlestown High squad. He did this through the annual Alumni Game, where the team faced off against a collection of his players from Charlestown's past. No event on the Charlestown calendar better reinforced the central message he embedded into the program: You will be rewarded for your hard work, and you'll always have a home.

An hour before tip-off, Zach pushed a mop and metal bucket across the court, cleaning off the grime. He couldn't have been more excited. "This is my favorite day of the year!" he announced to the people walking by him. "I'll take this over the state championship!" O'Brien, who was racing around the gym handling last-minute details, would have agreed, though his face, unlike Zach's, gave no hint of happiness.

He wore his usual game-day face of worry. But this game was anything but usual. For starters, there was the weather. During the regular season, the heat of the Charlestown gym was a welcome relief from the sub-freezing winter evenings outside. For the Alumni Game, the gym only made the 91-degree scorcher outside more unbearable. Yet the difference that meant the most to O'Brien was being able to watch thirty of his former players—the fruits of a dozen years of his labor—walk through the door.

Before long, the gym was packed more tightly than any regular-season Charlestown game. Students, parents, and friends plunked down a few dollars each to see the stars of the past defend their honor against the players of today and tomorrow. J-Rome, the student DJ who had spun hip-hop records at the team's home games for years now, would be heading off to Saint Michael's College in Vermont in the fall. Standing behind large speakers in the corner, he reviewed his playlist, which included 50 Cent's "Candy Shop." Some of the guys liked the tune because it was a four-minute metaphor for oral sex. J-Rome liked it because it was heavy on the bass.

Waiting for the noontime tip-off, women in sundresses sat in the bleachers, using their game-day programs to fan themselves, moving their forearms rhythmically to the beat of 50 Cent blaring from J-Rome's speakers. Middle school and high school kids looked for relief by congregating around the old metal standing fans that lined the perimeter of the court. Guidance counselor Kristyn O'Brien fanned herself as well, but used a stamped business envelope rather than the program. It contained Hood's application for financial aid. When she and O'Brien had sorted out Adelphi's final scholarship offer, it came up about $4,000 short. Kristyn had hurriedly put together an aid application but needed a signature from Hood's father before she could submit it. She knew she'd find him at the game. Kristyn had never met Jamie Cosgrove, the man who would be coaching Hood at Adelphi, but he too was in the crowd.

A group of players past and present stood by the bleachers. Ridley and Spot weren't among them. Word came back that they had been at Spot's uncle's place in Brockton and had missed their train into town. Alray Taylor, a beefy alum from the class of 2002 who had given Hood his nickname fours years earlier, was ticked because Spot had his gym shorts and he needed them to get changed for the game. After graduation, Alray had done a year of prep school and then earned a D-I scholarship to the University of New Hampshire. But after a season seeing little playing time, he transferred to a smaller college in southern New Hampshire, hoping for the kind of intense yet intimate experience he had found with O'Brien. He didn't find it. In the three months since his basketball season had ended, he had yet to hear from his college coach. Pointing to the Charlestown gym, he said, "There's nothing like this program anywhere out there. Coach cares so much, makes sure you get to college, works so hard. People criticize him around Boston, but they don't know all he does for his guys."

For the past few weeks, Alray had been coming to the Charlestown gym every afternoon. The place was such a home away from home for O'Brien's former players that many of them made it their first stop when they returned from college, walking through the blue doors and dropping their bags near the back wall under the red championship banners, before they even checked in with their families. All through May and early June, the former players would spend their afternoons in the sweaty gym scrimmaging against the guys on the current squad—all building up to today's showdown.

Glancing at his watch, O'Brien made clear his irritation with Ridley and Spot. He'd spent four years drilling these guys on the importance of being on time. You show up late for a job interview, he would tell them, and you might as well not show up at all, because there's no way you're getting the job. And yet they couldn't find a way to be on time for the final event of their Charlestown career?

Still, O'Brien had to admit tardiness was a pretty mild infraction. He wasn't letting Ridley's cousin Paul play after his suspension. He wasn't letting LeRoyal, the sophomore with the gorgeous jump shot, play because he'd been neglecting his schoolwork and O'Brien felt his up-and-down attitude had only gotten worse. The coach had also chosen to deny them the championship rings that everyone else on the team had received.

As the alumni began shooting baskets during warm-ups, a wave of familiarity crested over the gym. Rashid Al-Kaleem—the top scorer in Charlestown history, who put up 1,566 points and led the team to three straight state titles—had experienced a lot more lows than highs since leaving high school. The 6-foot–3 Rashid may not have returned to the Charlestown gym as the D-I star everyone predicted he would become when he left to play for the University of Florida. And his appearance certainly had changed, given the tattoos now blanketing his arms and torso. But as soon as the ball touched his hands, he began draining 3-pointers just like in the old days. In the crowd, the people began smiling and pointing like it was 1999. After he sank one lovely 3-pointer, someone in the stands yelled, "Cash!"—his way of labeling a money shot.

During warm-ups, LeRoyal, wearing street clothes, looked on from the bleachers. Sitting next to him was Lorenzo, the junior who had quit at the start of the season. When O'Brien's head was turned, Lorenzo bounded out of the bleachers, grabbed a loose ball, sank a jumper, and then raced back to the stands before the coach turned back around. More than anything, Lorenzo wanted to be out there playing with his former teammates. But what was done was done.

For LeRoyal, the jury was still out. But it felt as though the verdict could be announced any day now. Zach had been frustrated with LeRoyal for weeks, avoiding him until yesterday, when he pulled him aside to vent. "It's like if you wanna go out with a pretty girl and she doesn't want you," Zach said. "At a certain point, you have to walk away, even if she's really pretty. You're the pretty girl—but you don't like us, don't want to listen, so at some point we have to move on." In the Alumni Game program, which listed all the members of Charlestown's latest state-title team, O'Brien made sure LeRoyal's name was nowhere to be found.

Zach refused to let any of that dampen his enjoyment of the day. He bounded around the court during warm-ups, hugging alums and yelling, "My brother from another mother!" He ribbed the youngest guys on the current squad, the freshmen Shoddy and Day-Day, telling them, "You're scared!"—knocking his knees back and forth comically as he said it.

Ridley and Spot arrived just in time. After checking in with O'Brien, Ridley noticed his father in the stands. In one week, Ridley would be leaving for Toledo. Division I programs made sure their incoming players got off to a good start, having them take a few summer school courses before their freshmen year started to begin racking up the credits. Ridley walked over to McClary. "Hey, son," McClary said.

"Hey, Pops," Ridley replied warmly, putting out his hand.

When it was time, all the players left the court and crowded into a stairwell off the gym. O'Brien, sweating through his warm-up suit, walked to the center of the court and picked up a microphone. As the players waited for him to announce each of them by name, they joked and roughhoused. When Hood got bumped by an alum, he pushed him back—hard. The rest of the pack got involved, and the shoving cascaded along the stairs. But by the time O'Brien called out the first name, the calm had returned to the stairwell, the guys laughing and hugging each other. Despite their age differences, they got along like old teammates, brothers even. In O'Brien's world, that's exactly what they were.

Many of the alumni returned to Charlestown as success stories. They included an engineer, a finance guy, an assistant admissions director at an elite college. O'Brien had helped steer all of these alumni to college, but some hadn't lasted there and were now holding down blue-collar jobs doing security or installing insula-tion. Many others were still plugging away on campus. After O'Brien called out a name, that player would emerge from the stairwell, dribble toward the hoop and toss the ball in. One alum decided to charge in for a dunk, but the ball bounced out. O'Brien grinned, pulling the microphone toward his mouth and announc-ing, "That's just what happened when he was in high school!"

As per tradition, Zach, looking oddly relaxed by the time the game began, coached the alumni team, rotating two dozen players in and out of the game. Cassidy, looking as serious as a talking head on PBS's *NewsHour with Jim Lehrer*, coached the current squad. At the final buzzer, the score was 105–102. As the alumni left the court and headed for a pizza party in the cafeteria, they did so with their unbeaten record intact. Yet every year, the score was close, which is exactly how O'Brien wanted it. If one side ever threatened a blowout, the referees were encouraged to call enough fouls down the stretch to narrow the gap.

•   •   •

A S THE SUMMER WORE ON and Ridley and Hood began settling into their new lives as college basketball players, O'Brien made sure his current players' lives were packed with camps, summer leagues, and one-on-one time with him. But as he compared the success he'd had with Ridley and Hood with the frustration he'd ex-perienced with last year's sophomore and junior classes, he real-ized something important. He had begun working intensely, and individually, with Ridley and Hood as far back as the summer be-fore they entered Charlestown High. In recent years, as he'd gotten tied up handling one crisis or another, something had to give. Too often, that had been the individualized attention with the youngest

guys in his program. So he rededicated himself to that early inter-
vention. He'd hatched a plan with Harry Dixon, his wealthy bene-
factor, to create a mentoring program for the Charlestown players,
assigning the most inspirational mentors to work with the incoming freshmen. And he had assigned himself the task of working
closely with Tron Griffith, who, as an eighth-grader, had joined
O'Brien on the team bus ride to the state finals. Tron had a sort of
retro Afro, and he sometimes walked around with a comb stuck in
it. He wasn't a great student or tall or a dazzling shooter, but he
had real presence on the court, especially for a young guy. He'd
dribble toward the basket with his chin jutted up in the air, seemingly undaunted by the much taller defenders closing in on him.
Tron was one of those kids who could go either way, and in middle
school he had joined the wrong crowd. O'Brien took an immediate
liking to him, and all through the summer had ridden him hard, requiring him to read four books and write reports for him about
them. O'Brien read the books alongside him.

As much as O'Brien was frustrated and fatigued as he faced the
new school year, the experience of having worked with Tron all
summer had reassured him once again why he was doing what he
was doing rather than commanding more money and attention by
coaching at the college level. Working with teenagers, breaking
through to them before they became fully formed characters, before the mounting slights they encountered formed chips big
enough to make their shoulders sag—that was his calling.

When Tron was having some trouble with his foot, O'Brien took
him to see an orthopedic specialist. Riding down in the elevator
after the appointment, they were talking and joking around with
the ease they had developed over the summer. When the elevator
reached the lobby, a woman who had been riding in it with them
turned to O'Brien and asked, "Are you related?" As he recounted the
story later to his players, O'Brien still couldn't believe it. "Here I

am, a white guy. And here he is, a black kid—he's not even mulatto or anything! But she could tell how good we get along, how close we are."

The other big highlight of the summer had to do with the Charlestown gym. O'Brien had been nagging the headmaster for years to get the place fixed up, and finally it happened. The exposed insulation was patched up, the walls were given a fresh coat of paint, and, best of all, there was a gleaming new floor. O'Brien was particularly pleased to have gotten rid of the old center court, with the Bunker Hill Monument painted onto the floorboards and the word "Townies" underneath it. In its place, there was now simply a picture of a bright orange basketball. The spruce-up extended beyond the gym: The stalls in the nearby boys' bathrooms actually had doors now.

•   •   •

WHILE O'BRIEN WAS ENJOYING his new court, Michael Fung was busy preparing for a new school year. One day in July, he walked into Marshalls, a discount clothing store in Boston's tired Downtown Crossing retail district, carrying a pair of pants that didn't fit. When he approached the service desk, the clerk asked him, "Why are you returning them?"

He could see the words floating around in his head, yet he could not retrieve them. The clerk could tell he was struggling, so she asked him again, and then again. Each time she repeated the question, she spoke more slowly and loudly. Here he was, an MIT-trained headmaster about to turn sixty-two, and this minimum-wage clerk was feeling pity for him, assuming he was just some illiterate foreigner frozen in fear while trying to speak the local language. He didn't know whether to cry or laugh. But he did know this much: He was having a stroke.

Five times, her question went unanswered. Fung wished the clerk were Chinese. He recalled once reading an article about how stroke victims lost their second language but somehow retained their primary tongue. Finally, on the sixth try, Fung was able to muster a meek, "Not *feet*. Not *fit*." She slid the return authorization slip over to him and directed him to sign it. He could hold the pen but was unable to form a single letter. So he moved it across the slip, making an ink squiggle. That was good enough for her.

Suddenly, Fung was overcome with fear. It wasn't so much the likelihood of dying that worried him. It was the location. *I do not want to die in Marshalls*, he said to himself. *Somebody will take my wallet and then when they find my body they won't even know who I am.* So, in the middle of a stroke, he hopped on the subway and headed for home. He began humming his favorite song, Janis Joplin's "Me and Bobby McGee."

Fung had no idea if he was singing the lyrics and humming the *la-da-da* refrain in his head, or if the people around him on the subway could hear what he heard. It didn't really matter. There were always a few oddballs singing to themselves on the subway in Boston, and nobody paid them any mind, preferring instead to stare at the mini-billboards above the seats.

When Fung got back to his townhouse in the Longwood neighborhood, home to many of Boston's world-renowned teaching hospitals, his wife was not around. Fung led his life by logic, and a life-threatening crisis was no time to change his approach. His grandfather on his father's side died of a stroke in his sixties, and two of his paternal uncles had also died young of strokes. But on his mother's side, his grandmother lived to 103 and his grandfather lived to 107. So in the midst of watching his own body shut down, Fung glimpsed the worst possible outcome: That he would have a stroke that left him debilitated, and that he would live to be 107. No, he told himself, he'd rather die now. He climbed into bed and went to sleep.

When he awoke the next morning, the symptoms were gone. He figured he'd just pretend it never happened, but his wife insisted he go to see his doctor. A CAT scan showed severe blockage in an artery in his brain. The doctor told Fung he could put a stent in it, but it was such a delicate spot that his chance of survival would probably be less than 5 percent. Now that he'd had one TIA—the medical acronym for a stroke without permanent damage—he could live for many years more with no further problems, or he could have another episode and die tomorrow. The doctor told him the best thing he could do was change his lifestyle, starting by overhauling his diet, which was dominated by junk food.

Fung returned to his normal argumentative self, telling the doctor, "I don't smoke, I don't drink, I don't do drugs, I don't chase women. And you're going to make me change my diet?"

The doctor turned to Fung's wife and said, "Will you tell this man to begin chasing women so he can get some exercise?"

The first time O'Brien saw Fung after the TIA, he was struck by how much the headmaster looked and acted like his old self, as though the health scare had never happened. But Fung told him he had been changed by it. "This coming school year will probably be my last, Jack," Fung said. "After that, I think I will retire." As much as they had butted heads during the previous spring, on issues ranging from school discipline to class schedules, O'Brien had a hard time imagining Charlestown High without Fung in charge. Despite their sparring, he always knew he could count on the headmaster to support his program. But he didn't worry too much about a future without Fung. He knew how obsessed Fung was with moving Charlestown High forward, and O'Brien knew a thing or two about obsession. Provided the man remained healthy, he figured Fung was no more capable of walking away from Charlestown than he was.

●　　●　　●

THE CROWD RIMMED AN OUTDOOR COURT in Ramsay Park in Roxbury. On an August evening in the twilight of summer, a few weeks after Fung's stroke, the fans had shown up for the championship game of a summer league run by Boston's Violence Free Zone Initiative. The idea behind the league was to keep the peace throughout the long, hot summer by giving teenagers something constructive to focus on, rather than letting them get caught up in the housing-project turf wars. No one needed to look far for a reminder of how those wars too often ended. Beside the court there was a makeshift memorial for Biggie Gaines, a heavyset twenty-three-year-old coach who'd been shot to death as he was running his players through drills on the court during the previous summer. The park sat between two housing projects—Lenox Street and Grant Manor—and each project had its own gang. One was called Lenox and the other 1850, after the address of a Grant Manor building on Washington Street. A feud between the two gangs had been simmering for years. Police said Biggie, whose mother lived in 1850, had gotten caught up in the feud, and that was that. A week after his murder, an innocent eleven-year-old boy trying out for Pop Warner football at a park down the street was hit by a stray bullet, which tore through his lung and heart muscle and nearly killed him. By holding league games at Ramsay, organizers hoped to send a new message, the same one contained in the motto they'd come up for the program: "Books and Ball So the Streets Don't Call."

As it turned out, the two teams playing for the Violence Free Zone championship on this night in Ramsay Park both came from Orchard Park, or OP. Two of O'Brien's soon-to-be-sophomore players—Day-Day and Shoddy, whom he'd called up to varsity in time for the state finals—were playing. Around 8:30 PM, a kid wearing a black hoodie rode by the court on his bike. As Shoddy sailed toward the basket for a layup, the kid on the bike fired four bullets at the court. People in the crowd screamed and dove for cover. One of the bullets hit Day-Day on his foot. Another went right up

Shoddy's leg as he was in the air, then traveled up his back. Both kids were rushed to the hospital. Despite the fact that several cops were patrolling the area, the shooter managed to pedal away on his bike and was never caught. Police concluded that Shoddy and Day-Day hadn't been shot for any reason besides their address. The 1850 gang had just begun beefing with the OP gang. And when two teams from OP showed up to play on their turf, 1850 decided a message needed to be sent.

Day-Day and Shoddy were both rushed to Boston Medical Center. Shoddy's injuries were more serious, and he spent several days in the hospital recuperating. O'Brien sat with both boys in the hospital, trying to cheer them up, reminding them how lucky they were to escape without permanent injury. But inside O'Brien was shaken. Shoddy and Day-Day were two of his favorite freshmen from last year. Shoddy was only 5-foot-10, but he had been the sparkplug on the JV squad. And Day-Day had huge potential beyond just his height, which was 6-foot-4 and growing. After Day-Day had been threatened in the spring by a gang member wielding a knife at school, O'Brien had been relieved that his mother hadn't transferred her son out of Charlestown, even though O'Brien had been unable to persuade Fung to expel the gang member. But O'Brien feared the shootings would compel the mothers to want to do something, anything, to try to make their boys safer. He stressed that the shootings had nothing to do with Charlestown and there was nothing to suggest the boys would be safer at a different school. For the time being, both mothers kept their sons at Charlestown. But he had a feeling that wouldn't last.

For years, O'Brien had been offering his players the same social contract: Stick with me, listen to what I say, and you'll end up OK. But privately he was growing more worried about being able to hold up his end of the contract.

V

END GAME

16

THE
UNRAVELING

O'BRIEN BEGAN THE NEW SCHOOL YEAR the same way he had the last. But there was no denying that the true believer in him had, in important ways, been tamed. On a warm evening in the waning days of summer, he picked up the two seniors who would be his captains for the coming season's squad and took them to Oak Lawn Cemetery. As he stood with them before Richard Jones's black granite gravestone, he felt more detached than he had been the year before. He did not kneel down in front of the gravesite, did not let his finger trace over the laser-etching of Richard's smiling face at the center of the stone, did not offer a prayer, at least not out loud. He just stood and stared. He was equally restrained after leading his co-captains to Paris Booker's grave marker 30 yards away. Still, he ended by delivering a similar graveside message to the one he'd given Ridley and Hood a year earlier. "As hard as things might get this year," he said, "think about these guys."

In part, O'Brien's restraint was a product of his diminished expectations for the coming season. As always, he began the year by telling himself all the reasons his team could not hope to win another state title—the competition was too stiff, too much of his talent had graduated, the basketball gods just wouldn't allow Charlestown six championships in seven years. Usually this line of thinking motivated him to figure out a way to cheat the odds again. But this year the tally of all those daunting factors was less a psychological lever than a sober acceptance of reality.

His new senior co-captains, Bernard Coleman and Rashaud Skeens, were friendly, good-natured guys, but unlike Ridley and Hood, they weren't stars on the court. That, combined with their anemic academic transcripts, made their college prospects shaky at best. They were simply the last ones standing in a senior class that had, for O'Brien, begun four years earlier brimming with expectation. All the other promising players had over the previous three years quit, transferred, been tossed, or bombed out. Since Rashaud had joined the team as a junior, Bernard was the lone survivor from the original freshman class, and he had added incentive to stick it out, since his brother Hugh was the assistant coach. O'Brien's demanding program always had a fairly high attrition rate, but there had to be something else at work. He hoped it was an aberration, but other events over the past year made him worry that it might be a harbinger.

From Oak Lawn Cemetery, O'Brien drove his minivan through the heart of Boston, through traffic as slow as summer, until he made it onto the interstate. Then he headed north, so he could continue his tradition of treating his captains to burgers and mini-golf and get them pumped up about the new school year before them. At one point, he looked in his rearview mirror and spotted Bernard talking on his cell phone. "Bernie, no," O'Brien said. Bernard hung up.

O'Brien told them he'd heard a rumor that Lorenzo Jones, their classmate who'd joined the team as a freshman but quit at the start of the last season, had been caught with a gun.

"It's true," Bernard said, looking out the window. "He may be sent away."

"Imagine that," O'Brien said, shaking his head slowly. "He could be a team captain this year, poised to get a college scholarship."

The talk drifted to their arch-rivals from Eastie. David Siggers, the Eastie coach, had up and quit and moved to California. Eastie's star senior from last season, a lithe shooting guard whom Adelphi University had been scouting along with Hood, hadn't even managed to graduate. "Around Boston," O'Brien said, "the difference between getting a college scholarship and not graduating from high school is *so* small."

O'Brien mentioned that he'd received several voice-mail messages from Terry Carter over the summer. "I didn't return them because I wanted to see how hard he would keep trying to get a hold of me," O'Brien said. The messages stopped coming. O'Brien didn't tell his players about another call he had received about Terry, from his loyal guardian, Harry Landry. Harry said Terry had swiped his ATM card and stolen thousands from Harry's bank account.

When O'Brien had coached at Salem High, every year seemed to get a little easier. People assumed his life was even less strenuous at Charlestown, since he coached the most dominant team in the state. Instead, O'Brien found it to be a Sisyphean challenge; no matter how many times he rolled that rock up the hill, he still began every year at the bottom. It wasn't the loss of Ridley and Hood that bothered O'Brien. They were supposed to move on after moving up. What stung was how their potential successors had been lost, for a variety of reasons, none of them to O'Brien's liking.

Two 6-foot-4 players who should have been starting their sophomore years at Charlestown were instead repeating their freshman year at the private schools that had come along and poached them. It would have been one thing if O'Brien knew the players would do well in their new settings, improving as students and basketball players. But O'Brien couldn't shake the suspicion that these private schools were just using the players to upgrade their performance on the court. He'd seen players in the past transfer to prep schools, only to fail to graduate.

LeRoyal Hairston, who should have been starting his junior year at Charlestown, was instead attending John C. Fremont High School in a gang-infested corner of South Central Los Angeles. He had made a bizarre 3,000-mile move, along with his former teammate, Troy Gillenwater. LeRoyal had no family there. And as bad as the streets of inner-city Boston had become—LeRoyal had narrowly missed gunfire a few days before leaving his apartment in Orchard Park—South Central LA's were a whole lot worse. The *Los Angeles Times* once described Fremont High School, which had nearly 5,000 students and sprawled a full city block, as "a neighborhood fortress, its perimeter protected by an 8-foot steel fence topped by spikes, its windows shielded from gunfire by thick screens." Nearly a third of the school's 2,300 freshmen were reading at no better than a third-grade level. Two-thirds of its freshmen dropped out before reaching the twelfth grade. That is where LeRoyal and Troy flew to pursue their California dreams.

O'Brien eventually heard that Troy's Amateur Athletic Union coach had orchestrated the whole thing. The AAU was a sometimes shadowy world where some coaches struck contracts with sneaker companies and trotted hotshot players around to showcase tournaments all over the nation. AAU had no connection to high school teams, and AAU coaches didn't have to live by the rigid rules imposed by high school leagues. O'Brien knew he had no business bemoaning the loss of either Troy or LeRoyal. After all, he had kicked Troy off the team and put LeRoyal on notice, wiping his name from the Alumni Game program and withholding his championship ring. Regardless, he had hoped his tough stance at the end of the last year would have been enough to jolt LeRoyal back into compliance. And he couldn't believe the chutzpah behind these coaches who, he ·

believed, had moved two Boston kids clear across the country just so they could play basketball at a failing public high school. The kids were being treated like commodities.

In addition, O'Brien was bracing himself for two more names to join Charlestown's list of the disappeared. Ever since Shoddy and Day-Day had been shot in the summer antiviolence league championship, O'Brien had known their shaken mothers would want to do something to feel they were better protecting their sons. Deep in his heart, he doubted that by the time the first game rolled around, either player would still be on his team. As it turned out, by the end of the season many of O'Brien's plans for Charlestown had begun to unravel in ways he could hardly have predicted.

In October, as O'Brien had feared, Day-Day and Shoddy joined the exodus from Charlestown, driven out by hassles at bus stops and rumblings of gang beefs spilling over into the high school. Shoddy transferred to a Boston high school way across town and Day-Day to a school in Quincy, a neighboring city where a relative lived. O'Brien was so distressed at the turn of events that he didn't even talk about it to his assistant coaches. They sensed that what worried him most was the growing feeling that he was losing control.

He was. His diminished sense of control extended beyond his kids and the basketball courts. O'Brien found himself with a battle on his hands to preserve the career of one of his assistant coaches.

•   •   •

IN JANUARY, standing at the front of Room 512, Hugh Coleman adjusted his tie while a middle-aged, curly-haired man adjusted his video camera at the back of the room. The man was an education consultant. He and his partner ran teaching workshops all over the country, and they'd come on this January day to film a ninth-grade English class. Hugh was looking sharp, dressed in gray slacks, a yellow Oxford, and a blue striped tie. But the consultants weren't there to film him.

Twenty-five ninth-graders—mostly black and Hispanic, with a few Asians mixed in—sat at tables in groups of three or four. The lesson today had to do with sonnets. "Mr. Coleman, would you read the first one?" said a young woman with short brown hair and a set of keys hanging on a lanyard around her neck. After Hugh finished the sonnet, the woman snapped her fingers repeatedly and told her students to do the same, "Snap for Mr. Coleman."

The snapping was her substitute for applause. Clapping in a classroom could get raucous. Tracy Wagner did not like to waste time settling her students. Raised in the liberal university town of Madison, Wisconsin, she came to Boston to earn her master's from Harvard. She had heard that Charlestown High was an urban high school attracting a lot of young, smart, dedicated teachers, and she decided to join the pack. But unlike the many young teachers whose altruism got crushed by the grind of seeing kids mistake kindness for weakness, Tracy remained relentlessly cheery, mainly because she left little to chance in controlling her classroom.

The room was so vibrantly decorated that it approached sensory overload. On the back wall, student writing samples were posted. In the front of the room, the chalkboard was covered with so much chalk that it blocked out just about the whole board. There was the agenda for that day's class, a mission statement, and a "word wall." There were continual, clear updates on where each student stood with his or her assignments, so no one could claim ignorance at the end of the term. Above all, there was structure, structure, and more structure. She assigned kids roles like timekeeper, facilitator, and "volume control," the last one being someone empowered to say "Keep it down!" so Tracy wouldn't have to. In a school where some teachers used fear and intimidation to keep order and others let

their classrooms crumble into cacophony and chaos, it was re-
freshing to see a teacher maintain control without ever once raising her voice.

Hugh had gotten to know Tracy last year, when he taught in a
neighboring classroom. This year, he had been assigned to Tracy's
classroom to learn from her. But the stakes were higher than just
general professional development. How much Hugh learned from
Tracy over the school year might well determine whether he would
be allowed to keep his job.

O'Brien had helped Hugh get his position at Charlestown. What a
great catch he was, he'd told Fung: a young black male, who had
grown up in Boston, gone to Charlestown as a student, and then
earned his degree from one of the best small colleges in the country. He was married and raising a young daughter. He was bright
and charismatic. What more could you ask for?

Fung agreed to give him a teaching job. But after observing him
in the classroom, he felt there was something important missing
from the package. "He is not a good teacher," Fung told O'Brien. He
didn't feel Hugh had sufficient command of his material or the gift
for transmitting it in innovative ways that the headmaster demanded. He warned Hugh that there might not be a permanent slot
for him. Fung cited the new federal No Child Left Behind law, which
insisted all teachers had to have passed their certification test.
Hugh had failed his the first time he tried and wasn't eager to try
again. Fung had secured a waiver for him, but now, he told Hugh,
waivers were becoming much harder to come by. Along with
demanding that he get his certification, Fung advised Hugh to
enroll in a one-year teacher-training program at the University of
Massachusetts-Boston. If he did everything right, he could earn his
master's degree by the end of the year and, by being assigned as a
"resident" in an experienced teacher's classroom, gain valuable exposure to new teaching strategies. To do the program, Hugh would
have to give up his Charlestown job—and nearly $45,000 salary—

for a year, but the program offered a $10,000 stipend, and Hugh could do his residency right at Charlestown High.

O'Brien thought it was absurd to force a capable guy like Hugh to try to feed his family for a year on ten grand. "Look at how well he connects with the kids," he told Fung. The headmaster's teaching hires tended to be young white females, and O'Brien thought all the boys in the school suffered from having too few strong male figures, never mind strong black males. The coach was also worried about the ripple effect if Hugh wasn't able to keep his job. Over the years, whenever he asked his guys about how they envisioned their futures, he heard the same responses: playing in the NBA or "being an entrepreneur—you know, own my own business." The first one was, of course, a pipe dream. But the second one wasn't much better—a meaningless goal that probably came from watching too many NBA players talk on ESPN about all their off-the-court interests. O'Brien was, above all, a practical guy. Ever since Hugh had gotten hired, he was able to point to his example and tell his young students: Go get your degree; then you can come back and be a teacher. He knew the Boston school system was always looking for qualified teachers who were black. And he knew that for guys who grew up in neighborhoods battered by high unemployment and high crime, a steady salary approaching $50,000 a year could become their foundation for transforming their lives and breaking the cycle in their family. And now Fung wanted to mess with his model?

O'Brien knew Fung was just as stubborn as he was, and when it came to his pet subject of academic rigor, he wasn't about to take advice from the basketball coach with a degree in phys ed. "You know basketball; I know teaching," Fung insisted bluntly. So O'Brien did not dwell on his objections when Hugh had given up his teaching slot and enrolled in the teacher training program at the start of this year. As the year went on and he saw Hugh learning new teaching skills from Tracy, O'Brien had to wonder if maybe Fung had been right.

The issue of Hugh's teaching slot wasn't the only academic fault line between O'Brien and Fung, however. For a decade now, the coach had prided himself on being able to manage his players' academic paths, helping them build a record strong enough to get into college. But now forces were conspiring to make that much harder. Top of the list was something called MCAS, the acronym for the Massachusetts standardized test that students had to pass in math and English if they wanted to graduate. Because students were tested at the end of tenth grade, Fung now required all sophomores to double up on their math courses. He wanted them to be prepared for any kind of math problem they might see on the test. O'Brien hated this move because it meant elective courses, which Fung had already cut back severely to focus on the basics, were reduced even further. The coach had always used electives as a route to getting some A's and B's on the transcripts. Now, in addition to the double-math requirement, any student who failed math in the ninth grade was forced to take it again in the tenth grade. One of O'Brien's sophomores faced three math courses this year. It brutally reduced O'Brien's opportunity to turn a failing academic performance around if a kid who hated math was forced to sit through half his day in one math class or another. One math teacher, a young woman who had graduated from a well-respected college, had several of the basketball players in her class this year. She was failing 70 percent of her entire class. "How," O'Brien pressed Fung, "can that possibly be the kids' fault?"

• • •

IN LATE FEBRUARY, with the 2006 season building to its climax, O'Brien received a fresh reminder of how things had veered off track from the previous year. Troy and LeRoyal made an unexpected return, taking the reverse snowbird flight from California to the bone-chilling cold of Boston winter. It hadn't exactly been by choice.

Troy was taller and more muscular than when he'd left Charlestown in the summer. On the roster of his California team, he was listed at 6-foot–7 and 230 pounds, which came as a surprise to his former teammates. But there was no question that he had developed into the force that propelled his Los Angeles team's offense. Striding into the Madidome, the cavernous gym in Roxbury, Troy wore a black baseball cap on backward and busied himself checking messages on his Sidekick. LeRoyal, a small black knit cap resting on the top of his head, walked by Troy and took his place in the nose-bleed section of the bleachers.

They had returned to watch the rematch of Charlestown and Eastie in the City League finals. Charlestown came into the city finals after a much bumpier basketball season than the previous year, and two of the team's four losses had come at the hands of Eastie. Sitting in the stands, Zach's wife, Mandy, couldn't help but notice that no one seemed to be talking about the game at hand. Instead, there was a lot of indignant talk about how O'Brien had torpedoed Troy and LeRoyal's California adventure. The word coursing through the bleachers was that Troy and LeRoyal had lost their eligibility to play in California, and it had all been O'Brien's doing, which, in fact, was nonsense. Mandy had been coming to Charlestown games for a decade, witnessing heated battles in which it wasn't clear who would end up on top. But for the first time she worried about O'Brien's safety.

The Eastie players came out fired up, declining the traditional player introductions and opting instead to be announced only as a team, a maneuver the New England Patriots had made popular on their march to winning three Super Bowls in four years. But once the game got going, it was the Charlestown squad that hummed with the precision of a well-drilled operation, with both the offense and defense coming alive. With two minutes left and Charlestown up by 14, LeRoyal descended the bleachers and slipped out of the gym, Troy not far behind.

Their futures were uncertain. Had LeRoyal stayed with Charlestown, he would have probably been the one draining 3-pointers tonight. Yet he'd made little impact in Los Angeles.

Troy, however, had blossomed into one of the best players on the LA public school circuit. He was named MVP of the Pasadena city tournament and had led Fremont into the playoffs with a 22–3 regular season record. Helping in that effort was a 6-foot-8 Boston kid who'd also made the same curious cross-continental transfer at the beginning of the year.

Those kinds of statistics, achieved with a cluster of guys no one had ever seen around the city before, inevitably prompted some questions from competitors. After a *Boston Globe* sportswriter began making inquiries, the California Interscholastic Federation opened an investigation. In mid-February, the federation announced its findings: Troy, LeRoyal, and the 6-foot-8 Boston kid were among six players who had transferred to Fremont under fishy circumstances. Two other players had come from New York, and one from another part of California. Fremont was forced to withdraw from the playoffs and forfeit the season.

Because a Boston sportswriter had broken the story, word spread quickly that O'Brien, who was on good terms with the sportswriters on the high school beat in town, had been the tipster. In fact, O'Brien had been nowhere near it. The sportswriter had stumbled onto the story while researching a different piece.

•   •   •

FOR O'BRIEN, THE GAME THAT crystallized the notion that people around him were working against him, instead of with him, was the second-round game of the postseason state tournament. The first sign of trouble hadn't actually looked like much trouble at all. Heading into the state tournament in early March, O'Brien received a call from Ken Still, the athletic director for Boston schools, who was relaying a request from the coach of the team from the affluent suburb of Andover. That coach wanted their second-round playoff match-up moved from Charlestown High to a neutral site, arguing the gym would not be big enough to accommodate all the Andover fans. O'Brien laughed off the request. Why in the world would he agree to that? The league rules were clear that the team with the better record going into the tournament earned home-court advantage for the first two rounds, unless that team's gym was not suitable for playoff play. The recently renovated Charlestown gym had hosted playoff games for nearly a decade without a hitch. It could seat at least 800 people, and there were almost never more than a few hundred showing up to cheer on the home team. There would be plenty of room for the caravan of Lexuses that made the half-hour trip south from Andover to Charlestown. Besides, when the athletic director made his call to O'Brien on the first Thursday in March, Charlestown and Andover hadn't even won their first-round games yet. On top of all that, when Andover and Charlestown had played a few weeks earlier, Charlestown had been thumped by 12. So what was Andover worried about?

"No way," O'Brien said. The athletic director said he understood, and that seemed to be the end of it.

The next day, on Friday, March 3, a second, more urgent call came. The Andover venue change now had the backing of the Massachusetts Interscholastic Athletic Association, the state group overseeing high school sports—and, for some reason, the number 2 official in Boston Public Schools.

Michael Contompasis, the school superintendent's right-hand man who had scolded O'Brien in the spring for letting eighth-graders on the Charlestown bus, called up Michael Fung and told

him the score: The game would be moved, and O'Brien had no
choice but to accept it. Fung and Contompasis went way back, to
the days when Fung was one of the top officials in the school system and Contompasis, as headmaster of the elite Boston Latin
School, reported to him. Now their roles were reversed. Contompasis thought Fung was a clever guy who'd done a good job of improving academics at Charlestown High but didn't have sufficient
respect for the importance of order in a school, and in a school system. Fung considered Contompasis a capable and well-intentioned
administrator, but thought his acute desire to please the powerful
people around and above him sometimes got the better of him.

Contompasis made clear he had heard from two top officials
with the MIAA, and they had persuaded him the game should be
moved. "I made a judgment call," he explained later. He'd heard
the objections from Fung and O'Brien, but he gave special weight
to the opinion of the MIAA's executive director, for whom he had
"the utmost respect." For many years, Contompasis had served as
president of the MIAA's board.

As far as the standoff between Andover and Charlestown went,
Contompasis had heard enough. He wasn't blind. He could see how
the venue change appeared to be a pretty naked move by the Andover coach to improve his team's chances by stripping Charlestown of its home-court advantage. But Contompasis couldn't
concern himself with that. League rules allowed an opposing coach
to request a venue change if he felt the gym was insufficient, and
the league's executive director had seen fit to grant the request. The
game would be moved. "End of discussion," Contompasis told Fung.

Fung warned him that O'Brien might not accept a venue change
forced down his throat. "Jack may forfeit the game," he said.

"If he does, he may never coach in the city again," Contompasis
said. Then he added another warning: "If anybody goes to the press
on this, heads will roll."

Fung chuckled. "You think that's going to matter to *him*?"

When Fung relayed the edict to O'Brien, he could see that the coach found nothing to laugh about. In all their years together, Fung had never seen O'Brien look so despondent. He thought O'Brien might cry. Together, they tried to gauge why Contompasis, the number 2 official for *Boston* schools, would be taking the side of the wealthy suburb. If he'd chosen to play it the other way, he could be scoring some easy points in the press, an urban populist defending the rights of the powerless. Fung mentioned Contompasis's past with the MIAA and said he figured the man was just trying to please some old friends.

O'Brien looked over to Fung. "The worst thing about Boston is that no one goes to bat for you. They just roll over."

"It's your decision, Jack," Fung said. "But I think we should forfeit. It will really send a message."

O'Brien knew he was right about that. But he worried about what kind of message it would send to his players. They'd been screwed with before in life. They'd be screwed with again. How would walking away be the right lesson for them to learn now?

Readers around Boston picked up the sports section on Sunday, March 5, to find a pointed message from the Charlestown High School basketball coach: "Shame on Andover." O'Brien had gone to the media. He accused Andover of using its political clout to get the Charlestown gym declared unsuitable. "It's an injustice," O'Brien said. "Shame on Andover for trying to play politics. They're an affluent community trying to get their way."

Fighting words, for sure. And O'Brien meant every one of them. He'd never been close with the Andover coach, a tall, bulky white guy named Dave Fazio, who had a shaved head and spent most of his games ferociously stalking the sidelines. Still, even though he didn't respect Fazio's maneuver, O'Brien could understand it. Fazio had his best team in years, and he was simply doing everything he could to improve its chances of getting to the finals. O'Brien had been accused of similar aggressiveness in the past. What he couldn't fathom, or forgive, were Contompasis's actions. But O'Brien didn't say any of that to the reporters. He knew he was running a big enough risk by taking his beef with Andover public. He didn't think he could afford to take on his bosses downtown at the same time.

For the past few days, O'Brien had been careful not to reveal any of his angst to his players. With them, he simply dialed up the intensity of his team practices. He'd been bringing in a group of his former players—including Rashid, Alray, and Hugh—to scrimmage his current squad, killing the younger guys with college-level intensity in preparation for the Andover showdown. In particular the veterans drilled the young guys on how to shut down Andover's potent backcourt, the key to Andover's win over Charlestown a few weeks earlier.

After going to the media with his complaints, O'Brien made two related decisions. First, there was no way his team was going to forfeit. Second, there was no way his team was going to lose.

Before the Sunday practice, he pulled his guys together and delivered a motivational talk that was one part Tony Robbins and two parts Huey Long. Getting the game moved out of Charlestown, he said, was just the latest example of how fat cats in places like Andover were used to getting their way. "This is why you have to go to college, make a success of yourself, and get some power and influence." In the meantime, handing these well-heeled suburban kids a defeat sure would send a message that there are limits to what money can buy.

Later that day, O'Brien got a call from an old friend and veteran referee who was well known in basketball circles around the state. He had gray hair, a charcoal mustache, and a stomach that bowed his black-and-white vertical striped shirt. His name was Paul Campbell, but everyone called him Soup.

Soup had grown up with O'Brien on the basketball courts of Medford and the neighboring city of Somerville. He was white but was tight with many black coaches in the city. Over the years, he'd heard all the accusations about how O'Brien was bending the rules to win. Soup always tried to disabuse people of those notions. He'd done it so many times, he almost had a script. "Christ, would you look at how hard he works to make these kids wake up and see what life is like? How he makes them *men!*" He'd rattle off example after example. "Look at Tony Lee. That kid was a lunatic! He wanted to carry a gun. Now he's playing Division I ball at Robert Morris, and he's a polite kid. Jack changed his life." When people would ask why O'Brien seemed to have no life apart from high school basketball, Soup had an answer: "He had plenty of chances to coach college. But he chose to do the right thing and take care of his mother, which is the true measure of a man." Though younger people tended to raise an eyebrow at the idea of a middle-aged bachelor living with his mother, Soup found nothing unusual there: "Turning around kids' lives is all the self-satisfaction Jack needs."

It was Soup who was assigned to referee the game between Charlestown and Andover. Every once in a while, someone would question how a referee like Soup, who was always a character on the court, could be impartial when an old friend was one of the coaches on the sidelines. But the community of coaches and refs was relatively small, so everyone was used to situations like this.

O'Brien told Soup he was still furious about the venue change.

"Relax, Jack," Soup replied. "It's going to work in your favor." He speculated that when the Andover coach raised the stink about Charlestown's gym being too small, he expected the game would be moved to the UMass-Boston athletic center, which sat on the Boston waterfront, in a relatively neutral section of town. Instead, it had been moved to the Madidome, the giant gym smack in the heart of Roxbury. Soup predicted that the black community would be so ticked off by the suburban power play that it would coalesce to support its fellow city school from Charlestown. He also got a kick out of the image of all those rich white folks from Andover nervously driving their Lexuses and Audis into Roxbury, when they could have been driving to Yuppified Charlestown, where Audis were a common sight. Soup laughed, "The junk yards will be busy tomorrow!"

The night before the Andover face-off, Cassidy had ventured to the wealthy Boston suburb of Lexington to scout the playoff game between Eastie and Lexington. Climbing the bleachers, Cassidy had to laugh: The gym was much smaller than Charlestown's, but no one had raised any concerns about its suitability to host a playoff game. But he was more struck by how, all night long, Eastie coaches and fans kept coming up to him and saying they thought Charlestown had been wronged by Andover and encouraging him and O'Brien to fight the good fight. Soup's prediction had been right. Like Democrats and Republicans uniting to battle a common enemy in wartime, Andover's naked maneuver—and O'Brien's clever casting of it strictly in class terms—had done the impossible in bringing Eastie and Charlestown together.

Among the people Cassidy saw in the Lexington gym was Ken Still, the athletic director for Boston schools. Cassidy walked up to him and huffed, "Thanks a lot for selling out city kids!"

The next night, when the bleachers in the Madidome had filled up, the mostly white Andover crowd dominated the side of the gym where Fung was sitting, while the mostly black Charlestown fan base crowded on the other side of the court. With the black-white divide on display and the large battalion of cops lining the perimeter, the gym looked like something out of Boston's 1970s busing era.

O'Brien basked in the popular support that was pulsating through the place. This "home" game had ignited Charlestown's fan base like nothing else in years.

Watching stern-faced from the press table, surrounded by a thicket of reporters who were wearing jeans or sweatpants, Michael Contompasis sat wearing a distinguished navy suit. The ranking school department official who had forced O'Brien to accept the venue change was making a rare appearance at a high school basketball game.

Before tip-off, Soup and his two fellow referees walked over to Fazio, who wore a tie and a blue button-down shirt, and then to O'Brien, who wore his customary red sweater vest. Both coaches were known for their sideline dramatics, but Soup didn't want things to get carried away tonight, given how thick the tension was already. In past games, Soup had battled with Fazio to see which of them—alpha-males both—would call the shots. He wanted to make sure Fazio got the message right away tonight. He knew it was impossible to keep the two animated coaches in their chairs the whole game, but he wasn't about to see all their assistant coaches popping up to protest every call. He had better things to do than play whack-a-mole all night. "No nonsense!" he said, "The head coach can stand, but everyone else on the bench stays sitting down!"

Charlestown came out fired-up, quickly establishing its run-and-gun pace. Andover looked intimidated. Even the team's dynamic point guard, a 5-foot-9 redhead named Casey Cosgrove, who had been flawless the last time Andover played Charlestown, looked rattled. Charlestown took a 6–2 lead.

During the first timeout, the Andover cheerleading squad marched purposefully onto the court, a long trail of blonde and brunette ponytails swaying back and forth. The cheer, which predictably found girls with high-pitched voices trying to conjure the exaggerated bass of DJs from classic-rock radio, was almost beside the point. Quickly, the girls propelled the tiniest member of the squad up to the top of their towering formation. With fearless poise, she undertook a breathtaking flip to return to the earth. A black middle-schooler in the Charlestown crowd stared in disbelief, smacking the leg of his friend sitting beside him. "Man, you see that?" For all the loaded marveling from opponents about the athleticism of inner-city basketball players, cheerleading was a sport where urban schools like Charlestown had trouble competing. The

Charlestown cheering squad—a ragtag group of girls, several of them heavyset—were confident dancers, but flips they did not do. Anyway, there were seldom enough of them showing up to muster a quorum, never mind a pyramid, so the few who did come typically just sat in their uniforms and clapped from the bleachers.

Returning to the court, Andover's speedy point guard quickly found his way, draining jumpers and dishing no-look passes that sometimes were too dazzling for his teammates to catch. All of a sudden, Andover had a 1-point lead.

• • •

FAZIO WAS ON HIS FEET as often as he was on the bench. "Oh, *come* on, Soup! That's a terrible call!" The refs did seem to be calling an extremely tight game, refusing to let anything slide. That was partly because three refs, rather than the normal two, were assigned to playoff games. But as the game progressed, the Andover fans joined Fazio in complaining that every time Soup blew his whistle for a borderline infraction, it came at Andover's expense.

When Soup called a rare infraction against Charlestown, Andover fans cheered, "Finally!" Soup turned to face them and smiled, "That was a gift!"

As it turned out, Charlestown players didn't need any extra help from Soup. They had the only gift they needed in point guard Paul Becklens. Ridley's cousin, whose eyes often opened so wide that he gave the impression he had just discovered a jalapeño in his sandwich, had always been a good shooter and a steady presence on the floor. But on this night, he was on fire. He sank a series of 3-pointers, causing one fan to yell, "He's D–I, baby!" Paul put up 15 points in the first half, giving Charlestown a 41–27 lead.

The second half started the same way, as the Charlestown defense managed to close down Casey Cosgrove and the rest of the

Andover offense, while Paul continued to be unstoppable. Fazio, a sheen of sweat on his bald head despite his loosened tie, continued to stalk the sidelines, protesting the calls. But he seemed to be lodging his complaints for the benefit of Andover fans now, rather than Soup, who clearly wasn't listening. "This is a joke!" Fazio yelled, waving his hand in disgust.

With four minutes to go and Charlestown up 73–57, Andover fans accepted the inevitable and began to file out of the gym. Tony Lee, who had once again used his spring break at Robert Morris to return to Boston to watch Charlestown play, made eye contact with each Andover fan walking by him. "Where you going?" he asked. "It's a *great* game."

When the buzzer sounded, Charlestown players erupted in joy. So did the coaches. As Cassidy crossed the court, the dark-suited Contompasis made a beeline for him. Tapping him on the shoulder, he laid into Cassidy for his behavior the night before. The idea of an *assistant* coach dressing down the athletic director in a crowded gym was an affront to the organization that Contompasis had spent forty years serving. "If you ever want to coach in this city," he told Cassidy, "you'll never talk to an athletic director like that again!" Then he turned and joined the throngs leaving the gym. Cassidy stood on the court, frozen, as the Charlestown players continued to bump chests in celebration around him. It took Cassidy a full minute to process what had just happened, as his surprise boiled into fury. He stormed out of the gym to try to find Contompasis so he could deliver a rejoinder to his face. He returned several minutes later, his intention frustrated but his coaching future still intact.

17

THE TIPPING POINT

RIDLEY AND HOOD WERE, in very different ways, represented at the game against Andover. On the court, Paul Becklens had showed the kind of game-winning transformation that had produced his cousin Ridley's Division I scholarship and escape from the streets of Boston. In the stands were both Hood's father, Willie Barnes, and his college coach, Jamie Cosgrove, whose son was the star on the Andover squad. As Willie spotted the Adelphi coach from across the court, he thought back to a call he'd received from him in the fall. Cosgrove had grown frustrated with Hood leaving Long Island every other week, ever since he arrived on the Adelphi campus in the summer. Willie shared the coach's frustration. Hood had repeatedly told his coach that he had to return to Boston to handle his court case. But that was only part of the story.

Ever since Hood and Pookie had been arrested in May, Willie had been battling with his son over how to proceed: "Tell them it was Pookie's gun, and be done with it."

But whenever his father said that, Hood shook him off. "I ain't gonna be a snitch."

"This ain't about being a snitch. It wasn't like there was a whole bunch of guys in the car. It was only you and him. If he doesn't man up and take his gun, then give it to him."

Willie had grown weary of making the eight-hour roundtrip drive to Adelphi to fetch his son for court hearings, especially since many of them kept getting continued. But he could tell Hood didn't mind having to come home, because it gave him a chance to hang with his buddies. It was the going back that his son seemed to hate.

So when he heard from Cosgrove trying to confirm a call Hood's mother had made to Adelphi, saying her son had to come home, Willie had to laugh. "Nah, my wife didn't call. He must have had some girl make the call for him because he wanted to come home." Cosgrove said Hood would be suspended for two games. Willie knew Hood had been expecting Cosgrove to roll out the red carpet for him. Instead, the coach wanted his freshman recruit to commit fully to his new program and stop looking for excuses. Willie figured Hood would suck it up and then move forward, realizing he had the kind of situation all those kids leaning on the fence at Washington Park could only dream about.

But for Hood, who still felt he'd been misled about what costs were covered by his scholarship, the suspension was too much. Willie had come home from work one night in October to find Hood lying on the couch. No matter how many different ways he tried to dislodge him, that's where he'd remained ever since. Hood had dropped out of Adelphi, walking away from a precious four-year scholarship worth more than $100,000.

Willie struggled to get his son to reconsider. He tried encouragement, telling his son to go make his name at Adelphi, like he'd done at Charlestown. He tried rubbing it in a little, filling the glass bookcase near the TV with the reminders of Hood's glory days—the basketball he'd received after scoring his one-thousandth point, the trophies, the nomination letter for McDonald's All-American team. "All them trophies—you can't eat none of them," Willie told his son. "Now it's time to prepare yourself for your career." Finally, he moved on to tough love. He stopped giving Hood money and took back the keys to his car. Instead, he gave him a pair of work boots and a pair of gloves. "If you don't make a career out of basketball," he said, "you gotta go to work. It's that simple."

Things only seemed to get worse. When Hood wasn't sitting on the couch, he was hanging out with his friends from the neighborhood, tempting fate that he'd end up getting arrested again, or worse. Or he was out with other girls, once again ignoring Tia, his longtime girlfriend and the mother of his child, in pursuit of new fun. Before long, Hood was bringing another serious girlfriend around the house. He tried telling Tia, who treasured her time idling with Hood's mother and sister, that the new girl was just a friend. Tia knew better. She stopped coming by the house with Janijah. But she had trouble letting go. When Willie heard Tia had loaned Hood money, he dashed over to her house to talk with her and her mother.

"Tia," Willie said, pointing to her mother, "if you don't tell her, I'm gonna tell her."

"I don't know what you're talking about," Tia said.

"Bottom line, I heard you gave him money. It's OK to love him, but don't take from your baby's mouth to give to him when he ain't even trying to be with you. Wake up!"

Hood's situation increased the tension between his parents. Willie accused Pearl of coddling their son, making it impossible for his tough love approach to gain any traction. Pearl accused Willie of just being upset because he could no longer go strutting into gyms to watch his superstar son play. "That ain't it, Pearl. I just don't want him to make the same mistakes I did. You raise the daughter, let me show him how to be a man!" When she kept talking, Willie got so furious he worried he might do something he'd regret. So he did what he'd done several times before in their twenty-two years together. He moved out. He'd come back when things settled down. Until then, he took a basement apartment a few miles away.

Truth be told, he was happy to be away from all those trophies for a little while himself. When he looked at them, he couldn't help but say to himself, *Damn!* Still, he was a man of faith who believed his son's setbacks might just be God's way of making him come back even stronger. And he held out hope that as soon as Hood knew his court case was going to trial, he'd do the right thing and tell everyone whose gun it was.

But as he sat in the bleachers for the Andover game, watching the team his son had so determinedly co-captained just a year before, Willie Barnes had to admit that he had no idea what would become of Hood.

•   •   •

THE SAME WEEKEND that Willie Barnes was revisiting the ghosts of last year's team, Ridley was on a distant court, making a new name for himself at a higher level. During his first semester away, he had settled in well at Toledo—the coach had told his mother that he wished he had a team full of Ridleys. He'd been back to the Charlestown gym a few days before Christmas—like most of the alumni it was a place he turned to without thinking—and found Spot in the bleachers, watching O'Brien lead the team through practice drills. They dapped up each other. Ridley and Spot had kept in phone contact, but less so as the semester wore on. Instead, Spot had been talking more to Hood, who was bored just sitting at home. Ridley never heard from Hood directly, but Spot kept him posted on what his former co-captain was up to, which wasn't much.

Spot was wearing washed-out baggy jeans, a black baseball cap, and square zirconia earrings. Ridley's braids were longer and narrower than when he'd left for Toledo in the summer, and his muscles were much more developed. Spot was content to hang back in the bleachers, but Ridley was itching to play again on the Charlestown court. He took off his sweatshirt and grabbed a Charlestown T-shirt O'Brien had given him. He looked it over. Not quite right. "Hey, Spot, you got scissors?"

"No, man."

Ridley used a car key to poke a hole in the seam between the shirt's shoulder and sleeve. He tore one sleeve off, then the other. He held up the shirt. That was more like it. He put it on and began shooting.

Cassidy came over to talk to Spot, opening the conversation with academics. "What are you taking for classes?"

"Astronomy, Moral Philosophy, Discrete Math—it's like statistics—and regular English," Spot said. "I got three B's and a C in English. Shakespeare—I don't get that dude."

Cassidy laughed. "What class do you like best?"

"I *love* Moral Philosophy. We have debates. Socrates—now that's a dude I get."

Spot, a smart kid who had a tendency to blow off his schoolwork at Charlestown, was clearly blossoming in a prep school environment where there was no stigma attached to being smart. Blossoming academically, at least. The social and athletic scene at the private Westminster School in Connecticut was a different story. Spot had been the most sociable guy on the Charlestown team last year, and, unlike most of his teammates, he never had any trouble adapting to situations where he was one of the only black kids around. Still, the culture shock at Westminster was overpowering. "It's all spoiled rich kids, driving Benzes," he said. He was going stir-crazy, but it was tough to get away. "We got a curfew, ten o'clock.

Besides, there's nothing around the school, just a Domino's, a CVS, and a lot of trees."

Despite his solid start at Toledo, Ridley had to wait until March, when the season was hanging by a thread, to really prove his worth to the team. If Toledo won the last regular-season game, the victory would keep the team's winning streak alive and secure a crucial home stand going into the first round of its Mid-American Conference tournament. But Ridley knew the stakes were even higher than that.

Ridley had heard the rumored ultimatum from Toledo's athletic director—hell, it had been printed in the local newspaper—that if the team didn't make it to the MAC championship game this season, it might be the last one coached by Stan Joplin. Forget the fact that Joplin was synonymous with Toledo basketball and had been so ever since his buzzer-beating jump shot against Iowa in 1979 propelled the team into the NCAA Sweet 16. As a mid-level Division I basketball program, Toledo had never been to such a rarefied place before, and it hadn't been back since. But college basketball is a business, and for Joplin, business hadn't been very good this past year. The team had limped through much of the season, posting more losses than wins, and carrying an embarrassing 1–6 record in conference play. Yet having his job on the line had injected a new urgency into the even-keeled Joplin. Late in the season, he began benching star players when they failed to perform, turning some of their minutes over to Ridley and two other freshmen. The changes worked, as the team racked up six straight wins going into this final game.

Even this deep into the season, Ridley never really knew where he stood with Joplin, whatever charming comments he may have made to his mother. Whenever Ridley or one of the younger players asked Joplin a question, the coach delivered the same refrain, without even the hint of a smile. "I don't talk to *freshmen*." The veteran players had heard it enough to know he was joking, but Ridley couldn't be sure. He was still adjusting to not being a starter. When he missed a shot, he'd often see Joplin contort his face and tell one of his assistants, "Get him out of there." It was such a difference from playing for O'Brien at Charlestown. Even though he tired of O'Brien's unyielding criticism, Ridley had come to appreciate always knowing where he stood. Joplin's refusal to engage him left Ridley baffled.

Joplin's quick trigger finger after missed shots may have made Ridley gun-shy with his gorgeous jumper, but he had become a bankable performer with another part of his game: rebounding. That would have surprised O'Brien, who had often railed at Ridley to charge the boards rather than just hanging out at the perimeter. But Ridley's confidence in the paint had grown considerably in the last year, in direct proportion to the growth of his upper body. When he arrived at Toledo over the summer, he was a flat-chested kid whose 6-foot-3 frame had barely 180 pounds on it. The Toledo staff immediately put him through an intense workout program; among other tasks, he had to get down on his knees and repeatedly push a 100-pound weight up and down a long carpeted corridor. At first, the summer workouts were so grueling he threw up after nearly every one. But during his freshman year, he'd put on more than 15 pounds of pure muscle, gaining definition in his upper arms and chest.

Ridley may not have connected with Joplin yet, but he respected him and certainly didn't want him to be fired. He recalled Joplin flying to Charlestown to see him practice during his senior year, and then again to watch him lead the team to victory in the state finals. He had confidence their relationship would develop after he left the ranks of a lowly freshman. Besides, he'd heard that when a college coach got fired, much of his regime tended to be repudiated by his replacement—especially the guys he'd personally recruited.

Before he left Boston, Ridley and Ashley, his petite Cape Verdean girlfriend, had committed to try to make their relationship work long-distance. But like all similar commitments made since the invention of the dorm, this one had fizzled out before long. Quickly, Ridley made up for lost time, taking advantage of his athlete status that automatically made him stand out on a campus with 20,000 students. It was the dawn of the Facebook.com era, and Ridley had a nice face, so not surprisingly he found himself being "poked" all the time, getting messages from girls wanting to meet him. Ridley and his freshman roommate, Jonathan Amos, worked out signals when they wanted the room to themselves, from a subtle nod to the not-so-subtle comment, "Oh, Amos, you reading my mind?" By this point, midway through the second semester, the parade of girls was getting a bit tiresome for Ridley and he began cutting back—some. Also he'd joined a Bible study group. Back home, even though his mother regularly went to church, Ridley was too lazy to go, and she hadn't pushed. But now, on his own, he was finding a little religion. He found the vivid stories of the Bible much easier to relate to than all that "thy" and "thou" Shakespeare stuff he was being forced to slog through in his English course.

Toledo was a big campus, but its various communities made it seem smaller. Only about 15 percent of the student body was nonwhite, and the black students tended to hang out together. So did the basketball players. Ridley and Amos spent the bulk of their time with their teammates. When they weren't in class or practicing on the court in the 9,000-seat Savage Hall, they could often be found hanging out in the locker room. Sitting on the padded chair each player had in front of his locker, they relaxed—watching BET, talking about everything and nothing, and occasionally sharing tips, such as the benefits of using Jergens cherry-scented moisturizer on your legs after practice. Several of Ridley's teammates came from the toughest parts of South Side Chicago. While they swapped war stories about life in the hood, Ridley tried to chime in with his own. They laughed him off. Everything they knew about Boston came from those picturesque shots of Quincy Market and Beacon Hill that the sports networks showed between commercials when they were broadcasting from Beantown. Once when a friend from home came for a visit and hung out in the locker room, Ridley asked him, "Would you tell these guys that Boston is tough, got thugs and shootings in Dorchester and Roxbury? They don't believe it."

The other place where Ridley saw his teammates was Study Table. Six nights a week, he headed over to an academic center, located upstairs from the weight room, that was designed to remind the players that they weren't majoring in basketball. Joplin was proud of his team's graduation rate—it was among the higher ones in D-I basketball—and a big part of the success was the rigid academic support system in place. At the beginning of the semester, Ridley and his teammates were required to bring into the center a syllabus from each of their courses. Then the advisers would enter the assignments and due dates into a database, allowing them to keep tabs all semester long.

Mike Meade, a short, peppy guy with chubby cheeks, oversaw the academic center. He had gotten used to defending the academic hand-holding that only D-I athletes received. The student-athletes got more because more was expected of them, Meade would say. "They can't just blow off a practice if they don't feel like going." College basketball is a business, and the academic center was just an investment from which the college was expecting big returns.

When the final game of the regular season rolled around on the first Saturday night in March, Rose Arena was packed with fans decked out in the maroon-and-gold of the Chippewas of Central Michigan University. CMU was in last place in the conference, and Toledo had handed the team a blowout earlier in the season. This game started off in a similar fashion. Ridley had gotten some decent minutes off the bench, and had 6 points and 3 rebounds. With just under six minutes to go, Toledo had a 13-point lead. But then Ridley's teammates got sloppy, which led to a complete meltdown.

Helplessly, they watched as CMU came roaring back. With thirty-four seconds left, a CMU player bounded toward the hoop with a layup that tied the game. Ridley knew that if Toledo went on to lose the last game of the season to the last-place team, Joplin had probably better start packing his things. A spectacular late-game flameout like that could provide the perfect cover for Toledo officials to dismiss Joplin, however popular a local figure and former star player he may have been.

Toledo moved the ball down court. With thirteen seconds left and his job on the line, Joplin called a timeout. Ridley, who was on the floor at the time, did not even want to approach the huddle, because he was sure Joplin was going to yank him for a more seasoned player. But then he heard one of the assistant coaches telling Joplin, "Leave Ridley in!"

Joplin mapped out the play. Everyone would clear a path for the team captain to release a close-range jumper. They broke the huddle and headed onto the court. Everyone did what they were supposed to. The ball went to the captain, and he drove to the basket. With six seconds left, he fired his jumper from 10 feet away. It bounced off the rim. The game would go into overtime. All the momentum had shifted to CMU. But then Ridley faked out his defender and, out of nowhere, sailed toward the hoop, taking advantage of every inch of his vertical leap. As the buzzer began to sound, Ridley tipped the ball in.

Toledo won, 66–64. Ridley's teammates heaved him onto their shoulders and carried him off the court. He was rounded up for interviews with the smiling sportswriters. As he boarded the bus, Joplin was singing his praises. Ridley pulled out his cell phone and dialed up his mother, then his Aunt Emily, then his father, McClary, then Robby, who had remained his closest friend from Charlestown. Over and over again, he excitedly replayed every second of his buzzer-beating heroics.

Before hanging up, he reminded each of them, "If we get to the championship game, be sure to watch, because it's gonna be on ESPN."

Toledo did make it to the championship game. The identity of Toledo basketball would remain inseparable from the identity of Stan Joplin, at least for three more years—the length of the contract extension he would be granted. Ridley knew his coach was looking at him differently now, knew he could rely on him in the crunch. His feeling of elation didn't last long. During the championship game, as Ridley eyed his teammates cycling in and out, he began to burn inside. All his family and friends were home watching him do nothing but sit on the bench. At the buzzer, Ridley looked around and realized he was the only player that Joplin never put in the game. Toledo lost.

18

THE DECISION

CHARLESTOWN FOLLOWED UP THE WIN over Andover by beating the team from Lexington, an equally affluent suburb, to advance to round three of the state tourney. Once again, Tony Lee was in the stands, for the second year in a row using his entire college spring break to show his support for O'Brien and his squad. Sitting in the bleachers, watching Tony passionately cheer on the Charlestown guys, Michael Fung had to marvel again at the loyalty O'Brien managed to instill in his guys. But he also began to wonder if perhaps it was too strong.

Fung had just heard that Cori Boston, one of Tony's former Charlestown teammates who was also playing on scholarship at Robert Morris, was planning to leave, disillusioned by the lack of attention he felt he was receiving. "Why is Cori talking about transferring?" Fung wondered. "Why did Rashid drop out of the University of Florida? Why have others failed once they left Charlestown? I think maybe they're looking for another Jack O'Brien. But in real life there aren't many Jack O'Briens."

Three nights after the Lexington win, Fung was scaling the stands at the Tsongas Arena in Lowell to get to his lucky seat, when someone called out to him, "Hey Mr. Fung, are *you* staying next year?" As the year had worn on, the headmaster had shown more signs that he wouldn't be following through on the retirement plans he had announced after his stroke last summer. He looked up and smiled. "The team is going to be very good next year. I think I will stay."

The question circulating elsewhere in the stands was whether O'Brien would say the same. A year after Hood's heroics had propelled Charlestown over Eastie in the round-four game, Charlestown was back at Tsongas Arena, this time facing off against Central Catholic, a perennial powerhouse in the Merrimack Valley northwest of Boston. The parochial school's coach had announced he would be retiring at the end of the season, after a quarter-century in the job. Local basketball circles were abuzz with talk that Central Catholic was aggressively trying to lure O'Brien to take his place. O'Brien had politely but firmly turned down plenty of similar overtures in the past. But after his emotional season this year, when he'd felt drained and stymied and abandoned, the thinking was that O'Brien might be ripe for the picking.

During the game, Charlestown's hot shooting hand that had powered the team straight through the postseason finally dried up. Charlestown lost by 7 points.

"It's OK," Zach told the dejected players in the locker room afterward. "No one died."

O'Brien joined in. "Some of you, at the beginning of the year, weren't even friends. Now you're brothers."

Still, he felt bad. He knew that at most schools, getting this far into the playoffs would be cause for celebration. But in Charlestown, as much as he tried to avoid it, any season that didn't end with another state title was viewed as a losing season.

A couple of weeks later, O'Brien sat with Zach in the cluttered office off the Charlestown gym, contemplating whether they could bring themselves to do the unthinkable. Neither of them wanted to leave Charlestown and the family O'Brien had forged there. But they kept asking each other if they needed to heed the messages from the season that had just passed.

LeRoyal and Troy had been ensnared in an exploitative maneuver to get them to play ball in a high school clear across the country, but O'Brien was the one taking flak. The winner of the state championship, he nonetheless had had to start the season down six players who should have been back. Despite all of Charlestown's success, the team attracted precious little support from the community. Not only did O'Brien feel underappreciated by the central administration of Boston schools, but he had been left to wage his battle against Andover alone.

O'Brien got worked up just thinking about it. "Our program has helped reflect well on the city. You'd think the people downtown would want to share in that—everybody take a bow. But instead of getting a pat on the back, you're made to defend yourself for silly stuff. And then when something like the Andover thing happens, you'd think they'd be saying, 'Here's our chance to go to bat a little'—not hard to do. Instead, Contompasis yells at Cassidy! Heaven forbid something went wrong with our program. Would they back us up? No way!"

Zach contrasted their situation with what his wife Mandy experienced coaching a girls' basketball team in an affluent suburb. "They go 16-and-6, and the town gives them *everything*! Free dinner, free brunch, free banquet at a restaurant that charges 50 friggin' dollars an entree!" And the community support wasn't just for sports. Zach and Mandy's oldest would be in a talent show tonight, he told O'Brien. "There will be 2,000 people there. You go by the high school any night, and the parking lot is full!"

O'Brien had a tight if complicated bond with Fung, but even that had begun to fray. O'Brien knew he had a successful model for getting at-risk kids into college. But he saw it being threatened by Fung's decision to kill most electives and clog his guys' schedules in an effort to improve the school's standardized test scores. This strip mining of the high school curriculum to boost math and English test scores was happening in urban schools everywhere, as administrators tried to avoid the noose of the No Child Left Behind law, but O'Brien couldn't care less about schools in other parts of the country or benchmarks from Washington. He cared only about his kids and where they ended up.

As O'Brien catalogued his gripes again with Zach, he raised his eyebrows and bit his lower lip. "I don't think we'll be able to get our guys into college in the next few years," he said, "and that scares me."

The final indignity was Fung's refusal to guarantee a job for Hugh. Although Hugh had given up his position, taking a huge pay cut to enroll in a teaching residency program in the expectation of earning a master's degree and a warm welcome back onto the Charlestown High faculty, now he was learning he would probably end up with neither. Three months into the program, he'd found out that his low college grade point average disqualified him from getting on the fast track to earning a master's. Fung would not offer Hugh a full-time slot because he had narrowly failed his certification test once again.

O'Brien had bolted into Fung's office when he heard. "Hughie is a black male, exuberant, a family man, not running around, a Bowdoin graduate, inspirational, connects with the kids. Not hiring him—that's *insane!*"

"Tell him to pass his goddamned certification," Fung said, "or we have nothing to talk about."

After tallying up the bill of grievances, O'Brien compared it with what he was being offered elsewhere. He'd begun by talking with the people at Central Catholic, but then a new suitor emerged. Andy Fila, the no-nonsense principal of Lynn English High School in a struggling city on Boston's North Shore, told O'Brien he wanted him to replicate his Charlestown program in Lynn. He promised all the tools and support he needed to do it—and not just from him, but from all the power brokers in the city.

In a meeting two weeks after the Charlestown season ended, O'Brien told Fila and the Lynn school superintendent that, for starters, both he and Zach would need phys ed teaching jobs. "Done." That he would need four paid assistant coaches. "Done." That he would need extensive input into mapping out his players' academic schedules, to get them on the road to college. "Done." They even discussed a job for Hugh, if things didn't work out in Charlestown.

Recalling the meeting for Zach's benefit while he sat in the Charlestown gym office, O'Brien said, "I kept waiting for them to say no."

Still, there was a big difference between enjoying a flattering courtship and breaking with your family. Every time O'Brien tried to imagine a scenario in which he had to tell his guys he was leaving Charlestown, his stomach knotted up. As the violence in the streets of Boston got worse and the odds of these kids making it up and out grew longer, O'Brien knew his presence in their lives was more vital than ever. He'd been worn down at the end of previous seasons—last year in particular—but had always bounced back.

O'Brien walked out of the gym and climbed into his minivan. As he drove along Medford Street, a couple of his guys walking in the other direction waved him down and crossed the street. Tron Griffith, the freshman guard he had personally mentored, was part of the pack. O'Brien rolled down the window, and they all approached. After a little small talk about classes, O'Brien shook hands with each of the players.

"Nah, nah, you don't shake like that, Coach," Tron said. "Three fingers, man!"

"Huh?"

Tron showed him the private handshake the players had been using lately to dap each other up. He extended his hand, fingers out, but used his thumb to pull back his index finger, so only three fingers remained extended. He instructed O'Brien to do the same. The coach fumbled a bit, but eventually got it. In one quick, smooth move, Tron slid his three fingers across O'Brien's, and then pulled his hand away.

O'Brien chuckled. "What's that for?"

"It's the love, man—family."

Driving home, O'Brien replayed the moment in his mind, savoring this latest invitation into the world of his players. Then he thought to himself, *How can I walk away from that?*

•   •   •

AT 3:15 PM ON THE AFTERNOON OF Wednesday, April 5, O'Brien stood in a first-floor office of a gray, boxy building built in 1930. He was wearing a maroon Reebok nylon warm-up jacket, black nylon sweatpants, and white sneakers. The word "Charlestown" was nowhere to be found on his clothing. He was biting the fingernail on his left thumb.

He turned to Zach and smiled. "Think we can still change our minds? How about pulling a fire alarm?"

Ten minutes later, they were both led down a long corridor and into a large rectangular room lined with bookshelves. Their escort turned and said, "This used to be the gym. They called it the Rathole." Above the bookshelves, there was a row of trophies rimming the room. Many of them were dusty. Nobody'd had any reason to climb up there in a while.

At the front of the room was a table lined with cans of soda. At the back was a row of chairs where a half-dozen reporters sat. A short, silver-haired man with a tie descending below his high waist put down his can of Diet Coke and approached the podium.

"Jack O'Brien's prowess as a coach is unparalleled," Andy Fila said, speaking into a tinny microphone that was hardly necessary, given the size of the audience. "When Jack spoke with us the first time, he didn't mention anything about basketball, but he mentioned education—and that was important. In the last decade at Charlestown, more than forty of Jack's basketball players have gone on to college, and that's a tremendous achievement."

As principal of Lynn English High School, Fila had just gone through a charged political fight to dislodge the man who had been coaching the school's basketball team for more than forty years. The team hadn't won much in recent seasons. Fila didn't directly address that fight in his remarks, but it was hard to miss the allusion. "For some time, parents have complained, and I've said, 'Be patient.' Patience has paid off. We get the best."

When it was his turn, the new Lynn English basketball coach grabbed both ends of the podium and shook his head slowly. "It's been hard," O'Brien said. "It's been a rough couple of days saying goodbye to Charlestown."

One of the Boston sportswriters lifted his hand and asked O'Brien if the Andover saga drove him to leave the Boston school system.

"Not really," O'Brien said. Deciding there was no sense in fighting an old battle, he tried to deflect the question by drawing a laugh. "We kicked their butts!"

Lynn English's student body reflected the working-class city around it—it was 35 percent white, 38 percent Hispanic, 14 percent black, and 9 percent Asian. About two-thirds of the kids qualified for free or reduced-price lunches. The school played in the same conference as Salem, so for O'Brien and Zach, there were several familiar faces in the local reporting corps. Zach privately told one scribe that he and O'Brien felt good about the decision. "I know he's needed here. I know he's wanted here. In Boston, I know he's needed, but I don't think he's wanted."

•   •   •

THERE WERE PLENTY OF PEOPLE in Boston who would have disagreed with Zach's assessment, but they didn't get a vote in the matter. Actually, most of them weren't even old enough to vote. The day before the Lynn press conference, O'Brien had brought the Charlestown players up to Room 319. The guys had logged a lot of hours in that chemistry classroom, since that's where study hall was held every day before practice. But they almost never met there outside basketball season. O'Brien was such a creature of habit that very little changed on the team calendar from year to year. They realized something must be up.

He began with some perfunctory announcements about kicking off the fundraising effort for next year. Then he got more serious. He told them he loved them all, but there were so many haters out there making it harder and harder for him to do his job. When he said he and Zach would be leaving, it sounded so preposterous that some of the guys had trouble processing it. He tried to explain it another way. "It's like being a mechanic. You could have all the ambition in the world, but if you've got no tools, you can't fix the car."

Other guys in the room needed no analogies. They knew exactly what he was saying, and several of them began to tear up. O'Brien had expected that from some of the kids, especially Tron and a couple of other freshmen with whom he was particularly close. But when he scanned the room, he was surprised at some of the people he saw rubbing their eyes to hide the tears. O'Brien liked Ravon Dunbar, a lightning-quick sophomore, but he'd never felt a particularly tight bond with him. Yet here he was crying at the idea of O'Brien walking out the door.

The fallout continued the next day in school. Tron was absent, which was rare for him. Paul Becklens strolled in around 11 AM, telling his teammates he planned to transfer. Other players were skipping class, getting into arguments with their teachers, or just breaking down in tears while sitting in the cafeteria. And then there was James Rodriquez, a freshman with a faint mustache and the habit of wearing his Charlestown shorts so low during his JV games that you saw more underwear than uniform. All morning long, James sat sobbing in the tiny office off the gym, where O'Brien had long ago filled a bulletin board with clipped headlines like "Winning Is Only the Beginning." O'Brien tried to comfort him, putting his arm around him, assuring him things would be OK. Zach told him he'd be in a good place, since Cassidy was all but certain to become Charlestown's head coach.

During a free period, Hugh stopped by the gym to talk with O'Brien and Zach. He was wearing earrings in both ears and a striped shirt with a tie, and he was chewing a pink wad of Bubblicious gum you could smell from 10 feet away. All the tumult was causing Hugh to get philosophical. "Twelve years ago when I first got here as a freshman," he said to O'Brien, "you were just getting here. Look at where just my class ended up. You had Nick at Bentley, me at Bowdoin, Ed Walker at Bates, Ian at Skidmore. It's a proven system that works. But now the chapter's ending." He pivoted around the gym, pointing to all the red championship banners. In some ways, the banners were part of the problem. The team had just wrapped up a season by getting all the way to the sectional finals of the state tourney, but the only thing the coaches and players seemed to be hearing from people around the school and around the city was, "Hey, what happened this year?" A lot had happened this year to make everyone second-guess things they had taken for granted. Hugh, for one, never envisioned teaching anywhere but Charlestown. But unless Fung had a change of heart, he would be packing up as well. There were other changes in store for Hugh. His wife, Emily, had just found out she was pregnant with their second child. Hugh looked around the gym once more, as though taking it in for the last time. "It's a story you want to never end."

•   •   •

O N A TUESDAY MORNING nearly one week after the Lynn press conference, O'Brien walked into Fung's windowless office. Things
had been strained between the coach and headmaster for weeks.
And ever since O'Brien had announced his departure, they had both
been careful to keep their distance. The last time they'd spoken privately was the Sunday before the press conference, when O'Brien
had spent three hours in Fung's office, looking for Fung to persuade
him not to leave Charlestown. Though he didn't say it outright,
Fung was upset that the coach he'd bonded with for nine years had
waited until after he'd been in serious discussions with other
schools to come seeking his counsel. O'Brien laid out his grievances. They both knew the headmaster had no control over some of
the biggest ones, such as the lack of support from the community
and from the school system's central administration. So O'Brien
hung most of his frustration on academic matters: the loss of control over his players' schedules; the lack of cooperation from many
of the young, book-smart teachers; the lack of a job for Hugh.

"Michael, control is what I'm looking for," O'Brien said. "Not in an
ego way, but in an I-wanna-protect-what-we've-got-and-what-we-
know-works kind of way."

Fung sensed O'Brien had already made up his mind, and besides,
he didn't respond well to ultimatums. "Jack," he said, "I do not run
this school for the basketball team."

He hated to see O'Brien go, but he had resigned himself to the
likelihood. In some ways, he figured, O'Brien's departure might be
for the best. He didn't know why Michael Contompasis appeared to
be down on O'Brien and his program. Fung once told the coach his
larger-than-life ways violated the time-honored ethos for surviving
in the school system that Fung had been told many years earlier:
Say nothing, do nothing, and say nothing well. Then again, Fung
had himself violated that rule repeatedly.

Anyway, what was done was done.

But a lot had changed in one week. As O'Brien stood before him in his office, Fung saw none of the swagger in a sweat suit he was used to. Instead, he saw a distraught, vulnerable man. The coach admitted he was being torn apart by having to watch so many of his players fall apart in the days since he announced his decision to leave. He kept telling himself that the kids would rebound, that the transition was the toughest part. But what if they didn't? He'd been so busy cataloging the slights wearing him down in Charlestown, and soaking up the compliments coming his way from Lynn, that he'd missed the big picture: He had devoted himself to building trust with kids hardened by a life of broken promises. Could he now be giving them another reason to be mistrustful?

"Michael," O'Brien said, "I don't think I can go through with leaving. Could I stay?"

•　　•　　•

THE FOLLOWING AFTERNOON, O'Brien stood by the second-floor window in the stairwell beside the gym, gazing below at the track team doing its warm-ups outside. It was a perfect spring afternoon—sunny, 70 degrees, with a light breeze. O'Brien was wearing a heavy, all-black Charlestown sweat suit.

He spotted Ravon leaning against a cement wall, stretching his calf muscles. The hare-footed sophomore had helped propel the basketball team through the playoffs, something that wasn't lost on Cassidy. Now that spring had rolled around, Cassidy had shifted his focus to the track team, where he was head coach. One of his first moves was conscripting Ravon.

O'Brien watched Cassidy approach Ravon. He couldn't hear what they were saying, but he noticed two things. Ravon was smiling. Cassidy was not.

When O'Brien had called Ravon the day before, to let him know he would be staying at Charlestown after all, he could almost feel his player's elation flowing through the receiver. When he stopped Cassidy in the parking lot, he could see the disappointment—even anger—in his assistant coach's face. He gave Cassidy the same explanation he had given Fila, when he'd driven to Lynn to deliver the news. "I couldn't abandon these kids, who've been abandoned by so many others, especially males."

Fila and Cassidy were both upset, but for different reasons. After his big press conference, Fila had to go out and tell the rest of Lynn he hadn't reeled in the state's biggest-name high school coach after all. And then he had to go out and find a replacement.

Cassidy's feelings were more complicated. For seven years, he'd been O'Brien's loyal assistant. Shortly after he'd arrived to teach at Charlestown High, the young, round-faced teacher had approached O'Brien and asked if he could help out with the team. He didn't mind that there was no pay for him his first two years on the bench. He just wanted to learn from a pro. He turned out to be a good-luck charm; his first year with the team, Charlestown won its first state championship and never looked back. All along, Cassidy continued to spend every bus ride sitting right next to O'Brien, trying to get inside his head and learn from the best.

Still, Cassidy had his own ambitions. He was finishing up the coursework for his administrator's certification, with the goal of running his own school before long. He also wanted to run his own basketball team. Cassidy did not want to leave his Charlestown High teaching position just to take a head coaching job, but he assumed at some point one of those goals would have to give. After all, he never expected to see the legendary Jack O'Brien leaving his perch. When the unexpected happened, Cassidy thought it was kismet. He could build on the success of a program he believed in but put his own stamp on it, all without leaving Charlestown.

Suddenly, everything had changed. He compared it to the college application process. "It's like getting an acceptance letter from your 'reach' school, and then getting a follow-up note a few days later, saying, 'Sorry. Not gonna happen.'"

Gazing out the window, O'Brien felt bad for the position he'd put Cassidy in. But he knew Cassidy was a bright guy with a lot of options. Even though his flip-flop had brought himself some embarrassment, O'Brien had done it for all those kids who didn't have many options.

He walked down the stairs, through the gym lobby, and out the door. As he headed down the long cement ramp leading to the sidewalk, a young black kid, maybe twelve years old, was heading up. The boy was familiar to O'Brien, since he was one of the many young kids from the adjacent project who regularly hung out at the Charlestown gym, watching the stars practice while waiting for their turn. The kid tapped O'Brien on the arm, rolled his eyes, and said, "Hey, I didn't know *Lynn* practiced here."

O'Brien chuckled. Then he told him he wasn't leaving after all.

"For *real?*" the kid said, widening his eyes.

O'Brien nodded.

The kid dramatically looked up at the sky, held his palms out, and slowly mouthed the words, "Thank you, God!"

19

BLIND JUSTICE

AROUND THE SAME TIME that O'Brien was torturing himself with indecision over his future, Hood's was being determined for him. At 9:05 AM on April 20 a doddering court clerk held the docket list as far from his bifocals as his arm would allow, squinted and called out the first case. "Commonwealth versus Eric Barnes and Jason White." The judicial system, of course, declined to refer to the defendants by the street names everyone else used. Pookie and Hood both looked up but did not stand. Pookie had logged enough time in the system to know that nothing would happen until his lawyer showed up. Hood, a novice, had decided he was just going to watch Pookie and follow his cousin's lead.

Hood was wearing square earrings in both ears, a blindingly bright white polo shirt that hung below the knees of his baggy gray Dickies, and a pair of white Adidas sneakers that were even brighter than his shirt. He was sporting a new hairstyle. Instead of his usual cornrows lying flat against his head, he had narrow braids shooting out from his scalp, which lent him a mad-scientist-of-the-street look. Pookie knew a court date was something you dressed up for, as though you were headed to church. He wore a three-button navy suit too big in the shoulders, a powder blue shirt, and a blue-and-gray striped tie. The cousins were similarly handsome, but Pookie had a lighter complexion and a smaller build. He wore a thin beard and his braids tight and back on his head. Lounging on one of the dark wooden benches in the court gallery, he draped his arm around his girlfriend, who had a cute face and a nose ring. A female court officer walked over to him and tapped him on the arm. "This is a courtroom," she whispered. "Please put your arm down."

The prosecutor and Hood's court-appointed lawyer both informed the judge that Pookie's lawyer was not present. Judge Paul Leary, slumped in his tall leather chair with sunlight streaming through the half-moon-shaped window above him, shrugged his shoulders. "We'll wait."

For almost a year, the busted-windshield case involving Hood and Pookie had crawled through the district courts. There were delays prompted by Pookie's paid lawyer. There were further delays as a consequence of the rampant turnover in the district attorney's office that turned the case into a dreaded box of Christmas ribbon candy, passed from one underpaid, overworked prosecutor to another to another. Finally, there was the inertia and inefficiency of the court system itself and its hopeless indifference to other people's time.

But at last the case had arrived at a special "Gun Court" session of Boston Municipal Court. The court was housed in a structure not far from City Hall called the Edward Brooke Courthouse, which was named after a Massachusetts Republican who became the nation's first black senator elected by popular vote. In February, the district attorney had trumpeted the creation of Gun Court as a chief component of his plan to reverse the city's surging homicide rate. Cases involving dangerous criminals and their dangerous weapons would be prioritized and streamlined, so that both could be taken off the street promptly. In practice, Gun Court also spent considerable time on defendants like Hood, who was hardly dangerous and who may well have never even touched the gun in question. And far from the streamlined process promised by the district attorney at his press conferences, Gun Court remained remarkably tolerant of delay.

In case after case called on this morning in Courtroom 10, there were delays. Lawyers weren't there. Witnesses weren't there. Evidence wasn't there. Prosecutors flipped through bulging manila folders, searching for answers to even basic questions about the cases posed by Judge Leary.

Leary was the last stop before cases went to jury trials. Because neither the defense attorneys nor the generally underprepared prosecutors wanted the uncertainty and intensity of a trial, they proceeded to cut all manner of last-minute deals. Some of the arrangements seemed incredibly lenient, given the severity of the charges involved. Leary went along with just about every deal presented to him on this morning, his usual commentary being no more than a shrug of his shoulders. At one point, five Hispanic men in their twenties and thirties, who were charged with kidnapping and assault and battery with a dangerous weapon, were granted a plea deal that spared them all jail time in favor of supervised probation.

At 9:35 AM, Pookie's lawyer showed up. William O'Hare had a thriving practice on the North Shore, so he'd cut back quite a bit on his appearances in Boston courts. But he remained on good terms with the court personnel there. As he entered the courtroom, he patted one officer on the back and waved to another on the other side of the room. The officer walked over to embrace O'Hare, who had a goatee and balding light-brown hair.

For much of the past year, Hood's father, Willie, had felt his son was ignoring the advice he was getting from him and his court-appointed lawyer and instead was taking his cues from Pookie, who in turn appeared to be taking his cues from O'Hare. Willie had warned his son that Pookie would be concerned only about himself.

He knew Pookie was facing much more serious charges for an alleged supporting role in an unrelated masked armed robbery. He knew that a gun conviction in the busted-windshield case would make it a lot harder for Pookie to beat that armed robbery charge. And he knew that, with the panic around Boston over the rising homicide rate, there was no way two black kids caught with a loaded .38 were both going to skate. Willie figured Pookie's lawyer was angling to get his client off, even if that left Hood taking the fall. After all, Hood was the one driving the car.

All along, Hood had thought Willie was off-base. But as he watched the proceedings unfold in the courtroom, there was fresh worry on his face.

O'Hare had filed what was called a "motion to sever." Hood and Pookie had been consistently treated as two parties to the same case. Now O'Hare wanted the court to treat them separately.

Objecting to the move was Amanda Martin, the thin blonde prosecutor who was scrambling to get up to speed on a case that had literally just fallen into her lap. The judge asked her for the facts of the case. She began by telling him that one of the charges—the threat to commit a crime—would be dropped because the guy whom Pookie had allegedly threatened to put in a body bag had chosen not to testify. The case would be restricted to the charges of gun and ammunition possession and malicious destruction of property over $250, namely the windshield. When Martin told the judge that Willie Barnes would testify that he saw Pookie holding a gun as he headed toward the Mitsubishi, the judge asked, "Who owns the vehicle?"

"Willie Barnes—Mr. White's father and Mr. Barnes's uncle." There was some momentary confusion over the fact that Hood's father shared a last name with his nephew, but not his son. But arrangements like that weren't so strange in an urban court, and the confusion quickly cleared.

"Motion to sever is denied," the judge said.

O'Hare protested, using his reading glasses to gesture. "It's his *son*, your honor."

"I don't see any problem with that," the judge said, shrugging.

When Martin stressed that Willie was also Pookie's uncle by blood, the judge smiled. "So everybody's related—fine."

The judge flipped through Hood's file, surprised at how little was in it. "He has no record?"

Amanda Martin responded nervously, "Mr. White's is more minor."

The judge pressed. "He doesn't have anything really, besides this case, correct?"

"Yes."

He flipped through Pookie's file. There were a host of major charges—assault and battery, auto theft, armed robbery, and armed masked robbery—and a bunch of minors. The convictions were mostly for the minor offenses: refusing to identify himself to an officer, unregistered operation of a motor vehicle, operating a motor vehicle after suspension of his driver's license. Of the major charges, the masked armed robbery was still pending, but all the others had gone south. The district attorney's office blamed the failure of those charges to stick on the refusal of a victim or key witness to cooperate, saying those people were following the code of the street—the one summed up on those Stop Snitchin' T-shirts—rather than doing the right thing. In reality, the failure of the cops to solve most shootings, coupled with the failure of the district attorney's office to gain convictions in some high profile cases and stop intimidation, often left inner-city victims and witnesses feeling they didn't have much of a choice.

The judge was used to seeing bulging folders like Pookie's. Thin folders like Hood's were much less common, and when he did see them, a prosecutor was usually standing before him asking for his approval on a deal that would involve no jail time. That wasn't happening this time. Pookie's looming masked armed robbery charges in a separate case may have made it in his interest to try to beat the busted-windshield charges rather than agree to a plea. And Hood's refusal to break with his cousin put a plea deal out of reach for him as well.

Judge Leary, who had just signed off on a no-jail-time plea deal for five guys facing kidnapping and weapons charges, didn't know that back story. So he paused for a few extra seconds on Hood's curiously skimpy file. But given his lengthy docket, he couldn't afford to linger long.

He kicked the case over to a different judge. Hood and Pookie were going to trial.

•   •   •

A BABY'S CRY punctured the quiet of courtroom 20. Hood, sitting on the dark hardwood bench in the front row of the visitors' gallery, turned around and put a finger to his lips. "Shhhsh!" he said soothingly to Janijah, his nearly-one-year-old daughter, who was wearing denim pants, a hot pink shirt, and matching hot pink plastic balls at the ends of her braided hair.

It was Friday, April 21, Hood's second day of court, and the first day of the trial. Because the judge had yet to arrive, Hood and Pookie had yet to be moved to the defendants' table. Sitting beside Hood was his petite new girlfriend, who had large eyes and wore her hair pulled back tight. Behind them sat Tia, who had a round, pretty face and straight hair that she held up with her sunglasses. Next to her sat her best friend, who held Janijah on her lap. Behind them sat Willie, wearing a black suede outfit and red leather shoes.

"All rise," the court officer said as Judge Mark Summerville entered the room and took his seat on the bench. The courtroom was small but modern and well lit. The judge was a stocky guy with dark hair and boxy glasses. Unlike Judge Leary, Summerville had perfect posture and spoke in a booming, authoritative voice. There was some whispering in the gallery about whether he was black or not—his skin was light enough to suggest he might be Hispanic. Later, when the judge was out of earshot, a court worker cleared the air, saying Summerville was indeed black and had grown up in the South.

Whatever the judge's color, it was clear he had more of it than anyone in the jury. Though there were a couple of blacks in the thirty-person jury pool that had initially been led into the courtroom, by the time the winnowing was done and six jurors and two alternates were impaneled, it was a monochromatic bunch: six white women and two white men. That didn't worry Willie. "I don't pay no attention to that black-white stuff," he said. "It's more important whether people are naïve or know the real world."

During his discussions with the lawyers before the trial got under way, the judge grilled Martin, the prosecutor whom he referred to only as "Commonwealth," since she represented the Commonwealth of Massachusetts.

"Commonwealth, how are you going to sustain the charge of malicious destruction?"

Martin stammered a bit, saying she would be relying on police evidence.

"Any tests on the weapon?" he asked.

"Yes, your honor. No prints were found on the gun."

Before he'd been elevated to the bench, Summerville had been a low-paid prosecutor like Martin, working with the cops to put the bad guys away. But anyone who assumed that made him more sympathetic to the law-and-order side of the courtroom did so unwisely. Summerville set the tone that he was in control of his courtroom, and he demanded order and preparation from anyone doing business before him.

While Pookie had O'Hare, a paid lawyer, the state picked up the tab for Hood's defender, a sixty-year-old guy named Jack Miller.

Willie had been through the system enough himself to know that attorneys were like automobiles—you tended to get what you paid for. But since his son refused to go against his cousin, Willie saw no point in straining to pay legal bills. "If you ain't willing to fight for yourself," he told Hood, "you could have Perry Mason and it don't matter." Absent from the courtroom was Jack O'Brien, who, in addition to being Hood's former coach, was also his most effective advocate.

The prosecutor went first, outlining the case, referring repeatedly to her legal pad for reminders about details she was still learning. She struck a cordial but businesslike tone with the jury. Then came Miller, who had thinning reddish hair and wore half-glasses and a gray-green suit.

Miller had been making a living as a lawyer for three decades. He handled some personal injury cases out of his one-man practice, but a large percentage of his clients were poor criminal defendants the court assigned him to represent. When he'd begun court-appointed work, the pay was only $15 an hour. He made ends meet by working weekends as a doorman at the Ritz Carlton. Nowadays, the pay was up to $50 an hour—double if it was a murder case. Behind the scenes, Miller was friendly and funny, streetwise and smart. But once he stood before the judge, he sometimes came across as nervous and a bit unsure, populating his sentences with lots of "ums" and "ahs."

In his opening statement, Miller took the jurors back to the night of May 3, 2005. He recounted that Pookie had made a cell phone call, responded angrily to the news that his girlfriend had messed up his car, and told Hood to drive him to Bowdoin Park so he could mess up her car. He said they stopped at a crumbling parking lot and filled the back floor of the car with chunks of asphalt. They stopped by Hood's place in Academy Homes, where Pookie's car with the freshly flattened tires was parked, and Willie saw Pookie walking from that car to Willie's Mitsubishi holding a cell phone in one hand and a gun in the other. Miller described the stop to get sodas at a Walgreens, how Hood went in first, leaving Pookie in the car alone for several moments. And he said Hood was fully aware of what he was getting involved in. "Mr. White is driving the car; he knows he's got rocks in the car; he knows what's going on." Finally, he told the jury that after Pookie used the asphalt rock to smash the windshield of the black Pontiac, a cop pulled up and spotted him, prompting Pookie to throw the rock on the ground and hop back in the Mitsubishi, where Hood was sitting behind the wheel.

In emphasizing to the jury that it was Pookie's beef and it was Pookie's gun, Miller said more about the incident than Hood was prepared to. He wanted to insulate Hood from the most serious charge, since a gun conviction carried a mandatory minimum sentence of one year in jail. But in essentially having Hood cop to the charge of malicious destruction of property, he also said more than he needed to.

When it was his turn, O'Hare strolled over to the jurors with an easy smile. He sought to develop a rapport with them, referring to the "urban setting" that was presumably foreign to both him and the all-white jury. And he signaled what would be the key to his defense. The cops had absolutely no evidence that the gun was Pookie's. The only witness connecting his client to the gun was Willie, the father of the codefendant, who had only recently stepped forward to be a witness. "The gun is in the car owned by Willie Barnes!" he told the jury, striking a how-'bout-that grin. "Wait until you hear the definition of possession. You think he has incentive to finger my client?" He concluded by warning the jurors that the trial would be boring at times. "All I ask is that you pay attention."

Judge Summerville had been doing exactly that, and he didn't like what he'd heard. He smiled politely at the jurors and dismissed them for a short "comfort break." Once they were out of the room, he laid into the lawyers. Is this what he was being asked to preside over—a trial where one defendant points his finger at his codefendant, and the codefendant points his finger at the defendant's father? "Do we have a *Bruton* problem?" he asked, invoking a Supreme Court ruling that had become shorthand for trials of codefendants that get stuck in a goulash of blame.

Martin and Miller argued it wouldn't be a problem because Hood was not planning to point any fingers at Pookie. It was only Hood's father doing the pointing, and he was a witness for the prosecution.

"They're gonna blame my guy," O'Hare complained, faulting Martin for not letting him know earlier that Willie had "jumped on the team of the Commonwealth." O'Hare insisted this was exactly why he had filed the motion to sever the case, which Judge Leary had denied.

"At this point I feel boxed in," Summerville said. But rather than declare a mistrial, he determined the trial would go forward, but not before he chided Martin and warned her that he would give O'Hare "wide latitude" in cross-examining Willie.

During the break, Hood was standing in the sixth-floor atrium near a bank of elevators. Pookie marched over to him and fumed, "Dawg, your lawyer is fucking everything up! Why he saying all that? He supposed to talk about none of what happened before!"

Pookie's mother—who had stopped talking to Willie on account of her older brother's decision to testify against her son—was standing in the atrium, watching the heated exchange. Finally, she turned to Pookie and said, "You just gotta save yourself."

•   •   •

THE TRIAL SHOULD HAVE BEEN PRETTY STRAIGHTFORWARD. The prosecution had just four witnesses—the three cops who'd responded to the scene, plus Willie Barnes. The owner of the car whose windshield had been smashed wasn't cooperating, nor was his girlfriend, who was the cousin of Lei, Pookie's ex-girlfriend and the mother of his baby. There were no fingerprints on the gun, nor any other evidence to speak of. During one break, as O'Hare puffed on a small cigar on the steps of the courthouse, he complained that if only Willie had kept his mouth shut, he could have gotten the flimsy case tossed without even breaking a sweat. "Without Willie, the government had nothing. Two kids in a car." At least nothing against his client. He conceded that if the gun charge was going to stick, without Willie stepping forward, it might have been more likely to stick to Hood, since he was the one behind the wheel of his father's car, where the cops found the weapon.

Back in the courtroom, Hood's lawyer began cross-examining the uniformed cop who had been the first on the scene.

"Officer," Jack Miller said—except that his Boston accent made the word sound more like "offisah." "On May the 3rd at some point, did you go to the second-floor apartment of 10 Bowdoin Park?"

"Yes," said the young cop with heavily gelled hair. Earlier in his testimony, the earnest cop had replied to questions with "That's affirmative," until the judge told him to stop doing that and just say "yes" or "no."

Two young male prosecutors from Martin's office slipped into the back of the courtroom to take in some of the trial and lend her support.

"Now, officer," Miller continued, "without disclosing the contents of that conversation, who did you speak to in the second floor apartment at 10 Bowdoin Park?"

"Mr. Robert Williams."

"Did you also speak to a woman there?"

"Yes."

"Who was that woman?"

"She wouldn't give me her name but she said—"

O'Hare shot up. "Objection!"

Miller was trying to use this cross-examination to establish that Pookie was behind the fight that led to busting the windshield. To do that, he was trying to link Pookie to Lei's cousin. But because the woman wasn't testifying, her relationship and her statements to police weren't admissible as evidence. Miller had painted this connection to the jurors during his opening statement, but the judge had warned the jury that opening statements were opinion, not evidence, and they couldn't use them in determining guilt or innocence. Miller had to use great care now in trying to make the link between Pookie and his ex-girlfriend's cousin, but he was struggling.

He tried again. "Do you know who that woman was in relation to either of the defendants?"

"Objection!" O'Hare repeated.

"Sustained," Summerville said, summoning the lawyers to the bench for a lengthy sidebar.

Miller returned with renewed vigor. "Officer, when you went to the second floor apartment at Bowdoin Park, you spoke to a man, is that correct?"

"Yes."

"And, ah, at some point, did you speak to a woman?"

"Yes."

"And who was that woman?"

"Who was that woman?" the cop repeated, looking confused as Miller continued to ask him a question he'd already been told was out of bounds. "She was the—"

"Ob-*ject*-ion!" O'Hare shouted, with equal parts fatigue and fury. He decided to rephrase it, if Miller wouldn't or couldn't. "Can you be more specific? What was her name?"

Miller nodded. "Did you get her name?"

"No," the cop said. "She wouldn't give it to me."

"And how many women did you speak with?" Miller asked.

"One."

"And, ah, did you know who she was without knowing her name?"

"Ob-JECTION!" shouted O'Hare.

"Sustained," said the judge.

Miller looked down at his yellow legal pad, flipping nervously through it for nearly a minute.

"After you spoke to that woman in the second-floor apartment of 10 Bowdoin Park, did you put Mr. Barnes and Mr. White under arrest?"

"Say that again," the cop replied.

"After you spoke to that woman in the second floor apartment at 10 Bowdoin Park, did you put Mr. Barnes and Mr. White under arrest?"

The judge turned to the cop. "That's a yes-or-no question."

"No," said the cop.

Miller stammered, "Ah, had you put them under arrest prior to that?"

"Yes."

Miller looked again, flipping through his pad several times, appearing to be in search of inspiration that refused to come. Peering over his half glasses, he looked up to the judge. "I have no further questions, your honor."

One of the male prosecutors in the visitors' gallery leaned over to his buddy and snorted, "Brilliant cross."

• • •

"**Y**OU REALLY DON'T HAVE A GOOD MEMORY as to dates and occurrences, do you?" O'Hare asked pointedly.

Willie Barnes opened his eyes extra-wide and fixed them on O'Hare. "My memory is *fine*."

It was Monday morning, day two of the trial, and Willie was being cross-examined by O'Hare. Because he was technically a witness for the prosecution, Willie had already been cross-examined by Miller, but theirs had been a friendly exchange. Miller had given Willie a chance to talk about his work counseling addicts at the jail, thereby getting his own past addictions with drugs and alcohol out into the open. That denied O'Hare the chance to turn those past troubles into bombshells that might prompt jurors to question Willie's credibility.

Now O'Hare was looking for other places to raise doubts. He drilled Willie repeatedly on why he had rented an apartment in Mattapan when he claimed to be a family man living at home with his wife and kids. Willie, his complexion as dark as the bound law books on the shelf behind him, turned and spoke to the jury as easily as he might have once confided in a bartender. "In twenty-three years, me and Pearl been separated probably four times." O'Hare asked Willie how far he put the seat back when he drove, why he'd had a gun permit years back, whether his other sons ever got the keys to his car—all in an apparent effort to tie him or someone besides Pookie to the gun.

One thing was for sure: O'Hare, cool and capable, had done his research. That, Willie said later, was the biggest difference between paid lawyers and the overworked, underpaid assistant district attorneys and court-appointed public defenders. When Amanda Martin had questioned him on the stand, Willie told her, "You're like the fourth ADA I've dealt with on this case."

Yet Willie had been more prepared, or at least more at ease, on the stand than perhaps O'Hare had expected. At one point, O'Hare had pressed him on whether he knew where Pookie had been living on the night of the incident. Willie paused. To a layperson, it appeared that O'Hare was simply trying to raise doubts about how close Willie was with the nephew he had testified he loved, if he didn't even know where he had lived in recent years. But Willie saw it as a trap. He knew Pookie had spent some time in jail, and he suspected O'Hare was trying to get him to say that, a step that would have inappropriately introduced his nephew's criminal record and perhaps forced the judge to declare a mistrial. If it was a trap, Willie didn't fall for it. "I don't know where he's living right now," Willie replied.

With the exception of one juror, a heavyset woman who wore a magenta fleece pullover, long bangs, and a permanently confused look on her face, the rest of the jury seemed to soften their facial expressions the longer Willie was on the stand. He came across as a genuine guy trying to do the right thing, even though, as he told them, doing so had caused him a lot of grief with his extended family. Any juror who had gazed over to the visitors' gallery could have glimpsed some of that grief. A broad-shouldered woman wearing a black T-shirt that read "Girls Gone Wild Film Crew" sat rolling her eyes, shooting Willie a give-me-a-break look every time her brother said something about her son Pookie. Toward the end of the cross-examination, when O'Hare's questions had really piled up, Willie turned to the lawyer and said, "I'm saying what I seen is what I seen. You think I want this family strife?"

Willie didn't mention how serious the strife had become, how he'd heard rumors that Pookie's friends were going to come after him because of what he was doing. "That's the problem with our community," he once said off the stand. "No one see nothing, hear nothing, know nothing, so the kids control the streets. I can't live in fear."

•   •   •

WHEN HOOD TOOK THE STAND on Monday afternoon, he came across as polite and confident. Just a year earlier, he had mesmerized a banquet hall crowd with his public speaking. Now he was speaking to a smaller roomful of strangers as Miller asked him to go back to the night of May 3, 2005, a week after his banquet talk, when the trajectory of his life had started its dramatic change. The night had begun with Hood and Pookie dropping off Tia at her home in Columbia Point before returning to Hood's house in Academy Homes, where Pookie's flat-tired car was parked. Miller asked Hood, "Where does your girlfriend live?"

"Columbia Point," he replied.

From the gallery, Tia smiled and tossed Hood's petite current girl a look that said, "Take that!"

Miller asked Hood why they went to Bowdoin Park.

"We drove to Bowdoin to smash a window," he said matter-of-factly.

As Hood's testimony progressed, it matched the story Miller had outlined during his opening statement, with a couple of crucial exceptions. One of them Miller was expecting: Despite Willie's testimony about Pookie holding the gun as he got into the Mitsubishi, Hood insisted he'd never seen the .38 special until the cops pulled it out of the car's center console. But the other discrepancy seemed to take the lawyer by surprise. During his opening, Miller said that when the cousins pulled up to Walgreens to buy sodas, Hood went in first, with Pookie joining him a few moments later. It seemed like a minor detail, but it wasn't. Under that sequence of events, Pookie would have been alone in the Mitsubishi long enough to have the chance to take a gun out of his pocket and stash it in the console without Hood seeing it. But when Miller asked him about it this time, Hood testified that they'd both walked into Walgreens at the same time. Miller froze, asking again. After getting the same answer, he moved on.

O'Hare would have reason to prefer Hood's second version. When it was his time to cross-examine Hood, O'Hare was much more delicate than he had been with Willie. Since Pookie would not be taking the stand—doing so would allow prosecutors to ask him about his criminal record—and since Hood's testimony bolstered his client's case, O'Hare had an interest in helping Hood come across as sympathetic and credible with the jury. In fact, he spent considerable time trying to establish that Hood was such a promising young man that his father might have been motivated to do whatever he could to keep him on the right path. Everything, O'Hare would allege to the jury, including saying he saw his nephew holding a gun when in fact he hadn't.

O'Hare asked Hood about the Division II college scholarship he once had to play basketball. "Adelphi, that didn't work out, did it?"

"No."

"You said it was partly financial, but it was also something else, right?"

Hood nodded. "I was going back and forth to court, and the coach felt it was messing up the chemistry of the team."

He asked if Hood hoped to return to college. Hood said he had a good shot at getting a scholarship to play at Community College of Rhode Island.

After Hood's testimony, both defense lawyers rested their cases.

Before closing arguments began, Miller told the judge, "I'd like to be able to handle the firearm during closing."

"Fine," said the judge, shuffling papers on his desk.

"Is it properly disarmed?" Miller asked.

The judge seemed puzzled by the question. Then he smiled, perhaps at the image of Miller channeling Barney Fife, accidentally firing off a live round in the courtroom. "I sure hope so," the judge said.

During closing arguments, Miller, Martin, and O'Hare all hit their expected notes, with Miller blaming Pookie, Martin blaming them both, and O'Hare blaming Willie. Pookie's lawyer told the jury that Willie had decided, "I have a son who's a really nice kid; he's going to college, so I'll blame him," pointing to Pookie. O'Hare then directed his finger at Hood. "I hope you believe this guy, the good kid who had the basketball scholarship. He says his father didn't get it right."

Heading out of the courtroom, Willie pulled his son aside. They had been distant since Hood's arrest. The case had left Willie a lonely man, alienated from most of his extended family and forced to sit in a courtroom and watch a savvy lawyer pit him against his son. Hood had been so hard-headed lately that Willie started to wonder if a few months in jail getting "a cot and three hots" would do him some good. Still, he knew that no matter how thick Hood's street-life exterior might be, there was a vulnerable boy under-neath. During one break in the trial, he spied his son staring out the hallway window, tears running down his cheek. "I'm about to go off into the sunset," Willie told Hood now. "I think you handled this all wrong. But whatever happens, I'm there. If you get locked up, call me and I'll put some money in your canteen."

• • •

AS THE JURY DELIBERATED HIS FUTURE, Hood sat in a window seat in the bright hallway outside the courtroom, the petite new girl-friend beside him, braiding his hair. Across the hall and about 10 feet away, Tia stood leaning against the wall. She had put Janijah in day care. Standing beside her was Lei, Pookie's ex-girlfriend and the mother of his five-month-old son, Eric Jr., who was asleep in his car seat. Destiny, her two-year-old daughter by another father, was run-ning up and down the hall, going back and forth between Lei and Pookie, who stood at the other end with his new girlfriend.

There was a certain social order that everyone seemed to ac-cept, if not particularly enjoy. The guys were attended to by their new girlfriends. But not far away were their original girlfriends, who were now more commonly referred to by the term "baby's mamma," or BM. The BMs were less shapely and had more com-bustible relationships than the new ones, but they also had the deeper bonds. There was tension and a distinct wariness between the BMs and the girlfriends, but also a grudging respect for the fact that neither side could take down the other. So they tended to keep their distance, limiting their interactions mostly to rolling their eyes and drawing support from within their social caste. All through the trial, Tia and Lei had hung together, as had the new girlfriends.

Lei called over to Hood and, with a big grin, said, "Don't drop the soap!" She wore a lime-green shirt and pumps of exactly the same color, and her smile revealed the nineteen-year-old's mouth full of braces. "You made fun of me when I was getting my six months, so I'm gonna do the same." Lei had complained to Tia that she used to like Hood but thought he'd gotten too conceited. "All that Charlestown fame really went to his head." She also complained about Pookie. Once, she said, he had been a good boyfriend, taking care of Destiny from the time she was two months old, even though he wasn't her father. But since she had given birth to his own son, Lei said, "He ain't done nothing for me. No support." She knew some people might find it strange that she would be showing up every day at his trial. "I'm here to support him, even though he don't support me," she said. "And to see him go to jail."

Destiny came running down the hallway again, blurting out something Pookie had apparently coached her to say. "I pimp you!" the two-year-old said to her mother. "I pimp you!" Pookie laughed from the other end of the corridor. Lei yelled over to him to stop it. Then his new girl laid into him about something, and he yelled back at her.

But the tension quickly cleared, and soon there was laughter in the hall. In addition to the guys, their BMs, and their girls, several of Pookie's siblings and friends were crowded into the corridor, munching on the Fritos and Snickers they'd bought from the vending machine. Unlike the enforced quiet and stiffness of the courtroom, the mood in the hallway was light.

Hood's lawyer, Jack Miller, sat in an adjacent conference room, listening to the laughter fill the hall. "It's like a fucking party out there," he said, shaking his head. Hood, he said, "is either going to college—out of Roxbury—or he's going to jail. You know how hard it is to get a scholarship? You know how good you have to be?" He knew all about Adelphi University—he'd once taken his daughter there to look at the beautiful Long Island campus when she was considering where she would apply. Hood may have blown that scholarship, but if he managed to avoid jail time, he still had a shot at getting another. "That's the story of the inner city. You either go to college or, more likely, you do your one or two years at the South Bay jail. But these kids don't grasp the fucking difference."

Still, Miller got a kick out of the size of the crowd that showed up faithfully every day. "All of my clients have a BM, a girlfriend, and many of them also have a fiancée," he said. "When they go to jail, all three of them are visiting them. Jesus Christ, if I got sent to jail, I'd be lucky if my brother came to see me."

Miller recognized that the roots for this hallway behavior ran deep. In the great lottery of birth, it wasn't these kids' fault that they grew up in neighborhoods where there were always people getting caught up with the law. That early exposure to the criminal justice system made it seem less intimidating when they had their own run-ins with it. And if these kids sometimes appeared disrespectful, that didn't mean they weren't scared. On the streets where they lived, appearing soft could carry far steeper consequences than mouthing off in court.

Just after 4 PM, a new face joined the hallway party. Lorenzo Jones, who had been Hood's teammate at Charlestown before he quit over a lack of playing time, wasn't standing in the corridor to offer moral support. Much to their surprise, the two former teammates realized they were both on trial for gun possession charges in next-door courtrooms. Their arrests had taken place months and many miles apart—Hood's in Dorchester and Lorenzo just outside Charlestown High, when the cops had arrested him for allegedly running off with a gun. But here they were, each facing the fork in the road of his future, Hood in courtroom 20, Lorenzo in courtroom 21.

Lorenzo's trial had been a stripped-down, single-day affair—he was the only defendant, and the only witnesses against him were the arresting cops. But the case against him was stronger, given the cop's testimony that he had seen Lorenzo running away with the gun in his hand. Lorenzo had gotten a paid lawyer, picking up extra shifts at his part-time supermarket job to help his mother—a transit-system worker who showed up in court wearing her uniform—pay the legal bills.

The lawyer, a tall, chatty guy named Mark Griffith, couldn't get over Lorenzo's politeness. Most of his teenage clients never thanked him the whole time he represented them, but Lorenzo said "thank you" every time he met with him. Like Hood, Lorenzo was naturally smart, though his grades weren't great. In fact, he'd done so well on the state standardized tests that he qualified for a full scholarship to the University of Massachusetts. That endeared him to Fung, and the headmaster had given Lorenzo a letter of support to bring with him to his trial. But, like Hood, the scholarship offer had lost the battle to his court summons, and a conviction on the gun possession charge would kill any hope of ever getting it back. "Mandatory minimum of one year," his lawyer said, biting the side of his lip, "and not a day less."

At 4:45 PM, with no verdict, the judge in Hood's case told everyone to return the following morning. The judge in Lorenzo's case, hoping to keep the proceeding to just one day, kept the jury deliberating until after 5:30 PM, before they too were ordered back the next day.

• • •

TIA EXITED THE ELEVATOR and walked down the hall. Willie was already there, reading the Tuesday edition of the tabloid *Boston Herald*. "I've been coming here at 9 o'clock every day for four days," Tia told him. "It feels like I started a new job."

There were brief appearances in the courtroom before Judge Summerville, as he instructed the jurors to return to their deliberations, or answered questions they had posed to him in writing. But mostly, the day was filled with waiting in the hall. Hood and Pookie were still keeping their distance, as they had been since their heated argument in the atrium after opening statements.

At 1:05 PM, Lorenzo walked out of Courtroom 21, beaming a bright-white smile. He excitedly spoke into his two-way cell phone. "I'm out!" He found Hood in the atrium by the elevators, and they shook hands and smacked shoulders. Lorenzo left to start the rest of his life. Hood returned to the hallway to await his fate.

At 4:15 PM, the jurors filed back into the courtroom with a new note for Judge Summerville. They had agreed on four counts, but said they were hopelessly deadlocked on two. The judge gave them a don't-be-deadlocked pep talk that he had no doubt given many times before. "Don't assume any other six-person jury is going to be any more intelligent than you," he said, before sending them back to deliberate some more. After they had left, he told the lawyers, "I'm not going to keep the jurors past 4:30."

Outside the courtroom, the defense lawyers Miller and O'Hare began doing verdict math. Hood and Pookie had each been charged with a single count of gun possession, ammunition possession, and malicious destruction of property over $250 (the windshield). "We both pretty much conceded malicious destruction," O'Hare said. "That's two. The way the evidence went in, it seems likely that they're agreed on my guy." If the jury had likely found Pookie guilty on the gun and ammo charges, the deadlock, he guessed, was over Hood. The question was whether the deadlock could be dislodged within the next fifteen minutes. O'Hare didn't think that was likely, so a case he thought could have been closed in one day was now likely to stretch into five. "I suspect I'm going to have to come back here tomorrow to be told my guy is guilty."

•   •   •

A SMALLER CROWD SHOWED UP on Wednesday morning—Tia and Lei at one end of the hall and Pookie and his new girl at the other. In the middle, Hood sat with a few of Pookie's siblings. Even Willie was absent, deciding he'd already missed too many days of work. Hood's new girl wasn't there either, so Tia should have been feeling more relaxed. But she wasn't. She was still trying to get past the angry confrontation she'd had with Hood the day before. Log enough time together in the same narrow corridor, and pretty soon there are no secrets. Pookie's new girl had been talking loud enough for everyone to hear about how she was two months pregnant. And though she'd been less vocal about it, Hood's new girl had hinted she was in the same situation. Tia was angry. The accumulated slights of seeing her man with his arm around another girl all week, letting her braid his hair, was one thing. But finding out that he was going to turn her into a baby's mamma too, when he wasn't even taking care of the baby he already had—well, that was quite another.

Even though Tia prided herself on her even temper, she lost it, marching up to Hood and telling him, "You hurt me a lot. I hope you get sent away!"

Hood swore back at her.

Eventually they both realized they hadn't meant what they'd said. Tia knew that no matter what happened, she had a special bond with Hood, and he always called her first for help. The more she thought about it, the more Tia realized a part of her almost felt bad for the new girl. "If she think she gonna keep him because she's pregnant, she gonna end up in a worse situation than me."

Standing in the corridor now, Lei turned to Tia. "These niggas changed."

Tia nodded, "Umhmm." She grew nostalgic about Hood. "He was a good old boy. I don't know what happened to him. He used to stay in the house all day. I would sit there braiding his hair and he would massage my feet."

Later in the morning, when Pookie and Hood had both left the hall, Pookie's new girl sat chatting with his siblings about how Hood might fare behind bars. "He's never been incarcerated, so that basketball stuff don't mean shit in jail," she said. "Pookie be all right. He got a lot of friends in there."

At 12:30 PM, the court officers announced to the hallway that the jury was about to return to announce its decision. The judge sat at the bench, reading a folded piece of lined yellow paper containing a note from the jury. Hood and Pookie stood. The doddering court clerk held the verdict slips, squinting as he read each count.

First came the verdicts for Hood.

"In the case of Commonwealth versus Jason White, count one, unlawful possession of a firearm, how do you find the defendant, Jason White?"

The foreman, a young guy with light brown hair, said, "Not guilty." Hood looked down in relief.

And the ammunition possession? "Not guilty."

And malicious destruction of property? "Guilty."

Then the clerk called out, "In the case of Commonwealth versus Eric Barnes." The judge lifted the yellow piece of paper and read aloud the jury's note about Pookie's charges. "After extensive deliberation, we were unable to achieve unanimity with respect to counts 1 and 2 against Eric Barnes." Summerville declared a mistrial on those counts. On the malicious destruction charge, Pookie too was found guilty.

The lawyers had guessed wrong. The jurors hadn't been hung on Hood's gun charges after all, just Pookie's.

The judge announced, "Sentencing will take place at 2 o'clock. Until then, both defendants will be placed in custody." The court officers cuffed Hood and Pookie and led them out a side door.

Walking out of the courtroom, with Tia beside him, Miller said, "He dodged a bullet, huh?"

•   •   •

A FEW MINUTES AFTER 2 PM, Amanda Martin hustled into the courtroom, carrying a towering stack of manila case folders that seemed likely to topple at any moment. The prosecutor opened the folders for Pookie and Hood and hurriedly flipped through her notes and documents, which she had covered in green and pink marker like a college freshman who'd been given her first highlighter. Martin huddled with Miller and O'Hare and a probation officer who had arrived to give sentencing guidance. They swapped papers back and forth for a few minutes as they tried to gather support for the sentence recommendations they'd be making to the judge when he entered the courtroom. "I have a letter from his coach," Miller said. He gave Martin a note O'Brien had hand-written, extolling his former player as "a model citizen at Charlestown High School."

Months earlier, Willie had asked O'Brien to write the letter for his son. The coach had readily agreed and told Willie to let him know if the case went to trial, so he could be there to testify as a character witness. Willie assured him he would. But there had been so many delays and false starts in the case that Willie hadn't wanted to waste O'Brien's time until a firm trial date was set. Then, once there was one, things moved along so quickly that Willie never got around to giving O'Brien a call. But at least he had the letter.

O'Brien, though, was never a person who made his impact in writing. The earnest "to whom it may concern" letter from him captured none of his passion. He was a man who had to do his persuasion in person. And he, better than anyone, could help other adults look past Hood's scowl and self-defeating tendencies and see the good soul that O'Brien saw. Unfortunately, at the same time that the judicial system was determining whether Hood's future would be a college dorm or a jail cell, O'Brien was uncharacteristically caught up in his own problems, focusing on his own future for once instead of his players'. So, yes, Willie hadn't gotten around to letting O'Brien know when and where he was needed. But for perhaps the first time in his coaching career, O'Brien hadn't made it his business to find out.

A court officer led Pookie and Hood, still handcuffed, in from the side room. Hood, who had been wearing his braids flat against his head for the last couple of days, had let them out during the break. The cousins were talking to each other as they entered the room. The deep freeze between the two of them had thawed.

The judge entered and asked Martin to go first. She began with Hood. Noting that his record was clean, she said, "The Commonwealth recommends eighteen months probation, supervised." If the judge accepted her recommendation, for the next year and a half, Hood would have to meet regularly with a probation officer, pay a $65 fee each month, and get permission to leave the state. She noted that Hood appeared to have lost his Adelphi scholarship but now had a shot at one with Community College of Rhode Island. "I'd ask that if he does go to Rhode Island to go to college—"

She seemed poised to ask that the probation sentence not interfere with Hood's ability to attend college—a request Willie had made of her. But the judge interrupted her. "I can't do that," Summerville said.

Martin sat down.

Miller stood up and addressed the judge. After Pookie's tires had been punctured, he said, Hood and Pookie "decided to do a tit for tat. There's no excuse for it. It was stupid, it was wrong, it was criminal. Now he's going to carry a conviction for the rest of his life." From here on, whenever Hood would be asked on any kind of application—for college, for a job, for an apartment—"Have you ever been convicted of a felony?" because of this smashed windshield, he would have to answer, "Yes." Noting his lack of a prior record and his college potential, Miller requested a sentence of one year probation.

The judge now asked for recommendations on Pookie. Martin said her office planned to retry him on the gun charges. She noted his charges and convictions in the past, and one serious case that was pending, and requested a stiffer sentence. She wanted Pookie to serve as least sixty days in jail in addition to the probation. The judge chided her, "Commonwealth, I can't sentence based on an open case."

O'Hare asked for the judge's understanding, saying Pookie was a respectful young man who had two young children and another on the way.

Summerville had heard enough. He was ready to hand down his decisions.

A court officer tapped Pookie and Hood on the arm. "Stand up, gentlemen."

Summerville began with Pookie. "Mr. Eric Barnes, you've been convicted of malicious destruction of property over $250. You will be sentenced to 18 months in the House of Correction, one year committed, the balance suspended, and probation for four years." A year in jail and four years of probation was a stiff sentence for a busted windshield, but maybe the judge had decided Pookie's guilt ran deeper than some broken glass.

And then he turned to Hood. "Mr. Jason White, you've been convicted of malicious destruction of property over $250. Your sentence will be one year in the House of Correction, six months committed, the balance suspended, and probation for four years."

Miller could hardly believe what he was hearing. Often judges take note of the divergent sentencing recommendations made by the prosecution and the defense and then split the difference. But here the judge was ordering a sentence for Hood—six months behind bars—that was far stiffer than the one even the prosecution had requested.

Miller's outrage allowed him to summon an eloquence and fearlessness that had eluded him earlier in the trial. "Judge, this is his first conviction; it's a crime against property! That six months is going to take him out of the ability to get out of the street life. You're going to take this great opportunity away from this young man to get out of the ghetto life, to go to college in Rhode Island, to board there. The government's not looking for committal. He was honest about breaking that window. Right now whatever opportunity we have to get this man out of street life, committal will totally break that chance."

Judge Summerville stiffened his already perfect posture, and his nostrils flared. "Counselor," he shot back, "number one, I haven't heard anything about Mr. White being in a *ghetto* life."

"*Street* life," Miller said quickly, hoping to avoid seeing his appeal go down based solely on his word choice.

"Far from it!" the judge continued. "Far from it! The only reason he's in this position is he put himself in this position. My decision stands."

Miller lowered the ambition of his appeal, asking the judge to shave just one month off the six-month jail term. Doing that would prevent the sentence from bleeding into the start of the new school year in September.

"No," the judge said. "No. He made the decision to do what he did. He's paying the price."

Hood whispered something in Miller's ear.

"Your honor," Miller said, "my client requests a one-week stay of execution, to put his affairs in order. He's got a young baby daughter." Janijah would be turning one in a few weeks, and Tia had been planning a big party.

The judge shook his head. "There will be no stay of execution."

It didn't matter that the owner of the car whose windshield had been smashed had declined to press charges, or that its replacement would be covered by insurance. It didn't matter that Hood's entire life might well pivot on this one offense of busting a windshield, a fate that would have seemed inconceivable had he been a young man of means. Hood was being sent to jail immediately.

From her seat in the visitors' gallery, Tia began sobbing.

O'Hare conveyed a different request to the judge. "On the $7,500 bail, my client's mother has asked me if it will be returned."

"Yes."

Hood turned around to look at the gallery. He stretched his arms, but only so far, because his wrists were still cuffed. The cuffs would not be coming off anytime soon.

A court officer handed Pookie's mother a receipt to retrieve the bail money she had put up for her son. Riding down in the elevator, Pookie's sister was sobbing. "What you crying for?" their mother asked. "He was already prepared for this. Didn't you see him smiling?"

Pookie's mother turned away from her daughter to face the elevator doors, staring as the lighted floor numbers descended: 5, 4, 3, 2. She shook her head. "I've never seen nobody get four years probation for breaking a window! I think it's 'cause they couldn't prove the gun case, so he was hard on them." A bell dinged, the doors opened to the main floor, and her scowl turned into a smile. "But I'm gonna go get my check!"

20

REVISE
AND REVOKE

A T 10:30 PM, THE PHONE RANG. Anyone who worked with Michael
Fung knew the guy was a seven-day-a-week headmaster, but
that didn't mean he was a night owl. No one called him at home
this late unless it was an emergency. He fumbled for the phone,
trying to shake himself out of his slumber. The voice on the other
end of the line belonged to Jack O'Brien. At least that's what the
caller said.

It was a Thursday night in mid-April, nearing the end of one of
the most eventful weeks in O'Brien's life. On Tuesday, he had been
in Fung's office, fighting back tears, telling the headmaster how he
couldn't bear to leave Charlestown. On Wednesday, Fung had ventured over to the gym to let O'Brien know, in his classically unsen-
timental Fungian way, how happy he was that the coach had
decided to stay. He told O'Brien he would address the sources of
frustration the coach had laid out during their lengthy meeting before O'Brien had announced he was bolting for Lynn. Back then, the
grievances had sounded too much like ultimatums to Fung's ears,

313

so he'd resisted making any assurances. But as soon as O'Brien made the decision on his own to remain at Charlestown, Fung felt he could be extra-accommodating. Then, this morning, O'Brien had been absent from school. In a dozen years at Charlestown High, the coach and gym teacher had rarely missed a day of work. The late-night call explained where he'd been.

O'Brien told Fung he'd met for two hours with the Lynn superintendent earlier in the day. He was calling now as a courtesy to prepare Fung for the news that would be hitting the newspapers in the morning. "I think it's best for me to go," O'Brien said. "I need to do what's best for me."

Fung was completely confused, but he couldn't tell if that was because he was still bleary from sleep. The voice on the phone didn't sound like O'Brien's. The tone and cadence seemed different. For sure, the message was different. In all their years together, Fung had never heard O'Brien frame any discussion in terms of what was good for him. It was always about "the kids, the kids."

Once he was confident it was in fact O'Brien, Fung mumbled, "OK, OK," and then hung up. But he had trouble getting back to sleep. He struggled to make sense of what he'd just heard. Fung felt he understood O'Brien's initial decision to leave Charlestown, amid all the frustrations of devoting his whole life to serving a city that didn't really appreciate him. And he certainly understood his decision to return, after the coach saw how despondent his players became at the news of his departure. But for the life of him, Fung couldn't understand why O'Brien was now jumping back to Lynn. He thought to himself, "I don't think the gods are going to be kind to him." Fung was pretty much an atheist, but he wondered if a faithful Catholic like O'Brien noticed the symbolism of the day he had chosen for his second defection in a week: Holy Thursday, when Jesus turned to his disciples and said, "One of you will betray me."

•   •   •

WILLIE BARNES REMOVED HIS DIAMOND stud earring, his rings, and his bracelets in white and yellow gold and placed them all in a locker. Even without the bling, he still looked sharp, wearing a double-breasted suit that was as cranberry as a jug of Ocean Spray, with a pocket square, shirt, and leather shoes that were all the color of heavy cream. His braids were tight and flat on his head, with a sheen underneath them. It was 7 o'clock. In a couple of minutes, Willie would be addressing a crowd of nearly 200 men. But that's not why he was all dressed up.

The nice clothes were for after his talk, when he'd be going out to a few of his favorite clubs. Willie learned the art of flashy dressing from his uncle in New York, who had a distant past as a hustler, but who had settled down into a legitimate white-collar desk job. On the wall over his desk, his "Uncle Bump" kept photos of Hood powering to the hoop. The man kept his eyes peeled for sales, and when he saw good ones he told Willie to drive down to the city, so they could snag $300 shoes for sixty bucks. He introduced his nephew to all the fine-looking secretaries in his office, telling them, "This is the father of the basketball player."

An escort led Willie through a metal detector and then through a series of electronic security doors. At each one, Willie knew which buttons to press. He'd walked this route so many times before. A few minutes later, he was standing before his audience, row upon row of men sitting in plastic chairs. Judging just from their dress— blue scrubs and white sneakers—it looked as though he were addressing a convention of emergency room doctors. But the line of balconied jail cells behind them gave the setting away.

"I'm Willie, a recovering addict," he said.

"Hey, Willie," they replied.

For eight years, Willie had been running this weekly Narcotics Anonymous meeting in the drug unit of the South Bay house of correction. The inmates seated before him received a little time shaved off their sentences in exchange for coming. The benefit to Willie went much deeper.

"I only got one story, and it's mine," he told the crowd, "but I can tell it a hundred different ways." He described the many years when he struggled with addiction, booze mainly, but also weed and some coke. Mostly, he was addicted to the party life—going to clubs, looking good to impress the ladies, drinking and doing drugs, having fun. It took him a long time, but he'd found a way now to enjoy clubs without all that other stuff. He'd nurse a couple of bottled waters and have a good time just taking it all in.

"I used to be strung out on drugs," he said, pacing at the front of the room, perspiring at his temples. "I remember how hard it was to get off them. I would hide money on myself. Crazy!" he said, drawing nods from the crowd. "You can't hide from *yourself*."

A natural at public speaking, Willie managed to hold the audience's attention, even though most of them had heard his story many times before. He told them he had once sat in their seats, watching other people lead these meetings, ignoring what they were saying. But then one day a clean-shaven man came in to address Willie and his fellow inmates. It took Willie a minute, but he placed the face. "This guy was a bum living on the street. You step over him in Chinatown. He pisses on himself, got no teeth. The proverbial 'If I ever look like that I'll know it's time to quit.' The fact that he had used NA to get his life back to order," Willie said, "gave me my first vision of hope."

Still, he admitted that even after you quit the junk, life remains a daily struggle. He told the crowd about how, earlier that day, he came dangerously close to getting locked up. "I threw a punch toward Pearl," he said. "I touched her. I didn't hit her, but I touched her." He said his wife had made him so angry, but he had to be humble now to return to her good graces. When she called him later in the day, she said, "You got some decisions to make." Smiling, Willie told the crowd, "Now I know I'm in."

He handed out laminated placards that listed the twelve steps to recovery. He didn't need one himself. As the inmates began reading the steps aloud, Willie mouthed them quietly. He knew every word. When that was done, he said, "I'm in a deep, deep love affair with NA."

After several inmates had shared their stories, Willie wound the meeting down. "I won't be coming here for about four months," he said, with some sadness in his voice. "I'll have a replacement starting next week." He explained that jail rules prohibited someone from coming in as speaker if they were also coming in to visit an inmate. "My son got locked up," he said, prompting many inmates to shake their heads ruefully. "You've heard me say this before, recovery begins at home. So I gotta focus on that."

As he was led back out to the lobby, Willie asked a guard to tell Hood to call him. "I put $50 on his account," Willie said. He explained that this would be the last NA meeting he'd be conducting for a while, but that they'd be seeing him come to visit his son. The clerk asked Willie for his son's name and then looked up his card. Each inmate was allowed to list three people who could visit him, and that list couldn't change for six months.

The clerk looked up at Willie and said, almost apologetically, "You're not on his card."

Willie looked hurt, but he tried not to show it. "Maybe he got his girlfriend, his other girlfriend, and his mother on there. I'll talk to him."

On the bright side, he said, he wouldn't have to give up his NA speaking commitment.

• • •

A FEW DAYS LATER, Ridley was standing outside Terminal E at Boston's Logan Airport when his Aunt Emily pulled up in her black Ford Expedition. It was the first Wednesday in May, and Ridley had just finished up his freshman year at Toledo. He was wearing a gray Toledo hoodie, jeans, a gold chain around his neck, and a New York Yankees cap on backward. He had cleared out his dorm room, jamming his stuff into two large hockey bags, which he picked up now and tossed in the back of the SUV. Emily got out of the driver's seat, hugged him, and moved to the passenger's seat. He climbed in behind the wheel, moved the seat as far back as it would go, and put the car in gear.

"Where's Jordyn?" he asked.

"Day care."

"You should have brought her. I wanna see her!"

Emily asked how his finals had gone.

"Good. I think I ended up with a 2.8 GPA."

Emily reminded him of their deal: $3 for every A, $2 for every B.

Ridley smiled. "Add a couple of zeroes on that."

"How many A's did you get?"

"Two."

"Let me hear you got an A in biology, history, algebra, something like that! What you got an A in? Ping pong? I know they do that stuff in college."

Ridley chuckled. "Contemporary Moral Problems." Ridley had been navigating those for years.

Emily asked him about his gold watch, which had a huge face and diamonds. It had cost him around $400. He had treated himself to it back in November, on the occasion of his nineteenth birthday.

She started rummaging through his backpack, looking for evidence that her boy had changed. She pulled out a box containing several pairs of diamond earrings. "Look at all this bling-bling!" She pulled out a bottle of Insurrection perfume, which had an odd rectangular shape and an even odder dispenser. "Where's the cologne I bought you?"

Naturally, Ridley's first stop would be the Charlestown gym. Two blocks away from the school, he turned onto Elm Street. Always a narrow road, it turned out to be temporarily impassable. Three middle-aged white guys from Boston's public works department had their truck parked on the side, with an attached mini-trailer jutting out into the center of the street just enough to make it impossible for Ridley to maneuver the SUV past them. The workers were adjusting a street sign on the other side of the street—hardly a three-man, all-morning job—but they would not be rushed. All three made eye contact with Ridley but made no effort to let him get by. Finally, one of them let go of the sign, sauntered across the street to get to the truck, and appeared poised to move it. He didn't, choosing instead to saunter back across the street, standing next to his coworkers and doing nothing.

As she watched this scene, Emily began to burn up. "He just walked back across the street?" she spat, incredulous.

"Yeah," Ridley replied coolly.

Fuming, Emily went to lower her window to say something to them. Ridley reached across the center console and put his hand on hers. "It's OK," he said soothingly, "we're not in a rush."

"But c'mon," Emily protested. "That's not right!"

"You're right," Ridley purred reassuringly. "They're ignorant. I don't blame them."

Ridley's phone buzzed. "'Ello?" he said, and then smiled. "'Ssup?"

By the time he hung up, the workers had driven away.

Many other nineteen-year-old black males might have taken the bait, viewing the slight by a couple of middle-aged white guys as a provocation that demanded a response. Others might have fretted about the consequences and backed down. Ridley managed to float above it all, acting mature yet looking nothing but cool.

Perhaps that, more than anything, explained why Ridley was returning as a success story to Charlestown High a year after graduation, and Hood was returning to his jail cell. Ridley knew he had to rise above one world to get to the next. Hood thought he could straddle both. As Emily once said, "There's no such thing as an educated thug." Hood had always faced longer odds, since he came from inside a tough housing project, whereas Ridley only lived near one. The distinction seemed small, but it wasn't, given the baggage attached to residency, even in cases like Hood's where the project had been torn down and replaced with something shiny and new. "Living in the projects, a black male got a 50/50 chance of getting caught up in street life," Emily said, "no better than that."

In the gym, Ridley stood talking to O'Brien, who was peppering him with questions about his dramatic buzzer-beating tip-in. "So they carried you off the court?" O'Brien asked.

"Yeah. It was like a dream."

O'Brien was beaming. "Wow, down one, your freshman year—you'll never forget that!"

Just then Ridley got tackled from behind by Lorenzo Jones. Lorenzo, who had time on his hands since he'd beaten his gun charges, had headed to the gym as soon as he heard Ridley was back in town. He hugged him and planted a big kiss on his cheek.

Ridley smiled. "What up?"

A few minutes later, Robby walked in, wearing a Black Label T-shirt, Girbaud jeans, and a black baseball cap tipped just so. Of all the players who had graduated, Ridley and Robby remained the closest, talking all the time on the phone, even though Ridley was in Ohio and Robby at Radford University in Virginia.

They left the gym and headed into the main part of the school building, with Robby reprising his dead-on impression of O'Brien for Ridley's benefit. As they passed the main office, a clump of ninth-grade girls began squeaking, "That's Ridley! He's cute!" Like the lead singer of a boy band walking through the mall, Ridley smiled and waved. Robby shook his head. "You going to jail, man."

Kristyn O'Brien, their former guidance counselor, spied them from down the corridor and came over to give her boys a hug. "Ridley, you look so much bigger," she said, her blonde hair pulled back in a ponytail.

"No, he just got some facial hair," Robby said, tugging on the thick, scraggly hair descending from Ridley's chin. "Don't be juicing his head up."

Just then Fung walked by. "Mr. Fung," Kristyn called. "Look who's back!"

"Um, hi," Fung said, barely looking up as he continued walking.

Robby shook his head again. "That dude is just oblivious to the *planet*. He's just in his own world all the time."

Kristyn told the boys she wanted them to come back to speak to a group of freshmen she was working with. "They're a horror show—so lazy."

She asked if they had heard about Menda.

"Yeah," Robby said, "I talked to her."

"It's so awful," Kristyn said.

Menda François was one of the academic stars from their graduating class who was now on a four-year scholarship to Bryn Mawr. Ridley remembered her as the studious, sometimes annoyingly inquisitive girl from his AP history class. "When we used to go on a field trip to a bank or something, she was all, 'Why this?' 'Why that?' OK, we wanna *leave*, Menda!" But when he had seen her over Christmas break, he couldn't get over the change. She greeted him with, "Wassup, yo!" Ridley figured that was because she was one of the few inner-city kids at her elite college. "She from the hood, so she's playing that up."

But during the spring, when she returned home for Easter weekend, she got more than she bargained for. She was at a house party in Dorchester, when she stepped out onto the sidewalk to take a cell phone call. All of a sudden, someone started shooting. Menda, who was on Bryn Mawr's track team, took a bullet in her leg. She was going to be OK now, though she'd need crutches for a while. But the idea that a driven student like Menda could get ensnared in the madness of the streets gave everyone pause.

Between Menda's shooting and Hood's jail sentence, Kristyn said, "I'm so heartsick." Still, she told Ridley and Robby, "Seeing you two makes me so happy."

Outside the building, they ran into Cassidy. Robby told Cassidy he'd heard he was going to revamp the Charlestown team now that he, and not O'Brien, was going to be in charge. "You gonna get rid of the press?"

"Oh, yeah, everything's changing," Cassidy said, flashing an exaggerated smile. "I'm gonna bring in all white guys to play."

For the next few weeks, Ridley and Robby spent most of their time hanging out in Ridley's bedroom.

"Everybody been changed now," Robby said one afternoon, sitting on Ridley's bed.

Ridley smiled. "Not you."

Robby smiled back. "You're still gay." He laughed. "Serious, man, since I came home I noticed how Boston's changed. Now I see elementary school kids on the corner at 12 o'clock at night. *Twelve o'clock at night!* It's crazy! Where's your parents at?"

"The kids bad," said Ridley, who was staring at his Sidekick as he text-messaged someone. "They bad."

"All the people dying in the street," said Robby, who had been orphaned at fifteen, "and they just wanna be on the street more."

Robby was wearing a T-shirt that said "Dre Robinson," a rapper about to release his first studio album. Dre also happened to be Robby's older brother. Robby listened mainly to rap, and he was excited about his brother's chances for stardom. Still, he saw a direct connection between rap and those grade-school kids hanging in the street at midnight. "It's a double negative, man. You can't make positive music, or you'll be soft. You gotta keep making the bang-bang, but then you're influencing the youth to do the wrong thing. They can't distinguish reality from the facade."

Robby got down from his soapbox long enough to take in the irony. Here he was preaching about the dangers of rap and wayward kids getting seduced by the street. But when he was at college, he knew that most of the white affluent kids looked at him—with his cornrows, tattoos, and baggy jeans—and assumed he was nothing but a thug. "They don't want to look at me as a person. They just see this." He slowly ran his hands down from his shoulders to his knees, like one of those *Price Is Right* models showing off a new appliance. "They just see trouble."

Actually, he found the rich white kids easier to take than the rich black kids. The white kids were curious about his culture. "They want to be able to say, 'What up, dawg'—all that type of shit. The rich black people, they don't want nothin' to do with you."

Ridley nodded, "Yeah."

"Because they might have a side of their family that's like you that they just don't want to talk about."

He was surprised to find he bonded more easily with the poor white kids. "They know about having your lights cut off or having no hot water. They know what government cheese is."

Robby knew he could have made things easier on himself at school by dropping his cornrows and baggy jeans. "But this is an expression of me. I don't dress like this to be no gang-banger or no thug. The punks express themselves with the piercings and the Mohawk. This is how I express myself. This is where I'm from."

More and more, he was realizing what a tough line it was to walk. "You don't want to stray away from where your heart is, but at the same time you gotta leave some of it behind so you can get ahead," he said. "It's hard—you know what I'm saying—to try to walk that line. You don't wanna not be able to go back home."

Ridley brought up Hood and how he had heard he was in jail because he wouldn't say it was Pookie's gun.

"Yeah, you don't snitch," Robby said softly.

"Yeah," said Ridley. "But if it was you, Rob, I'm *telling*!" He laughed.

"If it was you," Robby said, "I'm showing them where you live, Ridley."

"We get stopped, the cop would be like, 'Hi, how are you?' and I'm like"—Ridley pointed repeatedly to Robby—"He got a gun!"

When the laughing subsided, Robby shook his head. "Damn! Why didn't he just stay in school? Dickhead! He lost that scholarship, huh?"

"Yeah," Ridley said. "He got his daughter, too."

"Now he gonna be one of those guys who walks around saying"—Robby narrowed his eyes and started talking in a cool, detached voice—"'Well, yeah, that didn't work out, but the coach from *here* called me. I'm supposed to be going up *there* to look at that school.'" Robby predicted Hood's future, figuring he would look a lot like the washed-up guys they had all grown up seeing around city basketball courts, talking about their glory days. "He'll be saying, 'Yeah, I got three rings. I'm a high school basketball legend.'"

To Robby, those guys never grasped the most important lesson of high school basketball: It's a means to an end.

"Without basketball, on hot summer days, you ain't got nothing to do but get in trouble."

"If I didn't play no sport," said Ridley, "I really don't know what I'd be doing."

"Sometimes sports is the only reason somebody goes to school."

"That's the only reason I went!" Ridley said. "If Coach wasn't that strict, forget about it."

Over time, O'Brien's relentlessness chipped away at Ridley's love of the game. It became more of a job. But now Ridley could appreciate that. It prepared him for college, where it was clear all ball players were cogs in a big-business machine. A romantic attachment to the game at that level could only do harm.

Walking out of the house, Robby stopped on the front porch and tapped Ridley on the arm. "You remember last year, when everybody used to be here?" he said. "When everybody was on the same team, you couldn't get them out of this little house."

Ridley nodded.

Robby continued. "Nobody calls you no more. Nobody cares how you doing."

Ridley admitted that Robby was the only Charlestown teammate who still kept in touch.

"It's amazing what a year away at school will do," Robby said. "It shows you what is real."

.   .   .

WILLIE CAREFULLY PLACED HIS SON'S 1,000-point basketball on the wooden railing in the courtroom, holding it there until he was sure it wouldn't fall. The court was quiet the last Friday in May. Beside the basketball, Willie put a weather-beaten football, a huge framed photo of Hood sailing toward the hoop, and an orange folder bulging with clippings from his son's previous life. Among the folder's contents were letters of praise from his Charlestown coach and guidance counselor, a letter listing Hood as among the 1,500 players nominated for McDonald's All American Boys High School Basketball Team, and an awards-dinner program that Willie had gotten the Boston College basketball coach to autograph for his son ("Best wishes, Al Skinner.").

Earlier in the morning, Willie had lugged a trash bag full of memorabilia on the subway with him, hoping it would do Hood some good when he stood once again before Judge Summerville. The gathering was officially called a Revise and Revoke hearing. Lawyer Jack Miller admitted to Willie that it would be a long shot, going before the same judge who had ordered Hood to serve six months in jail and four years of probation for the busted windshield, and ask him to change his mind. But he figured the odds were better than normal. Hood, who had been in jail for a month now, would be appearing before the judge without his cousin. Pookie was now in the process of cutting a deal with the district attorney's office over his charges in the armed robbery case. Miller hoped the judge could finally see Hood as an individual rather than some repeat offender's partner in crime.

The visitors' gallery was pretty empty. In the row behind Willie, Tia sat on one end, and Hood's new girlfriend, her belly showing a little more now, sat on the other.

On the other side of the railing stood Danny Ryan, a thin, friendly court officer who had earned the nickname "Red Skin" in his younger days when he hung out on Dorchester street corners and had a full head of red hair. Ryan slipped into an adjoining room and then reappeared a minute later, leading Hood into the courtroom, the silver cuffs around his ankles jangling as he walked.

Ryan was an easy conversationalist who called everyone "Budso," so much so that people began calling him that. You could meet him in line at the bank, and five minutes later he felt like a lifetime pal. It had taken him about that long to size up Hood's situation: a decent kid caught up in a bad situation, with a father trying to help him get out of it. Ryan wasted no time in deciding to help out Hood and Willie.

Hood turned around and made eye contact with Willie but didn't say anything. Ryan tugged on Hood's arm. "I didn't hear a 'Thanks, Dad,'" he said. Hood mumbled his gratitude and stuck his hand over the railing to meet his father's, while looking away.

Willie started right in on his son. "I hope you used all that time in jail to think about what a big mistake you made."

Ryan shot his hand out like a crossing guard. "Hey," he told Willie. "The kid don't need that fucking speech right now!"

Willie laughed and leaned back on the bench.

As everyone waited for the judge to arrive, Hood turned around to look at his new girlfriend, pulling on his lobes to ask her where her earrings were. The next time he turned around, he asked Tia if their daughter was in day care.

When Ryan walked to the other side of the room, Willie asked his son how it was going at the South Bay jail. "I'm in a three-man cell, with some white dude who's in there for kidnapping or something, and a Spanish guy who got caught with a gun. There are other guys doing six months for distribution in a school zone." Hood shook his head and laughed. "And I'm doing the same time for bustin' a window?"

That prompted Willie to resume his speech. "You should have listened to what I said and told the DA that it was Pookie's gun."

Hood shook his head slowly. "I got a life after this."

"Exactly."

"What's done is done," Hood told his father. "Nothing I can do to change that now."

"You can make sure you learned your lesson."

"I did," Hood said. "I'm never driving with anybody else again. From now on, I drive *alone*."

Ryan returned to hear the end of the snitching debate. "I agree with the kid," the court officer told Willie. "It's not like when we were growing up. All these guns. They're looking for a reason to shoot you. You snitch and that gives 'em one."

Ryan shut down the debate and got father and son to focus on what really mattered: getting the judge to agree to let Hood walk today. "I know this judge," he said. "He's a friend, but he's tough." Ryan had advice for everyone.

To Hood, he said, "Look humble."

To Miller, he said, "Jack, the most important thing that you can do is make sure the DA tells the judge why they think probation is *fine*."

The assistant district attorney who prosecuted Hood's case was tied up with another case. When Ryan spotted her substitute entering the courtroom, he bounded out of his chair and pulled the young, well-dressed guy out into the hallway, to make sure he was on board.

In his absence, the courtroom was silent, except for the repeated clicks coming from the mouse on the clerk's computer.

When Judge Summerville entered, Miller presented him with the letters supporting Hood.

"Counsel," the judge asked, "you want me to read them before you continue your presentation?" He took off his glasses and began reading.

When the substitute prosecutor weighed in, it was obvious that Ryan's hallway pep talk had worked. The prosecutor told the judge he served on a task force working to improve safety in Hood's neighborhood. "I see the bad decisions that people in that area are making every day," he said. Given his talents and college prospects, he said, Hood had tremendous opportunities that were simply unavailable to other kids from his housing project. "This young man is at a point in his life where he could go either way." The prosecutor encouraged Summerville to release Hood from jail.

Miller figured Summerville wouldn't relish having to admit he had been wrong when he gave Hood such a stiff sentence. So he made it easy on the judge, skillfully blaming himself for failing to have presented his client's case adequately enough during trial. "Judge, I wish I had been better prepared."

But Summerville was hearing none of it. "Mr. Miller, you and your co-counsel were *extremely* prepared and put forward a fine defense."

Miller tried again. "Maybe I was so focused on the trial I didn't do enough for sentencing, for you to understand what kind of kid he is." He continued, "I'd like to see *one* of my clients from Academy Homes break out of that syndrome. Instead of sending kids off to college, from there the kids are sent off to South Bay."

"I could have given him a two-and-a-half year sentence," the judge said. "I think I did give him a break."

When Miller tried once more, the judge shut him down, saying finally, "I believe he thought he was going to walk out of this courtroom. It didn't happen, and it's not going to happen."

The judge stood up and left.

Willie stood up, filled the trash bag with the basketball, football, bulging folder, and framed photos, and then he walked out of the courtroom.

•   •   •

IN EVERY COACHING JOB Jack O'Brien ever had, from Medford to Salem to Charlestown, his attachment to his players and his program was impossibly intense. It was hardly a surprise that his exits from those jobs turned out to be so dramatic and draining. Still, the fact that each departure devolved into a messy, tortured affair, generating headline after headline in the sports pages, led even some of O'Brien's friends to wonder if, subconsciously, he needed it to be this way. Was he so insecure that he needed a public testimonial to hear how much he'd meant to people? Or did he need a wrenching period of grief in order to let go of the old bonds before moving on to forge new ones?

In the days and weeks after Holy Thursday, O'Brien had repeatedly tried to explain his decision to colleagues and players past and present. He talked about how, when he'd announced he would be staying at Charlestown, he barely had a moment to savor things before teachers hit him with fresh complaints about how his players were failing in class. They didn't even begin with an obligatory "glad you're staying" icebreaker. Just laid right into him. What was he coming back to? It had made him wonder if he had acted too quickly. Perhaps it was true what so many people had told him a week earlier, as he panicked at seeing his young guys crying in the corridors: "Give it time, Jack," they said. "These kids will get over it, and so will you."

So he reversed his reversal, and the papers on Good Friday carried the news that he was headed to Lynn after all. In the nearly two months since then, O'Brien and Zach had been traveling to

Lynn several times a week to get to know their future players, preaching discipline in the classroom and on the court. Around Charlestown High, the post-O'Brien basketball future had begun to take shape. Even though nothing had been finalized, Steve Cassidy had assumed the role of head-coach-in-waiting, meeting with players in groups of two and three, getting them focused on summer leagues in preparation for next year's season.

At 6:30 AM on Friday, June 9, O'Brien loaded one last box into his minivan and began the drive from his home in Medford to Charlestown. The boxes contained thirteen years worth of surplus Charlestown memorabilia—T-shirts, calendars, photos, sweatpants. In a few hours, O'Brien's players from across the seasons would converge on the gym for the annual Alumni Game. In years past, O'Brien had gone all-out, printing up game-day T-shirts and programs. This year, he hadn't been able to summon the energy for all that. Instead, he decided to open up his boxes and let them choose their own keepsake from a happier time.

Around 9:15, O'Brien, wearing his red Charlestown sweatshirt and black sweatpants, walked into the headmaster's office. He needed to tell the secretary to expect the delivery of twenty pizzas he'd ordered for after the game. He bumped into Fung.

"You coming to see the game?" O'Brien asked.

Fung looked distracted. "What time?"

"Noon."

"I will try to make it, if I'm not too busy dealing with your guys going crazy."

O'Brien chuckled. Fung did not, and walked away.

A minute before noon, O'Brien leaned against the wall, under the scoreboard, and let his eyes scan the gym. He was happy to see J-Rome back behind the DJ table. Spinning a new tune by Mobb Deep called "Put 'Em in Their Place," Rome had just finished his freshman year at Saint Michael's College in Vermont. That made him a Charlestown alumnus now, so he liked the message the tune would convey to the upstarts on the team. O'Brien was thrilled to see Ridley looking like a star on the court, and his dad, McClary, showing up to cheer him on. "Ridley, he comes back with muscles!" McClary said, smiling, before flexing his own biceps and adding, "I guess he's trying to keep up with me."

O'Brien couldn't help but think about who was missing. Instead of sailing toward the hoop, Hood was sitting in a jail cell. O'Brien hadn't given up hope on Hood yet, but he knew a felony conviction and jail term would be especially hard for him to bounce back from.

Once play began, the alumni quickly took control. Ridley helped power the veterans to a 127–111 win. In the cafeteria after the game, the players wolfed down pizza. The mood was light, though there was a sadness hanging in the air. The alumni all told O'Brien they supported his decision. But privately, most of them still didn't understand it. They worried about what would happen next year. Would there even be an Alumni Game? Was their connection to a place or to a person?

O'Brien had invited a few of his future players from Lynn to watch the game and attend the pizza party. As a former player and assistant coach for O'Brien, Hugh pulled the visitors aside. Gesturing with a cup of grape soda in his hand, Hugh told them how lucky they were to be getting O'Brien, to be getting the best.

One of the Lynn kids nodded. "I've learned so much from him in such a short time."

At the next table, O'Brien made small talk with Hugh's wife, Emily, and her sisters—Ridley's mother, Rebecca, and Paul Becklens's mother, Joanna.

"Joanna, you've lost weight," O'Brien said. "What you been doing?"

Joanna smiled. "Nothing. I just been waiting for you, honey."

"Oh, God," Emily groaned, spooling out the possible outcome of this unexpected flirting with the man her husband Hugh considered his father. "I can't handle you being my mother-in-law as well as my sister."

Joanna laughed. "I need my lingerie on for him."

"The one with the basketball on the front of it?" Emily joked.

O'Brien took a sip of his Diet Coke and deadpanned, "That would get me excited."

The next morning, O'Brien awoke knowing he had to talk to Fung. It was a Saturday, so naturally he found the headmaster alone in his office. He told Fung he knew he was going to think he was nuts, but he was still struggling with the fear that he'd made the wrong decision to leave Charlestown. Every time he drove to Lynn, he said, he got a pit in his stomach. "What should I do?"

Fung was in no mood to rehash. "You never asked me the first three times for advice, so I'm not going to give you it now," the headmaster said. "Besides, I have a vested interest."

"No," O'Brien pressed, "I'm asking you as a friend."

"OK, Jack, if you still have second thoughts, after all this time, it's not a good sign." He told him that he had understood his first two decisions but never understood the third one, the one to return to Lynn. And he said he thought he knew what was nagging at the coach's conscience.

"What?"

Fung hesitated. He wasn't sure if he should introduce a deeply personal chapter of O'Brien's past. He'd heard about it from another member of the faculty, but he'd never before discussed it with O'Brien. He forged ahead anyway. "It's like a betrayal, Jack. Your father betrayed you. And now you feel you are betraying your players by leaving, because you are like a father to them."

O'Brien waved his hand dismissively. He wasn't about to open up to his boss on his father's case of matricide. But Fung thought he saw something registering in his eyes.

"If you want to come back, the job is still yours," Fung said, finally. "The school year doesn't end until June 30. You let me know by then."

•   •   •

IN EARLY JULY, Cassidy interrupted his summer vacation to stop by Fung's office. The headmaster assured him he would name him in the fall to be the head coach. After all, Fung's June 30 deadline had come and gone without any word from O'Brien.

Everything proceeded as expected until late August. That's when, once again, O'Brien showed up at Fung's office, telling him the pit in his stomach about leaving Charlestown had refused to go away. In fact, now he was racked by the kind of regret that makes your forehead scrunch up and your toes curl in your shoes. With the new school year about to begin, O'Brien felt the Lynn officials had begun to backtrack on some of the assurances they had made while recruiting him, and that gave him real pause. But more than anything, the source of his angst and insomnia in August was exactly what it had been in April. He just couldn't get over the feeling that he was abandoning the people who needed him most.

So O'Brien did what he had done back in April. He asked Fung for his job back.

"Jack, I already promised the job to Cassidy, and I cannot break my word," Fung said. Although he was losing patience with O'Brien, he still felt for him, knew his heart was in the right place. The only way around the impasse, Fung said, would be if Cassidy decided not to apply for the job. "Why don't you talk to Cassidy?"

O'Brien did just that, but the conversation, unsurprisingly, did not go well. Cassidy told O'Brien all his back-and-forth had simply gone too far. Everyone had to accept the consequences of his decisions and move on.

O'Brien was hurt, seeing disloyalty in his former assistant's refusal to yield. Cassidy was hurt, too, resenting his former mentor for putting him in this squeeze. He told O'Brien he had been in the running for an administrator job at a school in New York but had withdrawn when the Charlestown head coaching job opened up.

After O'Brien failed in his pitch to Cassidy, Zach approached Cassidy and gave it a shot. After they had spoken for about an hour,

Cassidy said, "Enough! I'm not talking about this anymore." He decided to put it all back in Fung's lap, confident the boss wouldn't break his word. "It's the headmaster's decision," Cassidy said.

Fung wouldn't go back on his word. He told O'Brien that even if he couldn't be coach, he should consider staying at Charlestown to teach, where he could remain involved in his kids' lives. "And who knows, maybe Cassidy will leave after a year."

So when the new school year began in September, O'Brien and Zach were back in their usual spot, teaching gym at Charlestown High after having declined the phys ed jobs at Lynn English. When anyone asked, they explained that they still planned to coach at Lynn when the basketball season began in November. Cassidy never asked. He was careful to avoid them, and they did the same.

O'Brien tried to make the best of the situation, but he felt embarrassed that he'd let his indecision drag on so long. To a man known for being theatrically resolute on the basketball court, this image of endless vacillation just didn't compute. He knew what people were saying behind his back. *What's going on with this guy? Just suck it up and move on!* On some level, he knew they were right. Then again, he had followed that advice once before, and his guilt had only grown.

•   •   •

AS THE MOURNERS SCALED THE STAIRS leading into the New Hope Baptist Church on a balmy Friday evening in early September, a tall woman stood outside the door, selling pins. Attached to purple ribbons, the pins featured a picture of a handsome young man over the words ONE IN A MILLION.

The church, a sprawling Gothic-style structure built of pudding-stone, straddled the South End, with its million-dollar condos and their alarm system stickers in the windows, and Lower Roxbury, with its flat-roofed housing projects where the emergency exits were usually left propped open. Inside the church, O'Brien, wearing a navy blazer and a dark tie, sat with Zach in a pew near the front, a few feet away from the open casket. Hugh and Emily were seated behind them.

As Cassidy filed past the casket, he walked right by his fellow coaches and took a seat toward the back of the church. The tension between Cassidy and O'Brien was still thick. In the last few weeks O'Brien had been preoccupied by all that off-the-court drama. But now it all seemed so petty. His presence in church marked the grimmest milestone of his coaching career. To the left of the mahogany altar and the enormous white pipes of the organ, there was a giant arched plaque with the Ten Commandments etched in gold lettering. O'Brien's eyes couldn't help but fall on No. 6: Thou shall not kill. In all his years of coaching troubled kids from high-crime neighborhoods, he had lost players to ailments and accidents but never murder. Yet here he was about to eulogize Alray Taylor, one of his own, gunned down a week earlier.

"There was no phoniness about him," said O'Brien, standing behind the lectern, addressing a crowd of several hundred with a voice that was uncharacteristically shaky. "He was sincere, and you could see that in his eyes. The people who are special in life are the ones who don't act special."

Just after 10 o'clock in the morning on the last day of August, Alray had been walking into Liriano's Spanish Market in the Hyde Park section of Boston. Known as a safe, family-oriented neighborhood, Hyde Park was where the mayor came from and still lived, less than a mile from the market. According to the story prosecutors would tell, the murder unfolded like this: As Alray was walking in, a twenty-year-old named Shane Sinclair was walking out. There was already some bad blood between the two of them. Standing just outside the doorway, they exchanged words, then threats, and then punches, with the fistfight eventually migrating toward Cleary Square. Losing the fight to the hulking Alray, Sinclair reached into his pocket and pulled out a gun. Prosecutors say he fired several times. Two bullets struck Alray in the neck and chest. Sinclair fled the scene. Alray collapsed in the middle of a busy street, where he died, three days shy of his twenty-second birthday.

Olivia Dubose stood up and walked in front of the New Hope Baptist pulpit to deliver a solo. The diminutive woman, elegant in dress and diction, begged the congregation's forgiveness if she didn't hit all her notes. Since she was the pastor's wife and a member of ministerial staff herself, she had experience presiding over plenty of funerals. But this one, she said, was different. She had grown quite close to Alray during his days at Charlestown High, where she had been assistant headmaster. Alray may have been nicknamed Horse for his powerful frame, but she remembered him for his sweetness—the same quality that had endeared him to the white Townie lunch ladies from Charlestown, who always slipped him extra desserts and now sat together in one of the pews, dabbing their eyes with tissues.

Dubose managed to hit all her notes. When her husband, the Reverend Willie Dubose Jr., delivered his eulogy, he smiled and implored the congregation to do the same. "Celebrate Alray's life!" he said. "Sing!" He led everyone in a rendition of "Blessed Assurance."

> Perfect submission—all is at rest,
> I in my Savior am happy and blest.

O'Brien sang along, but he could find no celebration in his heart. His mind flashed back to a conversation he had had with Alray a month earlier. He could tell his former player was struggling. Less than a year earlier, Alray had lost his father. A few months after that, his mother—who had long battled severe breathing problems

and who seemed to lose the will to live after her husband's passing—died in Alray's arms.

O'Brien could tell Alray was searching. He had squandered opportunities at two New Hampshire colleges. But instead of offering
him comfort, O'Brien had offered up a little tough love. "Hey, you
blew two college scholarships," he said. "Some kids never even get
one. Let's get going again." O'Brien wished he could take that conversation back. Of course, he knew he wasn't to blame for Alray's
death. Given how commonplace shootings had become in inner-
city Boston, O'Brien had been lucky to have gone this long without
seeing one of his guys gunned down. Still, he knew he could have
done more. And at a time of unspeakable sadness for the other
members of the Charlestown basketball family, O'Brien felt a new
rush of guilt at how his decision to leave for Lynn had shaken the
family's foundation.

When he looked over his shoulder during the funeral, O'Brien
spied Hood slipping into the back of the church. He had recently
been released from jail on account of good behavior, but his
searching had no doubt just begun. Not so long ago, O'Brien had
been able to hold up Hood as a role model and a reminder for himself that there was a real payoff for all the hours invested in other
people's lives. Now, with a college scholarship squandered and one
tour of the criminal justice system already on his record, Hood ran
a much higher risk of writing his own bad ending. His entire life
had pivoted on something as minor as a busted windshield.

The combination of Alray's death and Hood's descent forced
O'Brien to reevaluate his approach. He had long seen his job as
helping his players rise above their bleak neighborhoods and get to
college, positioning them for a better life. Yet maybe that wasn't
enough. Maybe he needed to focus more on follow-through once
they left his care. It took all the energy and perseverance in him to
help his young guys pry open the window of opportunity. But to live

in the inner city is to be forever at risk of a gust coming along and slamming that window shut. Those gusts could be so fierce that they sometimes reached as far as distant campuses. And once the windows closed, unlike the suburban world of second and third chances, they were usually sealed for good.

•   •   •

THE FIRST MONDAY after Thanksgiving was the official start to the 2006–2007 high school basketball season. Charlestown High was even more chaotic than normal, since a power outage had left about half the school without electricity and heat all day. Cassidy had just found out he would have to rearrange the tryout session he had planned, his first as head coach, and he was scrambling to get the word out to all his guys. O'Brien was expected in Lynn to run his first tryouts as head coach there. He stopped by Fung's office before leaving the building, and the headmaster pulled a book off his shelf and handed it to O'Brien. "Here," Fung said, smiling, "You need this." O'Brien glanced down at the title on the cover and chuckled. *Decision Making.*

He walked out of Charlestown High, hopped in his white minivan with the Evergreen air freshener dangling over the mirror, and began driving north. Along the way, he got that familiar pit in his stomach, but he was sure that, after today, it would finally go away. Half an hour later, he pulled the minivan over, cut the motor, and stared out the windshield. Then he grabbed his cell phone and di-aled the Lynn principal.

"Mr. Fila," he said, "it's Jack O'Brien. I'm sorry. I just can't do it."

He started up the motor, and drove back home.

EPILOGUE

One by one, they walked through the royal blue doors. More than twenty of Jack O'Brien's former players showed up at the Charlestown gym in early June 2007 for the Alumni Game. The turnout was somewhat smaller than previous years. But the biggest difference was that this time, O'Brien arrived as a guest rather than the host.

As he leaned against the wall, across the gym from where his five state championship banners hung, O'Brien's mind flashed back to more than a year earlier. Shortly after announcing he would be leaving Charlestown, he had begun making the regular drive to Lynn to get to know his future players. It was during one of those drives, as he tried to will away the pit of regret in his stomach, that it had dawned on him: Leaving Charlestown would also mean leaving behind the Alumni Game. The annual event was the embodiment of O'Brien's aspirations as a coach: to create a winning team that would turn strangers into brothers, transform rudderless boys into high-achieving young men, and provide a comforting place to come home to. He wondered if he would ever have accepted the Lynn job had he just remembered to include the Alumni Game when he was compiling the pros-and-cons list in his mind. The realization made him smack the steering wheel of his minivan. "Damn!"

It had been a painful year for O'Brien. He had been roundly criticized back in November after resigning as Lynn coach on the first day of tryouts. Many people, especially in Lynn, were not inclined to see O'Brien's enduring devotion to the boys of Charlestown as sufficient cause for leaving the Lynn players in the lurch. In reality, O'Brien had taken steps to see that the Lynn kids were left in good hands. He had made sure Zach was there to run tryouts that first day and had lobbied the principal, Andy Fila, to name Zach as the new head coach. It was clear Zach was a true talent in his own right, and Fila seemed open to the idea. But he was overruled. Lynn's superintendent of schools was so furious about O'Brien's last-second exit that he insisted on hiring an entirely new coaching staff. So for the first time in more than a decade, Zach, like O'Brien, found himself uncomfortably idle during basketball season.

O'Brien had hoped that by staying at Charlestown, even without the coaching job, he would be able to continue counseling, motivating, and shaping the boys whose lives he had become so invested in. Yet that never really happened. In part, that was because he didn't want to step on Cassidy's toes. But a bigger reason was that since his first coaching job in his hometown of Medford, his role as a driven basketball coach had given him the confidence, and perhaps the right, to dive into his players' lives without doubt or self-consciousness. Basketball was his vehicle for reaching these kids; it was what made him different from all the other adults telling them what to do. Without his whistle and clipboard, he felt ordinary and exposed—even a bit empty.

Time and again over the years, O'Brien had delivered the key assist that helped troubled boys turn their lives around. But it was a co-dependent arrangement. Without O'Brien's hovering presence in their lives, some of the younger Charlestown players had struggled to get through the school year. Without their problems front and center in his life, so had O'Brien.

Still, some good had come from his sidelined season. He was able to spend more time with his mother and be there for her when she suffered some health problems. And he became closer with his brother, who, despite living with his family upstairs from O'Brien, had previously seemed separated by the distance of too many basketball seasons and too many years.

O'Brien took some comfort from his past as well. The year after he had lost his dream coaching job in Medford had been crushing. But then he landed in Salem, where he made his name and won his first state title. The year after he lost his job in Salem had been excruciating. But then he landed in Charlestown, where he became a legend, winning five state titles in six years and helping transform lives by the dozens. He kept reminding himself: *Things happen for a reason.* He prayed that God would once again lead him to a place where he could do even more good. *Where do you want me, Lord?* The only problem was that this time, he couldn't imagine anyplace where he could do more important work than Charlestown.

O'Brien watched as Cassidy ran around the gym, overseeing his first Alumni Game as head coach. He knew Cassidy was a good man, so it was sad that circumstances had allowed their relationship to become strained. During the regular season, Cassidy had struggled to step outside of O'Brien's shadow. The team had won twelve games and lost seven. Perennial rival East Boston seemed especially pleased by O'Brien's absence, beating Charlestown in both of their regular-season match-ups and dominating the league in a decidedly O'Brien-like manner. For the first time in nearly a decade, Charlestown failed to qualify for the City League tournament. After winning its first game in the state tournament, Charlestown found itself up against Eastie in the second round. No one gave Charlestown much of a chance. But Cassidy's resilience rubbed off on his players, and his team ended up stunning Eastie with a 70–68 down-to-the-wire win. Even though Charlestown lost in the next round of the playoffs, the thrilling Eastie upset drew plaudits for Cassidy and spared him an off-season full of chatter from critics about how he didn't measure up.

As Cassidy prepared to make introductions, O'Brien surveyed the lineup of former players.

Ridley was there. He had made good strides as a player and student in his sophomore year at Toledo, designing his own major of sports management technology. In March, a year after Ridley's last-second tip-in had given his team the win over Central Michigan, Toledo found itself facing the same team. This time the victory was less dramatic, but more significant. With Ridley's help, Toledo won its first Mid-American Conference title in more than a quarter-century, and head coach Stan Joplin was named the conference's coach of the year.

Robby and Spot were also there. Robby had left Radford University in Virginia to return to Boston, and he was now working full time at a local Best Buy and contemplating a return to college. Spot had finished up a year at Massasoit Community College, averaging more than eighteen points a game and being named to the NJCAA's All-Region basketball team. He expected those big numbers would finally produce his long-awaited scholarship offer from a big-name program. When that didn't happen, he grew frustrated and lost interest in school. He had begun working full time as a bartender's assistant at one of Boston's top restaurants.

O'Brien was surprised that George Russell hadn't shown up, though he knew he was doing fine at Salem State College. He wasn't surprised by other absences, like Troy Gillenwater, LeRoyal Hairston, and Terry Carter, since they had long ago made their break with Charlestown. After their California adventure ended badly, LeRoyal had returned to Boston to attend a high school across town while Troy made his way to a prep school in California. There, he continued to grow—to 6-foot-8—and flourish on the court, becoming a highly ranked recruit pursued by top Division I college programs. Terry's addiction to drugs had put him and his faithful guardian, Harry Landry, through hell after he'd left Charlestown. But the kid had just emerged from a year-long, intensive drug treatment program, clean and ready to resume his life, with plans to go to a prep school in the fall.

Naturally, Ridley's cousin Paul was on hand. Because he had turned nineteen before the start of the 2006–2007 school year, Paul had been declared ineligible to play for Charlestown as a senior. So the star point guard had left Boston to attend Bridgton Academy, a prep school in Maine with a powerhouse basketball program. The move had turned out to be a good one, putting him on the radar of college scouts while allowing him to focus more on his studies than he'd been able to do in the hectic halls of Charlestown High. After being courted by several D-I programs, Paul had decided to follow Ridley's lead, accepting a scholarship from Toledo.

And of course, Hugh was there. Even though he had taken Zach's place as junior varsity coach and second-in-command on the varsity bench during the previous basketball season, Hugh always returned to the Alumni Game as a player, not a coach. He had retaken his teacher certification test, and once again failed one portion of it by a narrow margin. The exam's failure rate among minority teachers in Massachusetts was so high—more than 50 percent—that more and more education officials had begun questioning its fairness. Ever the optimist, Hugh refused to complain. The inspirational speaker became more active in his church and began to contemplate joining the ministry. With his wife, Emily, and their daughter and infant son cheering from the stands, Hugh drained a stream of three-pointers to give the alumni team a commanding lead.

If Hugh wanted to continue teaching at Charlestown High in the fall, he would need another waiver from the headmaster. And for the first time in a decade, that would be someone new. Michael Fung was finally making good on his threat to retire. Back in the fall, someone hanging out in the housing project next to Charlestown High fired a shotgun on a group of students heading to school. Thankfully, no one was hurt, but there was immediate political fallout. The mayor and Michael Contompasis, who was on his way to being named school superintendent, promised a round of aggressive new security measures. Those included the installation of metal detectors in Charlestown High. Fung had long argued that metal detectors sent the wrong message to students and staff alike and were ultimately counterproductive. For years, he had refused to allow them in his school, warning, "The day the metal detectors come is the day I leave." As it turned out, he would stay through the end of the school year, but no longer.

Of all his former players, O'Brien was least certain what the future held for Hood, who had missed the previous Alumni Game because he was sitting in a jail cell. So O'Brien was pleasantly surprised to see that Hood had shown up this year. As a senior, he had been so dominant on the court that none of his teammates complained when a few female fans hung a hand-drawn sign on the gym wall that read "Hood's House." But that had been two years and a lifetime ago. Now on the court, Hood looked out of shape and his game was off. If his once bright college prospects had become clouded before his trial, his stiff sentence of six months in jail and four years of probation for the conviction of busting a windshield had darkened his outlook. In recent months, O'Brien had tried to motivate Hood into getting back on the college track, reminding him that he hadn't lost any of his eligibility and making a few calls to coaches on his behalf. But Hood, now the father of two babies by two different mothers, had trouble seeing his future on some leafy campus. Instead, he saw it unfolding around the same pock-mocked parks in Roxbury where he had spent most of his life. "People think jail is supposed to change you," Hood said. "Jail don't change you. Jail just gives you something to talk about when you get out."

O'Brien sensed that Hood's reluctance to try again might have more to do with a fear of failure than anything else, and he refused to give up on his former star. But he had to admit his own confidence was still a bit shaken. O'Brien was a self-effacing guy, yet in his heart he knew people were right when they told him he had a rare gift as a motivator of young men, and it was to everyone's disadvantage when he wasn't using it. He also knew what it felt like to go an entire year without coaching, and he knew he didn't want to do that again. But neither did he want to repeat his mistake of jumping to a new school when his gut was telling him not to go. As a coach, he had always refused to live in the past and focused instead on preparing for the next fight. But, like Hood, he now seemed to have a longing to return to 2005, when, despite fatigue and pressure, he had no doubts about what needed to be done or how to do it.

Coincidentally, the head coaching slot at Medford High had become vacant, and officials in his hometown had approached O'Brien to gauge his interest. Two decades earlier, there was nothing he had wanted more than that job. And he liked the thought of the narrative of his life coming full circle. But ultimately he deferred to his gut, which told him it wasn't the right move.

Fung said that even though Cassidy had done an admirable job in his first year as head coach, he favored reinstating O'Brien for the 2007–2008 season. "When in doubt, you go with the more talented person, and in this case that is Jack O'Brien," he said. But because Fung was retiring, this time it wasn't his decision to make.

After greeting his former players with smiles and hugs, O'Brien leaned against the wall as the Alumni Game was about to begin. But he found it all hard to watch. A few minutes later, trying to avoid drawing attention, he slipped out.

By the time the royal blue door had latched shut, he was gone.

• • •

A FEW WEEKS AFTER THE ALUMNI GAME OF 2007, Michael Fung sat down with his replacement as Charlestown High headmaster, a personable woman named Margaret "Ranny" Bledsoe. A former college professor with a doctorate in mathematics, Bledsoe had come to secondary education as a second career. She had recently finished a Boston training fellowship for new principals. Charlestown High would be her first job running a school. In his typically blunt fashion, Fung told her what her three most pressing priorities should be as she prepared to take over the complex urban high school. One of them was deciding who would be the head basketball coach for the following school year.

"It's your call," he told her, before making his preference for Jack O'Brien clear. While he felt O'Brien and Steve Cassidy were both talented and dedicated, his view was that O'Brien's track record and willingness to build his life around his players simply put him in a league by himself and created an engine of excellence within the school that transcended sports. Whatever her decision, Fung encouraged Bledsoe to make it quickly, so that the person who didn't get the nod could try to line up a coaching position elsewhere over the summer. When Fung and Bledsoe met again later that summer, he was frustrated to hear that not only hadn't she come any closer to making a decision on that coaching position, but that she had also sought out the opinions of former top administrators, including Michael Contompasis, who was preparing to retire as school superintendent and become a senior aide to the mayor of Boston. In the city's schools, headmasters have the authority to select coaches on their own. "It's your call," Fung said again.

In the fall, after meeting with both O'Brien and Cassidy, Bledsoe informed them that she would keep Cassidy in the job for the year as she closely monitored the program. At the end of the season, she would decide on the coach of the future. O'Brien would be consigned to another year of waiting, itching to reclaim the job that was once inseparable from his identity. Fung, whose relations with his replacement had become strained, told O'Brien he didn't think Bledsoe was ever going to give him the job. But O'Brien remained upbeat. Through his lengthy conversations with the new headmaster, O'Brien sensed in her a sincere commitment to improve the school and a growing realization of how his approach could fit into her overall plan.

The year saw the return of a good deal of Charlestown's dominance on the basketball court. Cassidy adroitly guided his young team to an undefeated regular-season record and an appearance in the sectional semifinals of the state tournament, though Charlestown did lose that game in overtime. But in other respects, the ride was bumpier. Bledsoe complained about the off-the-court misconduct of some of the players, something Cassidy attributed to his having taken a chance on a few borderline kids at the start of the season. Accustomed to the freedom Fung had given him to run the program during his first year, Cassidy had to adjust to the heightened involvement of Bledsoe, someone he saw as well-intentioned but less familiar with the realities of urban schools. "She got very involved," he said later. "She wanted to know everything."

Cassidy and O'Brien would say hello to each other in the corridors, but otherwise kept their distance. O'Brien and Zach Zegarowski continued to work with students in the jobs as Charlestown phys ed teachers. The previous year, they had struggled to do their mentoring without the special authority that flowed from their roles as coaches. But this year, they found that process a bit easier. O'Brien worked closely with a few former players who were still at the school but no longer on the team, and reconnected with several alumni who had left college, trying to help them get back on track.

After the season, O'Brien intensified his effort to get his coaching job back, meeting often with Bledsoe. Several others joined in the lobbying effort, notably Hugh Coleman and his wife, Emily. Hugh, who had moved a step closer to full certification and had a temporary teaching post at the school, had just finished his second season as junior varsity coach under Cassidy. He was careful not to criticize Cassidy, but he lamented that the ball players were being denied what had made such a difference in his own life—O'Brien's round-the-clock, compassionate involvement and rigorous discipline. Emily spent a good part of the year working as a substitute teacher at the high school and had developed a rapport with Bledsoe. She was plugged into the Charlestown basketball network of alumni and parents, and told Bledsoe everyone she talked to wanted to see O'Brien's return as coach.

According to Emily, shortly before the school's April vacation week, Bledsoe told her there was resistance to O'Brien's reinstatement coming from forces above her, and she encouraged Emily to organize an effort to demonstrate just how strongly parents wanted him back in the job. Emily interpreted that to mean Bledsoe needed some political cover, and she was happy to oblige. She spent much of the vacation reaching out to parents and alumni, and the week after vacation a group of them showed up at Bledsoe's office. Among them was Willie Barnes, Hood's father. He knew what a difference O'Brien had made in his son's life, and he wanted other kids to have the same opportunity. However, when the group arrived at Bledsoe's office unannounced, she said she wasn't free and asked them to come back in a week.

Willie was put off. He'd sacrificed a couple of hours of pay in order to make it to the school on time for the meeting. Still, he felt strongly enough about O'Brien to do the same thing a week later, showing up in Charlestown on the first Monday in May. More than two dozen other parents and alumni were there with him this time, as well as a dozen current players. The extra week had allowed Emily to spread the word and draw a bigger crowd.

As he made his way into the school building, Willie spotted Cassidy outside. He walked over and chatted with him. Willie had no problem with Cassidy—he'd always liked the guy. It wasn't his fault that he wasn't O'Brien.

There was a bit of a standoff before the meeting began. Bledsoe said she didn't feel it was appropriate for the current members of the basketball program to participate. It was a matter for the adults to discuss. Anissa Booker—whose son, Paris, had been killed before getting a chance to play for Charlestown but whose gravesite O'Brien visited regularly—was among those who challenged Bledsoe. "Wait, this is their lives here," she said.

A compromise was struck. The current students were allowed to talk, and then leave the crowded conference room before the official meeting began. O'Brien, of course, was not there, but it wouldn't take long for him to get blow-by-blow accounts of what happened from many of the participants.

As Willie looked around the room, he took note of how the crowd represented the full span of O'Brien's tenure at Charlestown: from Shawn Brown, the star he kicked off the team during his first season as coach before helping him leave the street life behind, to Ridley Johnson, the co-captain (with Hood) of O'Brien's final Charlestown championship team.

Ridley had just finished his junior year at the University of Toledo, where he had been forced to watch another coaching drama unfold. He had continued to plug away academically, in particular enjoying a law course he took, and to improve as a ball player, doubling his scoring and rebounding totals in each of his three years at Toledo. In the 2007–2008 season, he started in every game and ranked second on the team in three-point shooting percentage. The highlight for Ridley came when Toledo traveled to Amherst to play the University of Massachusetts in the same arena where he had dazzled the crowd during Charlestown's state championship game. He drained four three-pointers and turned in the best performance of his college career. After the game, Toledo coach Stan Joplin joked that he was going to stack next year's Toledo schedule with games in Massachusetts if that's what it took for Ridley to dominate the floor. As it turned out, Joplin's future with Toledo ended when the season did. The athletic director fired him and replaced him with Gene Cross, a hard-charging former assistant coach from

Notre Dame. Coaching changes are usually bad news for scholarship athletes recruited under a previous regime, but, true to form,
Ridley quickly proved himself adaptable to the new environment
and developed a good relationship with the new coach. He was on
track to take on a leadership role for the team in his senior year.

As adaptable as he was, Ridley was also intensely loyal. He felt
indebted to O'Brien for having helped mold him into the player
he'd become, and he wanted to be there to back his high school
coach when he needed it most.

Although there had been a lot of talk about political pressure
above her, Bledsoe began the meeting by saying the decision
would be hers and hers alone. That point was affirmed by the rep-
resentative of the superintendent's office and the school system's
athletic director, who were both at the meeting. Paris's mother
said the parents had heard rumors that Charlestown might lose
funding or suffer other consequences if O'Brien was selected, but
the school officials assured her that would not happen.

When it came time, Willie said his piece, and he stressed that it
had nothing to do with basketball. "I'd see O'Brien's van parked outside my house at 11 o'clock at night in the summer," he said.
"There's no school in the summer, no basketball." Willie said that as
soon as O'Brien began working with his son, Hood stopped getting
suspended and started caring more about his school work. "O'Brien
was doing half my job." And unlike the other people pumping up
his son's head about his basketball talent, O'Brien was careful to
keep things real. After Charlestown, his son made some mistakes
that set him back, but Willie stressed that O'Brien wasn't to blame.
The coach had even begun working with Hood over the past year to
try to help him get back on the path. The bottom line was, O'Brien
had seen the good in Hood that so many other people missed, and
he'd helped put his son in a position to succeed.

One by one, people testified to O'Brien's impact. Shawn Brown,
who, as head of a well-regarded mentoring program, knew better

than most how easy it was to lose inner-city boys to the streets, talked about how O'Brien's willingness to be available to his players at any hour set him apart. And he stayed rooted in their lives long after they could do him any good on the basketball court. The presence in the room of the mothers of both Paris Booker and Richard Jones—members of the Charlestown family who were buried thirty yards apart in Oak Lawn Cemetery—spoke to that point.

Hugh talked about O'Brien's hand in helping him transform his whole family, how he graduated from Bowdoin College, how his brother Derek graduated from Robert Morris University, and how his brother Bernard was now headed to Salem State College. "I've been in this city my whole life," he said, "and I've never seen someone care as much as Coach."

Bledsoe said she had three options: keep Cassidy in the job, give it to O'Brien, or give it to someone else. She said she knew O'Brien was a special person who had touched a lot of lives. But she said that after researching the situation extensively, she had several general concerns with putting him back in charge. One was that he had burned bridges and caused resentment among some members of the Charlestown High community with his decision to leave Charlestown for Lynn, a tortuous period of indecision that left some students crying in the hallways. Another was her perception that O'Brien had received special treatment for his program and players during Michael Fung's tenure as headmaster. Her final concern was unusual enough that she clearly felt the need to offer a sort of "I know this is going to sound strange" preface: She felt the Charlestown team under O'Brien won too much.

That comment produced a cascade of double-takes across the conference-room crowd. *Win too much?* Tony Lee, who had the reputation as one of the toughest guys to have ever played for O'Brien and who was now about to graduate from Robert Morris University, piped up, "What do you want us to do, lose?"

Bledsoe tried to clarify things. Charlestown's dominance under O'Brien, she said, had stoked resentment from other city coaches and spawned complaints that Charlestown was hogging all the talent, stocking its bench with talented reserves who could have been starters for other schools.

Those packed into the conference room jockeyed to rebut each of Bledsoe's concerns. *He had burned bridges?* They could understand that argument if it was made by the higher-ups in Lynn, but hadn't O'Brien demonstrated his commitment to Charlestown by forgoing coaching just to remain at the school? Wasn't two years out of the game penance enough? And if the parents and players had forgiven him—a couple of the boys who had cried in the halls when he announced his plans to leave for Lynn were here tonight, arguing for his return—why couldn't the new headmaster and staff? *Special treatment?* No one was going to deny that O'Brien was zealous in advocating for his guys. But his players were generally standard-setters when it came to behavior in school, and he often pushed them to take harder classes in preparation for college. *Winning too much and keeping talented kids on the bench?* Many of the players who turned out to be stars for O'Brien were not viewed as great players in middle school. And O'Brien's all-game, full-court press approach meant that playing time was shared by a lot more players than on other teams. Hugh stressed that just because guys weren't starters didn't mean they weren't learning. He pointed to his brother Derek, who was also in the room. He hadn't been a starter until his senior year, but O'Brien helped him earn a Division I scholarship. Derek had just finished a season as a professional basketball player in Europe.

The longer the meeting dragged on, the more frustrated Willie became. When people were offering heartfelt stories, which were bringing tears to the eyes of some people in the room, Willie looked over at Bledsoe and the school officials. They seemed remarkably unmoved. And Bledsoe kept returning to O'Brien's negatives, particularly his original decision to leave the school for Lynn. Finally, he'd had enough.

"It seems to me," Willie said, "that you got your mind made up already."

When Bledsoe said that wasn't the case, Willie said, "I think you're wasting our time."

To him, the message from the parents was unmistakable: *We want O'Brien training our kids.* Yeah, he made some mistakes. But who hasn't? And didn't it say something about the depth of his commitment that he'd passed up opportunities to coach elsewhere so he could remain at Charlestown?

The meeting ended inconclusively. Bledsoe thanked everyone for their participation and promised to make a decision soon.

In the hallway, the parents and alumni chatted with each other, trying to sort out what had just happened and why there still seemed to be such resistance to O'Brien. Because the group couldn't conceive of the possibility that Bledsoe didn't see O'Brien as the most talented person for the job, speculation focused primarily on two possibilities: That she feared antagonizing powerful people if she gave him the job, or that as a new principal trying to gain control of the school, she didn't want to have to contend with someone who had his own intensely loyal fan base. Willie said that as frustrated as he was, he kind of felt bad for Bledsoe. "I think maybe somebody dumped this decision in her lap, not realizing how much support O'Brien had."

One other possibility some in the group allowed was that Bledsoe was reluctant to cause more dissension in the faculty by removing Cassidy from the post.

That risk was soon gone. The morning after Bledsoe's meeting with parents and alumni, Cassidy resigned as coach.

Publicly, he said he felt it was the right time to go. Privately, he told Hugh that the process had already dragged on too long, and he wanted to maintain control of his own fate rather than leaving it to Bledsoe.

Word quickly spread in the corridors, and many of the players headed straight for the gym to celebrate with O'Brien. But O'Brien had already seen plenty of painful twists in this two-year saga, so he cautioned against doing any celebrating until he actually had the job.

The caution proved to be prudent. For more than a month, O'Brien heard nothing from Bledsoe, who admitted she'd been caught off guard by Cassidy's resignation. O'Brien had made his case repeatedly, so he figured it would be better to keep his distance and let things take their course. Hugh took no chances, going in several more times to talk with Bledsoe and urge her to do the right thing.

Finally, with the school year about to end, O'Brien pressed Bledsoe for a decision. They agreed to meet in her office on a Saturday in the middle of June, nearly one year after Fung had first urged her to make a prompt decision on the coaching situation. Bledsoe began their meeting by thanking O'Brien for the enormous contributions he had made to Charlestown High. But she said she felt that the school needed to go in a new direction. This wouldn't affect his job as phys ed teacher, but she would be bringing in someone else to coach the team. She would decline to explain her decision publicly, beyond a written statement that said, in part, "After a good deal of investigation and reflection, I have concluded that all that has occurred in the two years since Jack resigned make moving in a new direction and hiring a new coach a better choice for the school."

O'Brien was determined not to give Bledsoe the satisfaction of showing the crushing disappointment he was feeling inside. He tried thinking of whose help he could solicit to reverse the decision. But for all the impossibly tight bonds he had developed with players and parents over the years, he had cultivated precious few alliances within either the school department hierarchy or the city's coaching fraternity. So once the views of the alumni and parents had been discounted, he didn't have anywhere else to turn.

On the Monday morning after O'Brien learned his fate, Hugh was checking in at the main office when he locked eyes with Bledsoe. "Dr. Bledsoe, you made the wrong decision," he said, before beginning to tear up. A few days later Bledsoe informed Hugh, whom she had previously warned of being too comfortable in the nest of Charlestown and under the wing of O'Brien, that he should look for a job at another school. She thanked him for all his service to Charlestown High, and offered to write him a letter of recommendation.

Many of the players, having glimpsed a future with O'Brien and Zach and Hugh, were left embittered by the turn of events.

There was no Alumni Game in 2008. Instead of facing off on the court, his players past and present—the family he had forged over the years—had crowded into a conference room to do battle for the man who had done so much for them. Even though they didn't win, O'Brien knew there was real victory in that.

ACKNOWLEDGMENTS

This book would have been impossible without the cooperation of the families of Charlestown, and I will always be thankful to them for their trust. But I'm also grateful for what good company they all were.

Top on this list is Jack O'Brien, a towering talent who gambled by letting me into his close-knit world. The players weren't kidding when they warned me early on that there was no such thing as a brief phone call from Jack. I've never met someone so committed to a cause, and what a great cause it is. He has a rare gift. Thanks also to his mother, Teddy, and his sister, Patty.

The rest of the extraordinary coaching staff, and their families, were essential and friendly guides for me, on and off the court. Zach Zegarowski and his wife, Mandy; Steve Cassidy and his wife, Nicole; and Hugh Coleman and his wife, Emily.

I spent time with all of the varsity players, as well as with many of their families. Even though I wasn't able to give most of them the space in this book that their stories deserve, I am richer for knowing them all. But anyone who has made it this far in the book knows there were two players whose families I ended up spending most of my time with: Ridley Johnson and Jason "Hood" White.

Ridley and his mother, Rebecca, are both warm-hearted souls who opened their home to the rest of the Charlestown team. I'm grateful that they welcomed me into the mix. I also enjoyed my time with Ridley's father, Ridley McClary Johnson; and Ridley's extended family, particularly Paul Becklens and his mother, Joanna; and, of course, Emily and Hugh, and all of Hugh's siblings, especially Bernard.

Jason's family was equally important. Although Jason took a while to open up, once he did, he was thoughtful and expansive. He has suffered some setbacks, but he is a genuinely good person, and I hope for and still expect great things from him. His dynamic father, Willie Barnes, was uniformly friendly, funny, and candid. Jason's mother, Pearl White, was always welcoming and genuine, as was his girlfriend Tia Martin. I'm also grateful for the conversations I had with his cousin Pookie's family during the many hours we shared a courtroom hallway.

Lamar "Spot" Brathwaite is a thoughtful, special person, as are George Russell and Ricardo "Robby" Robinson. Thanks also to Lamar's mother, Arnetta Clemons; his uncle Mark Brathwaite; his grandmother Roenita Harris; and George's mother, Lolly.

I learned about devotion from my time in the bleachers with Harry Landry and Harry Dixon, both class acts. I learned about friendship from my time off the court with Phil Jean and Jethro Trenteetun. Derrick Bowman, Terry Carter (who, I am happy to report, is doing really well now), Jerome Allen, Ravon Dunbar, Tron Griffith, Dean Lambright, Dashawn Matthews, Jeffrey Hall, Lance Green, Troy Gillenwater, LeRoyal Hairston, Lorenzo Jones, David Riley, and Rashaud Skeens were fun to be around, as were Charlestown girls basketball players Tawanda Brown, Teresa Pina, and Bie and Anim Aweh.

I was enriched by the time I spent with all of the Charlestown alumni, in particular Nick Souffrant, Tony Lee, Ian Urquhart, Shawn Brown, Tony Chatman, James Leveque, Basil Wajd, and, from O'Brien's Salem days, Rick Brunson. The late Alray Taylor was a gentle, kind soul. I'm grateful to all the wonderful people who joined me in the effort to create the Alray Taylor Second Chance Scholarship in Alray's memory, especially Heather Barry, Shawn Brown, Lisa Fliegel, Michael Fung, Lama Jarudi, Thaddeus Miles, Tom Nardone, Jack O'Brien, Nick Souffrant, Altia Taylor, and Michael Wanyo. The scholarship is designed to help promising Boston students who left college get back on track and graduate. The first award recipients were selected in 2008. For more information, please visit www.theassist.net. It was a pleasure meeting Delta Grant and Anissa Booker, the mothers of Richard Jones and Paris Booker respectively, and seeing the dignified way in which they keep the memories of their sons alive.

I learned from so many dedicated Charlestown High staff members, none more than the incomparable Michael Fung. He gave me sharp insights, unflinching candor, and lots of good humor. I was always impressed by Kristyn O'Brien and her commitment to the kids of Charlestown High. Thanks to all the Charlestown teachers who graciously opened their classrooms to me. Thanks also to Michael Contompasis for his time and insights.

Many at the University of Toledo were helpful during my time there, in particular Stan Joplin, Mark Vanderslice, and Mike Meade. Closer to home, I'm grateful to Paul Campbell, Jamie Cosgrove, David Siggers, and Danny Ventura for sharing their time and basketball knowledge. As guides to Charlestown's past, Arthur Hurley and Moe Gillen were knowledgeable and friendly. Staff members at public libraries in Medford, Salem, and Charlestown provided topnotch assistance. Thanks also to the many people around Boston who schooled me in important ways, notably Danny Ryan, Thaddeus Miles, Lisa Fliegel, Jake Wark, Jack Miller, Bill O'Hare, Gloria Bowers, and Jenry Gonzales.

Equally essential in this effort was the support I received from colleagues and friends. My brilliant agent, Sarah Chalfant, gave me crucial guidance and encouragement. She has a richly deserved reputation as one of the most effective advocates in her field, but what I found just as impressive was how much she genuinely cared about the people I was writing about. Her assistant, Edward Orloff, was first-rate in every way.

At PublicAffairs, I benefited from an exceptional team, led with great intelligence and enthusiasm by publisher Susan Weinberg. I was truly fortunate to have Clive Priddle as my editor. With smarts, wit, and high standards, Clive helped me reshape this book into something so much better than my first draft. He also had an uncanny ability to inhabit the world of Charlestown, as though he had been sitting there with me in the gym for years. I'm grateful to the talented Meredith Smith and Carol Smith for shepherding the manuscript through production with fine craft. Thanks also to Pete Garceau, Lindsay Goodman, Dan Ozzi, Niki Papadopoulos, Melissa Raymond, and all the dedicated people at PublicAffairs who helped in the effort.

I benefited from impeccable fact-checking assistance. Ann Silvio, my friend and best-in-the-business backstop for many years, kindly came out of research retirement to lead this effort, joined by Matt Mahoney and Stephanie Vallejo, who brought scrupulousness and sensitivity to their work.

There are so many people at the *Boston Globe* who deserve my thanks that I regret I have space to name just a few. Doug Most, my enthusiastic and inspiring editor at the *Magazine*, has been an incredible ally and friend. Marty Baron, the top editor at the *Globe,* is a gifted leader who brings rigor and excellence to everything he touches. Their support for this project was vital.

The book has its roots in a series published in the *Globe Magazine* in the spring of 2005, and Matthew J. Lee was the photographer assigned to that project. Matt became a surrogate reporter and a good friend. His superb photos live on in this book. Bob Holmes, the *Globe*'s local sports editor, gave me unerring guidance all along. Charlie Pierce has taught me so much by the way he makes words bend and sing. Early readers of the manuscript John Burgess, Barbara Pattison, Ann Silvio, and Ann Scales gave me encouragement and sharp advice when I needed it most.

Thushan Amarasiriwardena and Scott LaPierre helped guide me into the new multimedia world. Other colleagues who were particularly helpful on this project include Susanne Althoff, Alex Beam, Chris Forsberg, Stan Grossfeld, Tom Haines, Bob Hohler, John Koch, Suzanne Kreiter, Stephanie Kohn, Al Larkin, Toby Leith, Lauri Martignetti, David McCraw, Richard Pennington, Lisa Tuite, Mary Jane Wilkinson, and the entire staff of the *Boston Globe Magazine*. Colleagues who provided pivotal help early on in my writing career at the *Globe* include Tom Mulvoy, Peter Canellos, Helen Donovan, and Nick King.

Several of my richly talented writer friends offered key assists along the way, particularly Matt Bai, Josh Wolk, and BJ Roche. There are many writers from whom I drew inspiration for this book— some I've had the pleasure of meeting, such as Madeleine Blais, and others I know only through their words, most notably the late J. Anthony Lukas. I'm also grateful to a former professor and dear friend, the late Marjorie Pedersen, the first person who truly believed in my ability without the obligation of bloodlines. After my original Charlestown series was published, I received an e-mail from Adrian Wojnarowski. At the time, he was drawing well deserved raves for his unforgettable book, *The Miracle of St. Anthony*. Even though we'd never met, he saw something in what I had written and encouraged me to expand it into a book. Ever since, he has been generous with his praise and steadfast in his support, and for that I will always be grateful.

Finally, I could not be more indebted to the world-class extended family I've been blessed with, for their love, laughter, and unwavering support over the years: my parents, Samuel and Mary Swidey; my siblings and their spouses, Eric and Kristin Swidey, MaryAnn and John Jackson, Bob and Lynn Swidey, and Judy and Michael D'Angelo; my nieces and nephews; my in-laws, Herb and Sara Drower; and all my relatives, in particular Mary Hayes for leading the cheering overseas. In addition to teaching me all of life's important lessons, my parents read the manuscript and gave me invaluable suggestions. Thanks also to all those relatives here only in spirit, particularly my grandfathers, Saleem Swidey and Patrick Ridge, who came from different lands but shared a belief in the power of hard work and the written word to transform lives.

All three of my beautiful daughters—Sophia, Nora, and Susanna—patiently logged time with me in the stands for Charlestown games. Even when they were nowhere near the gym, they inspired me in more ways than they'll ever know, and never more than through their laughter and their hugs.

Most of all, I want to thank my wife, Denise, who radiates beauty inside and out. She has always been my best sounding board and first-line editor, and this effort was no different. Her ability to shoulder so much of our joint load over the past several years, and her willingness to do it without even a hint of complaint, was extraordinary. For this and so much more, she has all my love.

She didn't wait long to set the tone. On a sleeting Saturday night in 2004, Charlestown was scheduled to play its first game of the season, on the road in Salem. That day, Denise, who was nine months pregnant, began feeling some strong contractions. I told her I would skip the game, but she refused. Instead, we packed our two daughters into the car and we all went together. The contractions subsided during the game, so after the final buzzer, Denise encouraged me to go listen to Jack O'Brien's locker room talk. Since we were new to the Charlestown program, we both assumed a postgame talk after a blowout win wouldn't last long. When I emerged twenty-five minutes later, Denise's easygoing expression had changed. "We should go," she said. We raced back toward Boston, and the next day our youngest daughter was born.

Neil Swidey
September 2007

RESEARCH METHODS

This is my first book, but I approached it the same way I had all my previous writing assignments: as a reporter. All the characters, names, scenes, and events in this book are real. To keep the narrative moving, in a couple of instances, I slightly altered the placement of a minor scene within the chronology, without changing details or context. In every way, this is a work of nonfiction.

I first met Jack O'Brien in August 2004, at a Bickford's pancake house off the Southeast Expressway in Boston. When we reconvened at that same spot almost exactly three years later, we joked about how neither of us knew what we were getting into back then. But we both agreed we were happy we had taken the plunge. In truth, it was only a few hours after that first meeting when I realized how special the Charlestown basketball story was. Jack had invited me to accompany him that evening as he took a few players out for burgers and mini-golf. But the outing began with all of us standing with our heads bowed in front of the gravesites of two members of the Charlestown family. That scene, of course, became the Prologue for this book, and fixed in my mind the notion of how much bigger than basketball this story was.

I witnessed most of the events and interactions described in this book that took place after that cemetery visit in the summer of 2004. At the outset, there was some understandable wariness from

Jack, his players, and their families. But before long, they allowed me into their lives with warmth and trust, and for this I remain extremely grateful. As a magazine writer, I have always spent a good deal of time immersing myself in the lives of the people I am profiling, trying as much as possible to blend into the background. But for me this project set a new standard for immersion, as I spent countless hours with the people at the center of the story—at home, in school, in the locker room, and on the road. I got up at 5 AM and made my way to the house of one player or another, so I could experience the long commutes to school they made every day without complaint. I joined the team on the bus and in the locker room for most games and accompanied the players on visits to college and to court. But the most productive and enjoyable times for me were when we sat for hours in their rooms doing nothing—just talking over the chatter of ESPN and the sounds of PlayStation 2. Along the way, I found myself caring deeply about what happened to the players and coaches of Charlestown. Because of my regular contact with them, even in cases where I did not witness a scene, I was able to reconstruct it while everyone's memories were still fresh. I witnessed most of the dialogue quoted in the book; where that was not possible I recreated it based on the recollections of at least one—usually two—of the participants.

For events prior to the summer of 2004, I relied on the memories of the participants, as well as a host of supplementary sources. (More specific expressions of gratitude can be found in the Acknowledgments section.) A list of the materials I found particularly useful follows.

For the sections on Jack O'Brien's life before Charlestown, I relied on recollections from Jack, his family, and former colleagues, as well as the remarkably thorough coverage of him in the *Medford Daily Mercury* and the *Salem Evening News*.

For the sections on the history of Academy Homes, I benefited from conversations with longtime tenants and housing officials, as well as coverage in the archives of the *Boston Globe* and materials from the Department of Housing and Urban Development and other agencies.

For the sections on the history of Charlestown, especially during the most contentious years of busing, I relied on the recollections of people who lived through it, as well as the exhaustive coverage in the *Boston Globe*, and, in particular, the retrospective pieces on Ted Landsmark and Joseph Rakes written by Thomas Farragher. Books on the history of race in Boston schools that I found helpful include: Jonathan Kozol's 1967 book *Death at an Early Age* (as well as his 2005 update *Shame of the Nation*), Robert A. Dentler and Marvin B. Scott's *Schools on Trial* (1981), and Susan Eaton's *The Other Boston Busing Story* (2001). I marinated in the Charlestown history collection at the Charlestown branch of the Boston Public Library and lingered over WGBH's impressive online archive of footage from the busing years. Among the books on Charlestown and Boston history that I referred to were Nancy Lusignan Schultz's *Fire and Roses: The Burning of the Charlestown Convent, 1834* (2000) and Thomas H. O'Connor's *Boston A to Z* (2000). I turned to Omar M. McRoberts's *Streets of Glory* (2003) for an interesting exploration of the roots and range of Boston's black population, particularly around its churches. By far, the most valuable source for me when I was researching the chapter "Townies in Black and White" was *Common Ground* (1985) by the late J. Anthony Lukas. I am particularly indebted to Lukas for his meticulous reporting on the inner workings of Charlestown High School during the pre-busing and busing periods. When I first read *Common Ground* many years ago, I was awed by its breadth and intimacy. I've felt the same way each time I've reread it. I'm sure part of the appeal for me of writing this book was that I was able to revisit and update some of the same turf that Lukas had covered so unforgettably.

I also benefited from more contemporary writing, including coverage of Massachusetts high school basketball by Dan Ventura of the

Boston Herald and the high school sports staff of the *Boston Globe*, under the direction of Bob Holmes, as well as coverage of University of Toledo basketball by the staff of the *Toledo Blade*, particularly by Dave Hackenberg. In writing on LeRoyal and Troy's California experiences, I relied on coverage in the *Boston Globe* by Bob Hohler, who broke the story, as well as background coverage of Fremont High School by the *Los Angeles Times*, particularly by Richard Lee Colvin.

My understanding of trends in education and the nation's overall racial landscape was informed by numerous academic reports and independent analyses. Those I found most useful are listed here: three reports by the Lewis Mumford Center at the University at Albany, SUNY: "Separate and Unequal: The Neighborhood Gap for Blacks and Hispanics in Metropolitan America" (2002); "Choosing Segregation: Racial Imbalance in American Public Schools, 1990–2000" (2002); and "Segregation in Neighborhoods and Schools: Impacts on Minority Children in the Boston Region" (2003); analyses in 2001, 2002, and 2003 of Census and public housing data by the *Boston Globe*, in particular the 2002 piece by Scott S. Greenberger, "White is still the color in two neighborhoods"; two studies by Christine Rossell: "Controlled Choice Desegregation Plans: Not Enough Choice, Too Much Control?" (1995), and, with J. Michael Ross, "The Long Term Effect of Court Ordered School Desegregation on White Withdrawal from Central City Public School Systems: the Case of Boston, 1974–79" (1978–79); a report by Andrew Sum of Northeastern University's Center for Labor Market Studies, "Trends in Black Male Joblessness and Year-Round Idleness" (2004); and a study by the Center on Education Policy on the narrowing of the public school curriculum, "From the Capital to the Classroom: Year Four of the No Child Left Behind Act" (2006).

Ultimately, on everything that really matters in this book, I was schooled by the people at its center. Because many of them were minors, at least when I began my research, I tried always to be mindful of their interests, explaining the project and its implications to them and their parents and coaches. When, during the course of my three years of reporting, some of the players ran into trouble in their lives, I gave serious thought to changing their names in the book. In the end, I decided against that. Through our many conversations, I came to realize that they tended to have a level of comfort, or at least acceptance, with revelations that I assumed they would be most sensitive about. In the rare cases where one of the players asked me not to write about something—usually innocuous matters—I always tried to honor those requests. I think the players and their families recognized, even before I did, a message I hope that all readers take away from this book: The people described in the preceding pages may not be perfect, but there is real power and dignity in their struggle and in their stories.

A READING GROUP GUIDE

What attracted you to this project?

Initially, it was pretty basic. I wanted to understand what makes a high school basketball powerhouse tick. This was a team that had made history by winning the state championship four years in a row. But very early on I realized how small a piece of the story basketball was. It's really about an unlikely family and all the effort it takes to get ahead.

What surprised you most once you were on the inside?

I assumed that once you'd built a powerhouse, life would get easier each year. I was wrong. Inner-city life is full of such distractions, such minefields, that it's like starting from scratch every year. I came to appreciate the enormous energy it takes, on the part of both the players and their coach, to open up the window of opportunity, and the constant threat of even tiny missteps slamming that window shut.

How did you conduct your research for this book? Did you have to actually follow the players around? And if so, how did they react to that type of intrusion into their lives?

Unfortunately, I haven't figured out how to do the kind of writing I do without being there, immersed in the lives of the

369

people I'm writing about. So it takes a lot of time and patience on the part of my subjects. But over time, they get used to my being there, and it becomes more natural. I never want people to change their behavior because I'm there. And I have figured out when to put my notebook away.

Was it tough for Jack and Ridley and the players to open up to you?

I think everyone was justifiably wary at the outset. But it's amazing how quickly that changed. I learned from Jack's example in connecting with the guys. There are huge gulfs in their experiences. But he proved that if you dive in, and become invested in their lives, in their hopes and fears, they'll open up, and you'll find yourself doing the same with them.

What surprised you most about Jack O'Brien?

The fascinating mix that he is. On the court, he's this unbelievably demanding coach, who paces and pouts along the sidelines, even when his guys are up by thirty points. But off the court, he's this unbelievably devoted mentor, with almost maternal instincts, whether that's giving his players tips on how to wash their jerseys, or driving them to doctor's appointments, or picking up plastic produce bags at the supermarket because his guys like to use them to ice their sore joints.

You write that even as devoted as he is, "O'Brien is no saint. He needs his players and his problems as much as they need him." What you mean by that?

For me, this is what makes this story so different, and so much richer than the all too familiar tale about a tough-love white coach helping inner-city black kids beat the odds. O'Brien fills the space in his player's lives, and they fill the space in his. O'Brien needs to be needed.

You followed some guys who did very well, like Ridley, and others that got off track. Why do some succeed and others don't?

Part of it is luck. For example, Ridley lived on the edge of a housing project, rather than in it. In some ways, that made him less vulnerable to getting caught up in the turf battles that overlay public housing complexes. But I think a bigger part is the ability to make smart, fast decisions—hundreds of them every day. Ridley did this, and always managed to look cool.

Can you give us an example?

In the book I describe this scene where Ridley and his aunt are driving through a side street in Charlestown. Three middle-aged public works employees have blocked the street, for no good reason, with their truck, and are taking their time, not caring that they're making it impossible for Ridley to get the car through. His aunt fumes at this, and as she goes to lower the window to confront them, Ridley reaches across the console and puts his hand on hers and says, "It's okay, we're not in a rush." She says, "That's not right!" And he says, "You're right. They're ignorant. I don't blame them." Then he takes a cell phone call. By the time he's off the phone, they've cleared out. Now other kids may have taken the bait out of rage, or backed down out of fear. Ridley managed to float above it all.

You write about the absence of second chances for urban kids. What do you mean?

With a lot of hard work and some luck, these students can get some amazing opportunities. But if things go wrong, the safety net of the suburbs just isn't there. One of the players in this book sees his life pivot on something as seemingly minor as a busted windshield. That would be inconceivable for a similarly talented athlete in a typical suburb.

Is that why you set up a scholarship fund?

Yes. We've found that even after some of these guys get to college, there are so many places where things can go wrong, where little missteps can cascade into something far more serious. And when they do, there is much less support for helping them get back on track. So I've worked with a group of really dedicated people to put this fund in place. It's called the Alray Taylor Second Chance Scholarship Fund, named in memory of a former Charlestown player and gentle soul, and its aim is to help promising students who suffered a setback get back on the path.

For more information, please visit www.theassist.net.

DISCUSSION QUESTIONS

1. Jack O'Brien immerses himself in his players' lives both on and off the court, leading some people to comment that his method is unconventional, even controversial. Do you support his approach? Do the ends justify the means?

2. Do you think the "choice" system that the Boston Public School administration uses to assign students to high schools around the city works? Are the kids better off staying in their own neighborhood schools?

3. How do you think O'Brien's family history may have informed his career and his interactions with his players?

4. When Michael Fung, the headmaster of Charlestown High, hears that a former student is dropping out of college because he wasn't receiving enough attention on his college team, he asks, "Why have others failed once they left Charlestown? I think maybe they're looking for another Jack O'Brien. But in real life, there aren't many Jack O'Briens" (p. 267). How does O'Brien lead so many players to success?

5. In your opinion, what's the right formula for inspiring these kids from rough neighborhoods to graduate from high school and move on to college? Why do you think so many people failed to see the good in Hood that O'Brien saw?

6. O'Brien resigned in part because he felt abandoned—especially after the central school administration didn't back O'Brien when a team from a wealthy suburb requested a venue change in the state tournament. Was this a case of institutional racism? Or was O'Brien overreacting?

7. Why do you think Hood was ready to take the fall for Pookie in the busted-windshield case? Would you have done the same thing?

8. Were you surprised when the judge sentenced Hood to serve six months in jail for destruction of property? Do you think this was a particularly harsh sentence? Why or why not?

9. In the last chapter, Swidey says that Ridley's ability to stay cool "explained why Ridley was returning as a success story to Charlestown High a year after graduation and Hood was returning to his jail cell. Ridley knew he had to rise above one world to get to the next. Hood thought he could straddle both" (p. 319–320). Do you agree with Swidey?

10. When O'Brien tells Fung he's having doubts, for the second time, about leaving Charlestown, Fung tells him, "You feel like you are betraying your players by leaving, because you are like a father to them" (p. 336). Do you agree with Fung's assessment? Why do you think O'Brien struggled so much with his decision?

Read more at www.theassist.net.

Suzanne Kreiter / Globe Newspaper Company

NEIL SWIDEY is a staff writer for the *Boston Globe Magazine*. His writing has won the National Headliner Award and been featured in *The Best American Science Writing*, *The Best American Crime Reporting*, and *The Best American Political Writing*. He lives outside Boston with his wife and three daughters. For more information, please visit www.theassist.net.

PublicAffairs is a publishing house founded in 1997. It is a tribute to the standards, values, and flair of three persons who have served as mentors to countless reporters, writers, editors, and book people of all kinds, including me.

I. F. STONE, proprietor of *I. F. Stone's Weekly*, combined a commitment to the First Amendment with entrepreneurial zeal and reporting skill and became one of the great independent journalists in American history. At the age of eighty, Izzy published *The Trial of Socrates*, which was a national bestseller. He wrote the book after he taught himself ancient Greek.

BENJAMIN C. BRADLEE was for nearly thirty years the charismatic editorial leader of *The Washington Post*. It was Ben who gave the *Post* the range and courage to pursue such historic issues as Watergate. He supported his reporters with a tenacity that made them fearless and it is no accident that so many became authors of influential, best-selling books.

ROBERT L. BERNSTEIN, the chief executive of Random House for more than a quarter century, guided one of the nation's premier publishing houses. Bob was personally responsible for many books of political dissent and argument that challenged tyranny around the globe. He is also the founder and longtime chair of Human Rights Watch, one of the most respected human rights organizations in the world.

·　　·　　·

For fifty years, the banner of Public Affairs Press was carried by its owner Morris B. Schnapper, who published Gandhi, Nasser, Toynbee, Truman, and about 1,500 other authors. In 1983, Schnapper was described by *The Washington Post* as "a redoubtable gadfly." His legacy will endure in the books to come.

Peter Osnos, *Founder and Editor-at-Large*